Modern China

Modern China

An Interpretive Anthology

JOSEPH R. LEVENSON
University of California, Berkeley

THE MACMILLAN COMPANY
Collier-Macmillan Limited LONDON

About the cover: Lo P'ing, "Portrait of the Artist's Friend, I-an" dated 1798 (Ching Yüan Chai Collection).

"The painting contains so many levels of meaning as to invite one to read still more into it. Admitting this, we may still wonder, as we look at it, whether Lo P'ing was not conscious of standing near the end of a long evolution, contemplating the past with the same mild sadness as the figure he portrays. The painting sums up the special virtues of the last phases of the evolution, but also exemplifies the paradoxes and contradictions that had penetrated to the very heart of Chinese painting: awkwardness sublimated into a kind of skill, individuality manifested in archaism, straightforward feeling set forth through oblique allusions, serious points disguised as pleasantries. Every further degree of concern with such interplay of opposites, every additional layer of stylistic reference, had separated the artist that much more from the once-possible forthright approach to the world."

JAMES CAHILL, *Chinese Painting* (New York: Skira International, 1960), p. 192.

First Printing

Library of Congress catalog card number: 78–103692

THE MACMILLAN COMPANY
COLLIER-MACMILLAN CANADA, LTD., Toronto, Ontario

PRINTED IN THE UNITED STATES OF AMERICA

Foreword

On April 6, 1969, Joseph R. Levenson was drowned in a boating accident. This untimely death of so brilliant a scholar stunned his colleagues and grieved his family and close friends. For all of us Levenson came closer to the ideal scholar in humaneness and intellect than anyone we have known. His influence upon our own thinking and work has been great. Indeed for a whole generation of students of Asian history he brought not only great sensitivity and understanding to an analysis of the China of the past and the revolutions of her mind, but ability to make his students conscious of the sensibility of the Chinese past and of the sorrow and brilliance of her decline.

It is altogether fitting that this anthology is one of his last pieces of scholarship. Although it is precisely what it purports to be (a selection of readings skillfully tied together with Levenson's own remarks), it is also a reflection of Joe's own working style. One of his greatest gifts was his ability to read as much into a text as the author intended. Often, in fact, he saw implications of which even the original essayist was barely aware. These *aperçus* in turn, uniquely rewoven with other source materials, became integral parts of, and greatly enhanced, such works as his trilogy *Confucian China and Its Modern Fate*. In this set of readings we can join once again in the excitement of his understanding and the joy of his mind.

THOMAS R. METCALF
IRWIN SCHEINER
FREDERIC WAKEMAN

Preface

This anthology (like its companion volumes, *Modern Japan: An Interpretive Anthology*, by Irwin Scheiner, and *Modern India: An Interpretive Anthology*, by Thomas R. Metcalf) has four parts. The first asks, How does one define China—how have the Chinese defined themselves—as a vessel of history in modern times? The next, What was the role of the past, and of Chinese feelings for the past, in establishing definitions? Third, What made the old order seem threatened, what made men feel the urgent need to threaten it? Lastly, What were the goals (and why were they goals) of the bearers of the threat? The selections that follow do not comprise a flowing narrative. They offer, instead, connecting links of interpretations of the evidence of the senses.

Contents

PART THREE
The Sense of Urgency

PART FOUR
The Sense of the Future

Contents

PART ONE
The Sense of Identity

In the first selection (patronizing home industries), we range over our whole period, from the early seventeenth century to the 1960s, late Ming to the "Cultural Revolution." All the other selections find a place or point to a place on this arc of time. And this selection, on the sense of identity, rings changes on the other themes, the other senses—of the past, of present urgency, and of the future.

The Past and Future of Nationalism in China

JOSEPH R. LEVENSON

MING AND MAO

I N the sixteen-thirties and forties, the native Chinese Ming dynasty was hit by peasant rebels on the inside and aggressive Manchus on the outside. In 1644, a Ming general went over to the Manchus and helped them ruin both the dynasty and the rebels.

Three centuries later there was a similar constellation of forces. For Ming, the rebel Li, the Manchus, and the puppet Wu, read Kuomintang, Mao, the Japanese, and Wang Ching-wei. Established authority, social protest, invasion, collaboration: the analogy seemed perfect, as though China were indeed the land of eternal yesterday, with an *historia perennis*. It would be history not as development but as a vessel of fixed forms —political science teaching by example.

One of the modern protagonists seemed to see it that way. In 1933, Wang Ching-wei condemned Mao as the new 'bandit Li,' tearing the nation apart in a class interest while a national foe was marshalling in the north. And Wang, defending a soft Kuomintang policy towards Japan, denounced the Ming for scorning peace with the Manchus while the divisive peasant rebels remained unconquered. The modern rebels, the communists, repaid Wang in the same coin of invective. The Kuomintang (and the puppets like Wang who later hived off from it) were said to be

Joseph R. Levenson, "The Past and Future of Nationalism in China," *Survey,* No. 67 (April 1968), pp. 28–40. Reprinted by permission of the editors. Footnotes omitted.

selling the nation, in late Ming style, rather than yield their class supremacy.

But between the Sino-Manchu and the Sino-Japanese wars there had, of course, been development, historical process, not stasis. The analogy was not perfect: paradoxically, there had to be something new in modern times, impairment of the analogy, to make the analogy plausible. The nationalist mentality, an historically new ingredient, obscured historical change. Nationalism—only in modern times—had come to have an un-questioned moral claim on the national. Hence (for the present, and anachronistically for the past), the mutual charges of monstrous ethical behaviour—splitting the nation in face of the enemy, or letting the enemy in to save a class position. To say that Mao's China is essentially communist *or* essentially nationalist, to imply that this means 'new' or 'old,' is to miss the point of the modern debate about rebels, invaders, and puppets. When the debaters, by emphasizing nationalism, missed the point about the end of the Ming, they were trying to score points off each other.

In 1644 neither side was choosing between nation and class. They were choosing between dynasties, not nations. Though the Manchus were beset by anti-foreign feeling, anti-foreignism is not the same as national-ism. The Manchus were Chinese enough, Confucian enough, culturally, to become a Chinese dynasty, widely accepted as such within a Manchu reign or two. The issues in the seventeenth century were economic and cultural, not economic and national. If nationalism is a serious issue now, it has not been a perennial issue. Its past is the modern past, and its future lies in a 'People's China' (or in some successor regime), not in a 'People's Middle Kingdom,' a perennial China, perennially self-absorbed. Now and in the foreseeable future, Chinese self-absorption or self-assertion —translated as 'nationalism'—is not just the old Adam (or the old Con-fucius) coming out once more.

CH'ING AND MAO

Communist China: '. . . a reviving Chinese power under a leadership driven by an ancient national-cultural chauvinism and a modern ultra-revolutionism. The first demands restoration of China's greatness and the regaining of its place at the centre of the world. The second . . . some ultimate global triumph.' Let us worry about the first (plenty of people are worrying about the second). True, most recently in the eighteenth century, China was unmistakably 'great,' and it saw itself at the centre of the world. Indeed, it was a world itself, a world whose values were Value, whose civilisation was Civilisation, a trans-national antithesis to barbarism. Confucian 'culturalists' in China-as-a-world had traditionalism as a world-view. But Chinese nationalists, in the twentieth century, were iconoclastic. Either they were avowedly new men, in the 'May Fourth' spirit,* or, if conservative, they transvalued old values in their very affirmations of the old. If they tried to retain Confucius, for example, in China as a nation in the world, they were traditionalistic, not traditional —they had a relativistic concept, 'national essence,' not an absolute conviction.

National feeling, then, wherever it was going in the twentieth century, was going forward from the nineteenth, not backward to the eighteenth. An 'ancient national-cultural chauvinism' is not quite the spectacle that China affords today. For after 1839 and the Opium War, China's humiliations were distinctly modern. When China was beaten before, her 'place at the centre of the world' had not been jeopardised. No one had moved the centre away; the conquerors simply moved into it. They borrowed the mantle of greatness, the mandate of Heaven. Mongolia was not the centre of the world for the Yuan dynasty of Mongols (1260–1368), nor Manchuria for the Manchu Ch'ing (1644–1912). China was the prize, and China remained the centre, even among—especially among—those victims of barbarians who resented the conquests most. And resentment turned to acceptance, as the barbarians' sins were bleached (more or less) in sinification. China was still the still point, the Middle Kingdom, in the turning world.

But the Manchu conquest was the last of its kind. In the nineteenth century, the old recurrent form of Chinese weakness—a dynastic disarray that tempted the foreigners in—was complicated by new disabilities: inadequate technology and social vulnerability. China could be manipulated from a distance. Unlike the Manchus, modern Europeans had no need to assimilate to China. And the Chinese, unable to take them in, were just as unable to throw them out so long as the technological gap endured. The road to hell—and to *national* resurrection—was paved with new inventions. Thus, from the eighteen-forties on, a line of 'self-strengtheners' brought western technology more and more into their circle of acceptance, and they were drawn inexorably through merely military science to the industrial and political. The perimeter of the purely indigenous values shrank, even for bureaucratic Confucianists who longed to keep their social prominence and cultural distinction. While they defended the ever more narrowly defined 'Chinese essence,' the same West which gave them the insidious tools of defence—a merely useful technology, as it was supposed to be—was transforming an old social type, the agrarian rebel, into a proto-revolutionary, and creating a new social type, the legally protected capitalist, in the treaty ports. New roads to

* The May Fourth Movement of 1919 politically was a surge of feeling against the Japanese expropriators of Shantung province, their World War allies, and their Chinese official creatures; and culturally, against the temper and institutions of China which had allegedly made her such helpless, easy game.

social prominence, new content to cultural distinction began to threaten the old elite, even as the latter, in its own right, was shifting the ground of Confucianism, converting it from substance of education for life and action to symbol of China's individuality.

The agrarian rebels were the Taipings (1850–64). They flouted Confucianism with a garbled Christianity, part of the western intellectual penetration. And they were pushed over the edge of rebellion by western economic penetration, which aggravated endemic social bitterness to a new intensity. Intellectual apostasy underscored this bitterness. Literati-officials and landlords, almost unanimously loyal to the Manchu dynasty, damned the rebels as seceders from cultural China. For what the Taipings proclaimed was a national China, in which an ethnically foreign dynasty, however Confucian in its sympathies and culturally legitimate, was nationally illegitimate.

The dynasty survived for a while, the Taipings went down. But the intellectual revolution of the twentieth century was anticipated in the Taipings' fusion of cultural iconoclasm and political nationalism. And their fusion of cultural iconoclasm and rudimentary class-analysis (the Taipings' animus towards landlords being inseparable from their anti-Confucianism) foreshadowed the fate of that revolution: preemption by the communists.

MAO AND THE SENSE OF MISSION

In former days, the old Confucian fiction about 'beckoning barbarians from afar by civilised example' had covered a harsh politics of beckoning by weakness. But in the latter days the cover was stripped away, and the new conquests meant deflation of China, not inflation of the conqueror by his becoming quasi-Chinese. Ever since the early nineteenth century, foreign intrusion could nurture only resentment—against others, and against the self—not self-esteem.

From its beginnings in the May Fourth Movement, Chinese communism reflected that resentment, with both its targets. 'Anti-imperialism' struck at the foreign foes of the new or would-be nation; 'anti-feudalism' hit the domestic foes of the new culture. The combination released Chinese feeling against the Confucian past, which, though moribund, had still invited acceptance, as Chinese; and against a western present, which, though rejuvenating, had still invited rejection, as alien. To be both Chinese and fresh instead of either foreign or stale: that was the communist promise. Chinese nationalism, in both its affinities—with political self-assertion and cultural revolution—was bound to pervade communism and make China new.

Where was the novelty, really? If Chinese communism is strongly nationalist, a universal creed in a particular vessel, how does a communist China differ from a Confucian China? The latter, too, had an ecumenical spirit and a well-developed sense of Chinese selfhood. But it had no sense of *mission,* which communist China has.

Christian Europe had had it, too. In the Pauline spirit, Christian universalism was supra-cultural, trans-historical. It fostered expansion out from Christian lands to newly discovered lands of potentially Christian souls. Confucian universalism, however, was supremely cultural, invincibly historical. Its values were universal, like the Christian, but Confucian universalism was a criterion, a standpoint, not a point of departure. It applied to all the world (all 'under-Heaven': *T'ien-hsia,* both 'the Empire' and 'the world,' where the 'Son of Heaven' ruled); and it was open to all. But Confucianists as pragmatists accepted cultural differences as the way of the world, always producing candidates for the title of barbarian. From the point of view of normative Confucianism, wedded to culture and history and anti-messianic to the core, the barbarians are always with us. From the point of view of normative Christianity, transcending culture and history (those marks of distinction between 'Jews and Greeks'), the pagans are not always with us: they can be sought out and converted. The Kingdom of Heaven was nowhere in the world. But the Middle Kingdom, the point of balanced perfection in the world, under-Heaven, was at home. Though Chinese left home in great numbers, no one had any Confucian pretensions to be bearing out a Word.

Now, however, the new China has a Word for the world, beginning with all its Bolivias. China commends itself as a model of revolution. The model applies, allegedly, because all 'peoples' (i.e., all victims of imperialists) are brothers. But the model is political and economic. *Culturally* —with reference to specific, historical Chinese culture—Mao has no message for the world. Old China claimed to be exemplary because others were different and therefore lower. New China claims to be exemplary because it identifies affinities, a common plane of victimisation and a common destiny, so that the Chinese mode of liberation should meet the needs of others.

At the end of the eighteenth century, in that other age of claims to central greatness, a (Manchu) Chinese emperor dismissed the English blandishments: rudiments of Chinese culture could hardly be transplanted to a distant barbarous land. Ch'ien-lung's edict, of course, was universalist; China's civilisation was the touchstone for the barbarousness of England. If England was a backwater, it was the distance from China, in every sense, that made it one. But this older universalism allowed for, even demanded (as the fuel for condescension), the fact of western ignorance of China. That was the traditional situation. Next, transitionally, between the Ch'ien-lung and Mao eras, China became the backwater—an object of western influence, not a source of inspiration or of Chinese condescension to the hopelessly uninspired. And now, as China seeks to be the fountain-head again, the central source of world values, there is a different world from Ch'ien-lung's and a different China. 'Substructure' (a general social system), not 'superstructure' (a special Chinese high culture), serves as model. And the world's attention, not its inattention, ministers to China's self-esteem.

NATIONALISM AND INTERNATIONALISM

Peking neglected to send George III an English version of the Confucian classics. But Peking thoughtfully broadcasts far and wide, in English, Spanish, Arabic and everything else, the 'thoughts of Mao Tse-tung.' Perhaps the balance of payments is meant to be restored, with an outflow of influence after a century of inflow. There can be nationalist satisfaction in this presumption of Chinese leadership. But it depends on an internationalist premise. Mao, quite unequivocally, represents himself not as a Chinese sage prescribing for the world, but as a world sage in a line of sages (Marx, Lenin, Stalin), bringing China—agreeably, to the nationalistic spirit—to the forefront of history, everybody's history. To the culturalistic Confucian spirit (Ch'ien-lung's), Chinese history was the only history that mattered. To the nationalistic communist (Mao), the satisfaction comes in having Chinese history matter to the world.

For 'restoration of China's greatness' required an end to a century's ravages in the confidence in Chinese continuity. 'Westernisation,' the spectre since the Opium War, threatened to divert Chinese history into the western stream, as though the West, spreading over the world, had the only line from past to future. Mao, no Boxer xenophobe, is ready to tap the western line; but Mao, no 'rootless cosmopolitan,' is not prepared to cut himself off from home. And so he arrives at a modern synthesis, not an 'ancient national-cultural chauvinism.' He sees that a considerable Marxist-Leninist ancestry might establish China's leadership, not its dependence. To restore the continuity of Chinese history, Mao insists on the continuity of Marxist history. Aspiring to a world leadership that would reflect glory on China, Mao contends that he has creatively enriched in China what he has nevertheless drawn openly from international sources. The alternatives of 'Chinese' (nationalist) or 'communist' (internationalist) are misconceived. Mao has consciously lodged himself in Chinese history by drawing materials from histories outside China. He is not Chinese in the sense of presiding over the restoration of old China. He is Chinese in wishing to extend Chinese history, not to repeat it (for one must be anti-feudal), nor to end it (for one must be anti-imperialist).

Mao, then, has meant to be Chinese nationalist and Marxist theoretician. He united the two personae in moving from a westernising to a modernising zeal. In 1919, in a westernising vein, Mao inveighed especially against the backwardness of the Chinese social system. Confucian intellectual life was stale, Confucian society unravelled and unappealing. But westernisation could hardly hold him or many of his countrymen, for what led them to disaffection was their identification with China. As modern, but not as 'western,' China could still be 'theirs' without still being traditional. With the aid of a Marxist time-scale, China might own its own share of modern time—a huge share for a huge country—instead of deferring to the West. Class-analysis identified the stages of progress, class-struggle provided the motor: Marxism, especially Leninist anti-imperialism, would implement Chinese nationalism. Marxist and national fervour seemed to reinforce each other.

Today, what makes China seem so ominous to the West and the Soviet Union is Mao's last turn of the screw: Chinese nationalism has come to the fore to implement Marxism. If China could be free of 'antagonistic contradictions' internally, China would finally become what Mao's mentor, Li Ta-chao, had called it in 1920—a proletarian nation. *The* proletarian nation, with the other 'victims of imperialism' in tow? As Stuart Schram has remarked, if the Chinese people is a revolutionary class, then nationalists and revolutionaries are one and the same. The Chinese, by contriving a classless society in their nation, would constitute a class, or the vanguard of a class, in the society of the world. This fancy has nothing to do with any Confucian eternal return. It derives, however eccentrically, from a world-view that compensates for Confucianism lost. Just like the modern West, old China would be laid away in history. And so would Soviet Russia, while the *new* proletariat, new China, assumed for itself the grace of the *quondam* saviour. *Caveat redemptor.*

If Russia has to beware, it is not because Imperial Russia, with the Soviets as legatees, had taken land from Imperial China. Nationalism, for communist China, cannot be reduced to an irredentist organic nation against all comers. The Kuomintang's nation (not its state) was *min-tsu*, an organic community of integral nationality, and it made for a concept of national essence—transcending individuals, but an individual itself, a folk, in its resistance to cosmopolitanism. *Min-tsu*, perhaps, is most aptly conceived with the indefinite article: *a* people, like the Chinese, set apart. The communists use the term, too. But what they conceive of as *the* people is not *min-tsu* but *jen-min* (or the Chinese *min-tsu* as *jen-min*), not organic, collective life but a collectivist abstraction—and not single and self-contained, but cosmopolitan. Kuomintang nationalists could talk unambiguously about the Chinese nation against Russians or Japanese. As we have suggested, in the nineteen-thirties they could damn the communists as anti-nationalist, anti-*min-tsu*, for allegedly following Russian orders and sundering the nation with their class animus. But the communists, in reply, added *jen-min* to *min-tsu*, and claimed that the Kuomintang (with its appeasement of Japan, its priority for 'bandit-suppression') did violence to both. As an opponent of 'the people,' the masses, it betrayed 'the (Chinese) people.'

That is why, when they opposed a united front against Japan in the early thirties, or allegedly subverted it in the forties, the nationalist credit of the Kuomintang, the ostensible 'Nationalists,' was impugned. They became nationally suspect in suspecting revolution. The communists pre-empted nationalism during the Sino-Japanese war, but they did not do it, really, by abandoning their call to revolution. This they only muted for a while, to establish their own nationalist credit and to drain their rivals' account. The fact of revolution was suspended, but the promise lingered, as a lever to pry the Kuomintang loose from 'the nation.' For the Nationalists, it seemed, were only a class—the wrong class—ready to squander the Chinese people's sovereignty if this would buy them protection against the people. Perhaps (in the softest insinuation), they really opposed the Japanese while China stood alone. The invaders threatened, after all, to usurp power from the Kuomintang and communists alike. But when the United States became committed to finishing off Japan, the united front was finished. One could plausibly suggest that the Americans were welcome to win the war for the Kuomintang (so that the latter could break the peace with the communists), and then to abort the people's justice that the Kuomintang deserved.

The communists still claim to stand for both *min-tsu* and *jen-min*. Soviet 'revisionists' and United States 'imperialists' call to the Chinese bourgeois remnants, who still disfigure the *jen-min* People's China. Chinese bourgeois, if they seem determinedly unaffected by 'the thought of Mao Tse-tung,' can be denounced as denationalised. The internationalist term, *jen-min* (for there are 'the peoples of the world' on China's side), becomes the vindicator of nationalism.

PROVINCIALISM AND COSMOPOLITANISM

An earlier generation of radicals, the leaders of the 'Chinese Renaissance' (around *New Youth,* founded 1915, certain other periodicals, and the May Fourth Movement of 1919), were avowedly nationalistic, by and large. This meant that they were, both literally and figuratively, anti-provincial, with a cosmopolitan cultural drive that distinguished their cause, as nationalist, from a Boxer anti-foreignism. They took Europe as a model for China (reversing the eighteenth-century tack of western cosmopolitans): 'Chinese Renaissance' was plotted as a counterpart to the Renaissance in Europe. Science, vernacular literature, and national identity were supposed to be the common issue of western and Chinese histories, periodised in parallel lines, ancient, medieval, renaissance modernity. But the parallel, while it had to be sought, was unconvincing— just because it had to be sought.

For the substitution of national loyalty for cultural loyalty was implicit in the young Chinese nationalism; the new cultural values did not spring from native ground. Chinese Renaissance men were taking a

European line, not really coasting parallel down history. Uncomfortable in space (Chinese space, impinged upon by western), they were driven to seek comfort in time, the modern time that ticks away for everyone. But cultural evolution, the European process, was not the same as cultural transformation. There was a difference between Renaissance and Chinese Renaissance, between articulating nations out of Christendom and transmuting Confuciandom into a nation. If the analogy were valid, this would invalidate the analogy: the same process that created nations in Europe would have fragmented China into provinces. The nationalist pretext for cosmopolitan sympathies made the Chinese cosmopolitans (in the new cosmos, not the old *T'ien-hsia*) still see China as a whole. It was true of China, but not of Europe, that unity—all-inclusive nationhood—was required as compensation (and as a prescription for cure) for a cultural debacle. For China to be both culturally cut down and politically cut up was too crushing to contemplate. And the second of these conditions promised to perpetuate the first.

A cosmopolitan culture, then, for national enhancement and defence: these went together, in some few minds. Why have they been so few? The 'Great Proletarian Cultural Revolution' suggests why, and suggests where Chinese nationalism is going.

In the nineteen-twenties, especially in Shanghai, there was a cosmopolitan Chinese fringe. It had the tinge of revolution in its obvious anti-feudalism. Yet it seemed as though it might be imperialist-puppet, or at least semi-colonial if not semi-feudal. Detached from 'people' as *min-tsu*, it had no saving character of 'people' as *jen-min*. It was incorrigibly bourgeois, and while for classical Marxism the bourgeoisie was nationalist, for Chinese communism, ultimately, the bourgeoisie was internationalist in a reactionary way.

How could Shanghai or Peking types be 'national,' much less 'popular,' when they translated Pirandello or Schnitzler, just to have the fresh air of 'advanced art' in China? What did even the western art of social and political protest have to say? Imagine Shaw's *The Devil's Disciple* as the tutor for China in 'the spirit of resistance and self-sacrifice . . . the essence of success in the American Revolution.' Think of Byron as China's patriot bard, with at least five translations of 'The Isles of Greece': '. . . I dreamed that Greece might yet be free. . . .' What could a Marxist revolutionary mentality make of the bourgeois 'revolutionary' mentality that offered Barrie to China, with his pink-tea *The Admirable Crichton* as the clarion call to revolt? How could a Chinese radical, looking for a Pasionara, take Paula Tanqueray for his 'fearless social criticism of a conservative society'?

Ibsen was stronger medicine, as well as better art. There was a translation of *A Doll's House* back in 'Renaissance' days, and it kept its relevance to the plight of Chinese women. The translator of *The Lady from the Sea* [Shen Tsu-fu] let a woman friend have a look at his manuscript. 'She wrote in amazement that she discovered herself in *The Lady from the Sea*.'

This was all very edifying, and even close to revolutionary. But not close enough. In the nineteen-fifties there were many translations under communist aegis that testified to a communist cosmopolitanism. Even a play of Goldoni, for example, written not in his own Italian language but in French—and to celebrate the wedding of Louis XVI!—was published in Chinese as a tribute to a 'hero of world culture,' and to 'realism.' 'Realism' legitimised many a foreign dramatist in the fifties, from Shakespeare down, and realism meant 'the style of the age and place.' It was progressive, then, and international to praise the art that celebrated nations and limned the ages of progress (as from feudal to national consciousness) in everybody's history. History (and not just Chinese history), class-powered, was the realm of realism; idealism, anathematised, was the bourgeois concept of a timeless and classless 'universal human nature.'

What happened in the sixties? 'Universal human nature' continued to be assailed. But the old realism ('critical realism') became 'bourgeois,' as it was taken to imply description of individual subjective states. This was the theme (alleged the Cultural Revolutionaries) of cosmopolitan coterie art, egoistically unconcerned with the collective. That lady who saw herself in *The Lady from the Sea*—she could only be bourgeois, she and the others who seemed to deny class character, and national character, too, in their search for 'all-mankind' (*individual*) universal themes. Empathy was out; not the agonies of transitional man, caught between the old society and the new, but the glories of the hero, unambiguous and unambivalent and larger than life, made the subject-matter for art.

Cosmopolitanism, that is, was out. Sophistication, nuance, were out. The Cultural Revolution had a provincial cultural spirit, and the sophisticates, detached from the *jen-min* by their culture, were detached from the *min-tsu* by their world-wide affinities with fellow cosmopolitans. Specialities, expertise, know no national boundaries. The red-and-expert would still be with 'the people,' in the *jen-min* sense, and could thus still be certified in the ranks of the Chinese people. But the only-expert, experts of the wrong hue, bourgeois, not popular, had left the Chinese people; and the latter should struggle against them, in class struggle, in the name of the *min-tsu* nation. The Chinese nation had a new relation to China (to what China had been), and to what the world might be.

CULTURAL REVOLUTION AND THE STATE OF THE NATION

There were signs in the early sixties, and the Cultural Revolution was formally proclaimed in 1966. Why should a communist movement that once had cosmopolitan associations have become so especially nativist then—not just politically prickly (no problem there), but culturally so anti-western? And why, just then, should a nationalist movement have been so harsh with the national culture, the heritage of the past?

The last shall be first. Partly it was a matter of balance. The very intensity of the anti-westernism compelled a corresponding antagonism to traditional Chinese forms. Otherwise it would have been merely xenophobia, a throwback to the anti-foreign Boxer movement of 1900. And while the communists granted an honourable place to the Boxers, it was a place in history only. The Boxers were harbingers, not proto-types, of the communist fighters for Chinese independence. For Boxer anti-foreignism, while commendably anti-imperialist in political intent, was reactionary in its defence of 'feudal' culture. Chinese communists were nationalist enough to seek deliverance from traditional imperatives, and Marxist enough to see history as a linear process: it is evolution through revolution; the *past* does not revolve.

Yet the problem of the Cultural Revolution's special iconoclasm remains. Early twentieth-century radicals were generally hostile to the old values, and Chinese anti-communists have always seen their enemies as destroyers of Chinese culture. But once in power, the Party seemed to confound them. Iconoclasm was not a revolutionary prerequisite. Restoration was not a counter-revolutionary prerogative. The communists themselves were 'restoring' (in a way), not scuttling the past. Their way was the museum way. The restoration—of imperial palaces or classical reputations—was not a restoration of authority but of a history which the Chinese people (under *new* authority) could claim as its national heritage. Their historicism enabled the communists to keep the Chinese past as theirs, but to keep the past *passé*: the communists owned the present and would preside over the future.

In the Cultural Revolution, however, the museums, literal and meta-phorical, were ransacked. Old books, once assumed to have been sterilised by history of the power to harm, slipped into obscurity, if not into the flames. All kinds of relics were treated as ominously significant for the here and now; they seemed no longer safely dead, or simply historically significant. Even as they threw off the hand of the past, the communists had once retained the priceless advantage of conserving traditional culture to better effect than the modern conservatives did. Then why should Peking have thrown the traditional game?

It was because the modern game was a tricky one to play. Especially in China, where the Confucian amateur ideal was uncongenial to science, the advancement of science had revolutionary implications. It led to specialisation, the cultivation of experts. But these were suspect in com-munist China—which nevertheless, unlike Confucian China, was abso-lutely committed to the celebration of science.

It was not just that 'scientific socialists' (hardly humanist literati) could scarcely condescend to science. Marxists traded on the prestige of science, and they knew quite well that in everyone's modern world (quite unlike the Confucian world), in bourgeois countries and anti-bourgeois alike, science had prestige. When the Chinese communists put scientists down they acknowledged that prestige, they did not impugn it; its very universality, its apparent transcendence of ideology, was a threat to the masters of ideology. Science had to be mastered by the ideologues, or their own occupation would be gone. In a world where science could not be gainsaid, mere experts, practitioners of science, had to be bent to Marxist authority, or Mao, the latest Marxist in line, would have lacked authority himself. Ideology, the correct ideology, must dominate the ostensibly non-ideological expert. Politics must take command. For, as Mao proclaimed in his *Problems of Art and Literature*, the very profession of ideological unconcern ('art for art's sake') was a classic product of bourgeois ideology.

In spite of the common 'generalism' of the communist cadre and the Confucian official, the latter never believed what the former held as an article of faith: that one of the reasons for demeaning expertise was the need to erase the distinction—a crucial Confucian distinction—between mental and physical labour. Just as the Confucianist, with his amateur ideal, had displaced the old aristocracy, and then taken on an aristocratic aura (with licence to condescend to the technical professional), so the professional in the modern world, having broken the amateur ideal, had the status pride of the aristocrat today. Therefore, the Party had to trim him down ('first red, then expert'), to vindicate its own version of autocratic rule.

It is this that created the impression of a wilful cultural provincialism. The experts were China's 'rootless cosmopolitans'—*rootless*, since the peasants were the roots (whence the Red Guards, as a counter-weight to the urban, university types); and *cosmopolitan*, since, with universal science, the experts might see their association with professional col-leagues on the other side of national and ideological walls. And so winter came for the cosmopolitan scientists. But though many were cold, few were frozen. The armies and industries needed them, after all. The ones who were really blasted by the anti-cosmopolitanism were the expendables in the arts, dispensers of English literature, French music, Hong Kong haircuts. Any mute inglorious Schnitzlers or Pirandellos were well advised to stay that way.

Yes, the armies and industries needed the fruits of science, maybe to throw at the Americans. But the armies and industries might be hostages to science and technology, as well as beneficiaries. A war with America would certainly ravage the scientific complex, and exclusively expert advisers would have to counsel peace. Did the deep freeze of the experts, the coldness towards western culture (which was the source of the

expertise), mean that the risk of war was acceptable, that merely pru-
dential, technical-expert arguments might be overruled? Then the old
spirit of the Long March and the Yenan days, when the stronger battalions
were on the other side, would naturally be invoked, and they were. Not
senile nostalgia, nor a general taste for spiritual athletics, but a conviction
of present crisis may have been driving the train of events. If the weight
of weapons was against China, and yet the weapons might come into
play, man's spirit (a good Maoist anti-expert shibboleth), not weapons,
would have to be decisive.

For spirit, read ideology, the fantastic drenching in ideology that China
began to take. It came from a sense of danger, the danger of a war that
could not be left to experts, because they would not choose it and could
not win it with their expertise alone. And it was this danger that gave
the Cultural Revolution its dual targets, the two cultures, western and
traditional. The concurrent attack on the latter confirms danger as the
source of attack on the former, on the cosmopolitan spirit which the
experts represented. For the tendency to 'museumify' the past, instead of
rooting it out, belonged to the age of self-assurance. It had not been
there in the early days of struggle, when the communists had the passion
of engagement; and it vanished now in an embattled age of possible
destruction. The god of history was a hidden god again. Relativistic historicism, coolly accounting for one-time foes by giving them their niches,
went out of fashion. The dead were no longer monuments, but ghosts and
monsters to be slain again.

When they had confidence in historical progress (confidence in their
own success in moving from strength to strength), communists could
patronise their Chinese cultural past. But if the pastness of the past was
not so certain, because the future was so uncertain, if regress seemed
possible, then the communists would cease to be patrons, encouraging
curators to restore; they would be out of the gallery, at action stations,
finished with contemplation for a while. And regress was the spectre,
regress seen as furthered by Russian action (like the withdrawal of technicians) and dramatised by Russian example (revisionism). If the essential
Marxist notion of progress was not to be abandoned in a general failure
of nerve, revolutionary voluntarism, not evolutionary determinism, had to
be brought to the fore again, and the past be, not relativised, but seen as
all too possibly present. Absolutes took command. Impending crisis put
the expert under the gun, with the foreign cultural borrowings that made
him. And crisis, too, stripped the national cultural heritage of its protective
historical colour. China was not listening much to ancestral voices. But
someone in China was prophesying war.

Chinese national war or 'wars of liberation': realism is not so dead
that Mao's China cannot see the present possibilities. The sense of

peoplehood is strong—in both senses. The national people rebuffs the West, but not as Confucian China did. For the people (in the other sense), claiming the nation, against bourgeois, as its exclusive class preserve, aspires to lead the peoples of the world, or at least to inform them with the thought of Mao Tse-tung. And this thought rebuffs the old thought from the old culture, the centrepiece of the 'centre of the world.'

2

"The national people rebuffs the West, but not as Confucian China did. . . ." And so the sense of identity had changed. Ming China, facing foreigners, was a different China, not just an earlier China, from Mao's China facing foreigners. Who were China's foreign foes in the seventeenth century? What was the Manchu identity, and how did the latter, in relating to China's identity, reveal the Chinese quality before the modern change? Interestingly enough, as the next selection indicates, the Manchu conquest dynasty filled Chinese roles and fulfilled Chinese purposes, by and large. When the dynasty floundered it was all of China, not just its Manchu component, that was implicated in the crisis of identity.

FROM

The Significance of the Ch'ing Period in Chinese History

PING-TI HO

THE general significance of the Ch'ing period is that chronologically it falls between what is traditional and what is modern. However much the new China changes in the future, the Ch'ing period, the last phase of China's *ancien régime*, has left important legacies. The Ch'ing period will continue to serve as a datum plane from which to study either the earlier periods or to analyze the heritage of present-day China. To understand more fully both earlier and contemporary China, therefore, the Ch'ing period is crucial.

The Ch'ing period is significant for a number of more specific reasons. First, geographically China could never have reached its present dimensions without the laborious, painstaking, and skillful work of empire building carried out by Manchu rulers between 1600 and 1800. Since much of present-day China's impact on the outside world is due to its size and the location of its frontiers, the contribution of the Ch'ing period to the formation of modern China as a geographic and ethnic entity is of the greatest significance. Simple statistics will tell part of the story. The area known as China proper, which throughout much of the imperial age

Ping-ti Ho, "The Significance of the Ch'ing Period in Chinese History," *The Journal of Asian Studies*, XXVI, No. 2 (February 1967), pp. 189–195. Reprinted by permission of the editors. Footnotes omitted.

represented the limits of effective Chinese jurisdiction, amounts roughly to 1,532,800 square miles, which is about one-half the area of the United States. By late Ch'ing, when the Manchu empire had shrunk considerably from its fullest extent (reached by the end of the eighteenth century), China still embraced an area of approximately 4,278,000 square miles, which is 606,000 square miles larger than the area of the People's Republic of China.

It is true that at the peak of the Han and T'ang dynasties the Chinese empire reached as far west as parts of present-day Russian Turkestan, and that the Mongol empire is the largest in the annals of man. But the westward expansion of Han and T'ang was ephemeral at best, and the Mongol world empire was too loosely organized to leave any permanent imprint. In contrast, the Manchus alone were able to work out long-range policies of control and to design complex administrative and military apparatus by which to make the largest consolidated empire in Chinese history endure.

With the exception of the Mongol Yuan empire and such earlier non-Chinese empires as the To-ba Wei, the best that any Chinese dynasty could hope for was to make the Great Wall an effective front line of defense against the northern nomads. Thanks to their geographic propinquity to the Mongols and especially to their farsightedness, the early Manchu rulers had worked out, even before 1644, a basic long-range policy towards the Mongols of Inner Mongolia, which was continued and amplified down to the very end of the dynasty. The policy consisted of perennial intermarriage between the imperial clan and Mongol princedoms; periodic conferring of noble ranks on various strata of the Mongol ruling class; the endorsement by the imperial government of Lamaism as the religion for the Mongols; the setting-up of administrative machinery from *aimaks* (principalities), *chigolgans* (leagues), down to *hoshigo* (banners), which not only suited Mongol customs but also allowed the Manchus to follow a policy of divide and rule. All these, and much else, were supervised from Peking by *Li-fan-yüan*, or the Court of Colonial Affairs. In addition, a significant number of Mongols were incorporated into the Eight Banner system and into the central and provincial administration. Although early Ch'ing statutes prohibited the Chinese from entering the domains reserved for Mongol nomads, the imperial government from the late seventeenth century onwards connived at Chinese migrations to Inner Mongolia, especially in times of famine. Chinese immigration also received the tacit blessing of Mongol nobles who found their new role as *rentiers* profitable. Wherever sizable Chinese agricultural colonies were established, the imperial government set up regular local administrations, that is, counties and prefectures. Since by late Ch'ing times Chinese migrations to the northern steppe had become large-scale, Inner Mongolia had become increasingly sinicized. The integration with the rest of China of the Inner Mongolian steppe, which prior to the advent of the Manchus had always been outside the pale of Chinese civilization, was exclusively a Ch'ing contribution. Similar Chinese migrations to Manchuria, especially from the middle of the nineteenth century onwards, have made Manchuria thoroughly Chinese, despite the onslaughts of Czarist Russia and Japan.

The need in the late seventeenth and early eighteenth centuries to defend Khalkha (Outer Mongolia) from the warlike Dzungars of Northern Chinese Turkestan led the Manchus to a long series of wars which resulted in the establishment of Chinese suzerainty over Outer Mongolia and Tibet and the conquest of Kokonor and Chinese Turkestan. The effectiveness of Manchu control of these far-flung regions varied inversely in proportion to the magnitude of such difficulties as distance, terrain, transportation of men and supplies and financial resources. That the complex Ch'ing system of control of these outlying areas was by and large ingenious and viable may be evidenced by the well-known facts; namely, that Chinese Turkestan and Kokonor were made into new provinces of Sinkiang and Chinghai respectively in 1884 and 1928, that the imperial resident and garrisons in Lhasa were not withdrawn until after the fall of the dynasty in 1912, and that Outer Mongolia did not legally secede from China until January, 1946.

After 1842, the Ch'ing empire was compelled to learn the harsh realities of modern power politics. Step by step, Russia, Britain, France, and Japan reduced the question of the legal status of China's outlying regions and dependent states to an almost purely academic one. Every party had learned from *Realpolitik* that the true status of any of China's peripheral areas depended on China's ability to exert effective control. It is this rude historical lesson that prompted the People's Republic of China to seize the earliest possible opportunities to rush its army into Sinkiang and Tibet.

Before summing up the Ch'ing territorial bequest, it should be pointed out that the extension of China's internal frontiers in Ch'ing times, if less spectacular than empire-building, is historically equally important. Although the history of the extension of China's internal frontiers is almost as old as Chinese history itself, it was from the Yung-cheng period (1723–1735) onwards that a more energetic policy of sinicization was directed against the various non-Han ethnic groups who constituted the majority in the hilly enclaves of Hunan, the highlands of Western Hupei, and a number of mountainous districts of Yunnan, Kweichow, Szechwan, and Kwangsi. The core of this policy was to replace the native tribal system with ordinary Chinese local administration. Between 1723 and 1912 this policy was applied also to parts of Kansu, Kokonor, Chinese Turkestan, and eastern Tibet, which was made into Sikang province between 1928 and 1949. It is worth mentioning that even the last few years of the

Manchu dynasty witnessed a recrudescence of this policy in Sikang. Without the extension and consolidation of the southwestern internal frontiers,
it is doubtful that the southwest could have served so well as China's last
territorial base of operation against Japan during the critical years from
1937 to 1945. Externally, as well as internally, therefore, the Ch'ing period
is of greatest importance to the formation of modern China as a geographic
entity.

A second important inheritance that modern China has received from
the Ch'ing is her large population. Prior to the Ch'ing the peak officially
registered population of China was 60,000,000, although there is reason
to believe that during certain earlier periods, such as latter halves of
Sung and Ming, the population may well have exceeded 100,000,000.
The basic fact remains, however, that a preindustrial population could
not as a rule grow at a sustained high rate unless the combined economic
and institutional factors were unusually favorable. As has been discussed
in my *Studies on the Population of China, 1368–1935,* such a combination of favorable economic and institutional factors did exist in the
century from the dawn of domestic peace and prosperity in 1683 to the
late Ch'ien-lung era when China's population had shot up to 300,000,000.
Even an increasingly unfavorable population-land ratio and deteriorating
economic conditions could not prevent the population from reaching
430,000,000 by 1850 through sheer momentum. While modern China
had unquestionably been plagued by overpopulation and mass poverty,
her present estimated population of 700,000,000, when ruthlessly regi-
mented by the most Spartan state in history, cannot fail to make its
impact felt. To understand the historical roots of this impact of numbers,
the Ch'ing period is again crucial.

Thirdly, the Ch'ing is without doubt the most successful dynasty of
conquest in Chinese history, and the key to its success was the adoption
by early Manchu rulers of a policy of systematic sinicization. The Ch'ing
period thus provides an excellent case study for the complex processes of
acculturation which in turn helps to sharpen our perception of the inherent strength of traditional Chinese institutions and culture. Space does
not allow a systematic explanation of the reasons why early Manchu
rulers had to adopt such a policy. Suffice it to say here that for a conquering ethnic group so vastly outnumbered by the Chinese, the most effective
long-range policy was to sponsor the very institutional and cultural system which the Chinese nation, especially the key social class of scholars
and officials, regarded as orthodox. The systematic sinicization of the
Hsiao-wen emperor of Northern Wei late in the fifth century and the
conversion to Catholicism of Henry IV of France in 1598 were dictated
by similar political necessities.

Systematic sinicization of the Manchu imperial clan, nobility, and officials may be evidenced by the following facts: the adoption from the beginning of the dynasty of the Ming government system *in toto,* which, with a few Manchu innovations, was improved and rationalized; the ardent endorsement by the K'ang-hsi emperor and his successors of the conservative and passive aspects of social and political relationships in later Sung Neo-Confucianism as official orthodoxy; the unprecedented homage that the Ch'ing emperors paid to Confucius (two kneelings and six prostrations in Peking and three kneelings and nine prostrations in Confucius' birthplace, Ch'ü-fu); the designing and maintaining of the strictest education for imperial princes in Chinese history based largely on orthodox Confucianism; the utilization of Confucian orthodoxy as a justification for abolishing the various layers of feudal relationships within the indigenous Manchu Eight Banner system; the large-scale printing and dissemination under imperial auspices of ancient classics and Neo-Con-fucian writings of the Ch'eng-Chu school and literary reference tools and anthologies which culminated in the compilation of the *Ssu-k'u ch'üan'shu;* and the increasing addiction to Chinese literature, calligraphy, painting, and entertainments.

It is true that such unusually able rulers as K'ang-hsi, Yung-cheng, and Ch'ien-lung did not fail to realize the importance of preserving certain Manchu traits and customs. But so effective was the crucible of Chinese culture that by the latter half of the eighteenth century the imperially exhorted Manchu nativism had boiled down to little more than a legal obligation on the part of imperial princes and Manchu examination candidates to practice horsemanship and archery and to study the Manchu language, although Manchu Shamanism seems to have survived till the end of the dynasty. There is definite evidence that even for imperial princes, Manchu had become a dead language by the beginning of the nineteenth century at the latest. Furthermore, there is ample evidence that interethnic marriage went on throughout the Ch'ing period, especially during the long reign of K'ang-hsi and toward the end of the dynasty. The fact that Manchu Bannermen suffered progressive impoverishment as a result of their prolonged mingling with the Chinese in both urban and rural areas is too well known to need any elaboration.

In fact, so sinicized were the Manchus that much of what we regard as the orthodox Confucian state and society is exemplified not by earlier Chinese dynasties, but the Ch'ing period. We need mention only that in its formative stage the Sung Confucian state is known for its remarkable diversity of thought and policy and for its absence of officially endorsed orthodoxy. In spite of the Ming founder's choice of the Ch'eng-Chu school as orthodoxy, none of his successors showed any real concern for ideology. Even as gifted a Ming ruler as Hsüan-tsung (1425–1435) sent an official and his family to prison upon the latter's remonstrance that certain erudite officials should be appointed to help the emperor to study the Sung scholar Chen Te-hsiu's *Ta-hsüeh yen-i* (Systematic Exposition of the Book of Great Learning). In contrast, from K'ang-hsi's majority to the end of Ch'ing the officials selected to serve as imperial tutors and as special lecturers on Confucian classics for the emperor in spring and autumn were all scholars of the Ch'eng-Chu school. For good or for evil, it was under the alien Manchu rule that China became a strictly conformist "orthodox" Confucian state. In no earlier period of Chinese history do we find a deeper permeation and wider acceptance of the norms, mores, and values which modern students regard as Confucian.

Despite its inevitable cost, the Manchu policy of systematic sinicization and Confucianization served dynastic interests extremely well. The Manchus ruled China for a period of 268 years, as compared to a mere 89 years of Mongol rule of all China. For all their shortcomings and repressive measures, the eras of K'ang-hsi, Yung-cheng and early Ch'ien-lung constituted one of the rare periods in Chinese history in which the majority of the nation enjoyed peace, prosperity, and contentment. When the supreme test came in 1851 with the outbreak of the Taiping rebellion, the majority of the Chinese nation, especially the key social class of scholars and officials, fought loyally for their Manchu masters because the so-called alien dynasty had been, in fact, more Confucian than previous Chinese dynasties.

Fourthly, despite the collapse of the old order by the end of the dynasty, the Ch'ing period on the whole must be regarded as one in which traditional political, economic, and social institutions attained greater maturity and the economy and society achieved a greater degree of interregional integration.

As to political institutions, the Ch'ing definitely benefited from the prolonged trial and error of such earlier periods as Sung and Ming. A comparison of the administrative law of various dynasties since the T'ang reveals that in matters such as jurisdictions of and the interrelations between various offices, the classification and transmission of documents, the procedures by which decisions were made and subsequently executed, and a wide range of regulations on appointment, discipline, etc., the Ch'ing system appears to have been more meticulous, regularized, and rational.

It is true that few if any social and economic institutions originated in Ch'ing times. As is well known, merchant and craft guilds can be traced back at least to the T'ang, the modern type of patrilineal clan to 1050, private academies and the system of community chests for examination candidates also to the Sung. Likewise, various nongovernment benevolent institutions ranging from orphanages and community cemeteries for the poor to fire-squads and life-saving boats had all originated in earlier periods. Whereas during earlier formative periods they may have been sporadic, inadequately supported, or of limited geographic distribution, by the Ch'ing period they reached fuller development and became more common.

An excellent example by which to illustrate the maturing of economic and social institutions and to indicate greater interregional economic and social integration is the multiplication in Ch'ing times of various types of voluntary associations based on common geographic origin, generally called *hui-kuan* (*Landsmannschaften*). As far as can be ascertained from extant records, the *hui-kuan* made its debut in Peking in the early fourteen twenties in the form of an exclusive club for *Landsmann* of Wuhu, Anhwei, who served as officials of the central government. From 1560 on, some regional merchant groups began to establish their *hui-kuan* in the nation's capital. By the late sixteenth and early seventeenth centuries, *hui-kuan* established by merchants and craftsmen of various geographic origins began to appear in major cities and a few prosperous towns of the lower Yangtze. During Ch'ing times, however, the city of Soochow, southern Kiangsu, boasted as many as 41 *hui-kuan* and many more guilds established by various *Landsmann* groups who came from virtually every part of China. In late Ch'ing there were nearly 400 *hui-kuan* in Peking alone which represented all the provinces and scores of prosperous prefectures and counties and which served mainly as hostelries for *Landsmann* candidates for the metropolitan examinations. From my recent book, *Chung-kuo hui-kuan shih-lun* (*An Historical Survey of Landsmannschaften in China*), it is shown that by late Ch'ing times, *hui-kuan*, whether open to all social statuses or only to members of *Landsmann* guilds, existed in all provincial capitals, major and minor coastal and inland ports, certain subcounty towns, and many obscure inland counties noted neither for their trade nor crafts. The highest density is found in Szechwan, where practically every county had at least a few *hui-kuan* established by immigrants from afar and some counties had as many as 40 or 50.

In Szechwan and elsewhere in major cities where detailed local history or new inscriptional data are available, we learn that various *Landsmann* groups tended to merge into what in modern terms may be called chambers of commerce, and to take part in matters concerning the welfare of the entire local community. Constant contacts between various *Landsmann* groups and natives often resulted in intermarriage and brought about social assimilation. Contrary to the impressions of various Western and Japanese scholars that the prevalence of *hui-kuan* in Ch'ing times reflected an unusually strong local particularism in China and hence has retarded the modernization of Chinese economy and society, the existence of thousands of *hui-kuan* in all parts of China and the coexistence of various *Landsmann* groups in the same major and minor cities could not but have facilitated interregional economic and social integration—a process which went on apace even during the late Ch'ing and early Republican period of political disintegration.

Fifthly, in material culture and the arts, the Ch'ing period may be regarded as one of leisurely fulfillment and enrichment. One basic reason for the remarkable advancement in material culture which in turn stimulated broader cultural growth was the rare century of prosperity and benevolent despotism following the dawning of *Pax Sinica* in 1683. The field of Ch'ing material culture is obviously too vast to enable us to make any tentative generalization. For the present purpose, we can only surmise from better-quality local histories that the division of labor in trades and crafts became increasingly minute and that the range, variety and volume of articles for mass and elite consumption became even greater. While the merchant princes of the lower Yangtze set new standards of conspicuous consumption, a rising standard of living was nevertheless enjoyed by substantial segments of the population.

This century of peace and prosperity witnessed, among many things, an unprecedented demand for and supply of books and the rise of great bibliophiles and art connoisseurs. Led by the imperial court which since K'ang-hsi's majority had begun to compile, edit, and print books and to collect art on a grand scale, the merchant princes of the lower Yangtze and many officials and well-to-do scholars followed suit. While the vogue of cultivating scholarly and artistic avocations by the elite was a national phenomenon, the lower Yangtze area remained throughout this century the center of Chinese cultural activities. It was largely the wealth, leisure, great libraries and art collections, and the over-all sophistication of the lower Yangtze area that provided opportunities for the rise of research scholarship as an end in itself; for the flowering of the wonderful school of expressionistic painters led by Shih-t'ao and the Yang-Chou masters, who, along with the hermit Pa-ta-shan-jen, inspired such modern giants as Chao Chih-ch'ien (1829–1884), Jen I, better known as Jen Po-nien (1840–1895), Wu Ch'ang-shih (1844–1927), and Ch'i Po-shih (1862–1957); for the maturing of various schools of opera, including the one which was later somewhat erroneously called Peking opera.

After the decline of lower Yangtze merchant princes by about 1800. cultural activities became geographically more evenly spread and reached a wider public. In terms of the range of cultural activities and of their degree of permeation, there is little reason to agree with the erstwhile influential view that the Ch'ing period was one of cultural and artistic stagnation.

Lastly, an attempt shall be made to point out certain basic factors which appear to me of primary significance in accounting for the decline and

fall of the maturest empire in Chinese history. To begin with, thanks
to the existence of unusually favorable economic and institutional factors
during the century of *Pax Sinica,* by the late eighteenth century the
population explosion had reached unprecedented proportions and created
a set of new economic problems with which China's existing fund of technological knowledge failed to cope. Second, for all its outward grandeur,
the era of Ch'ien-lung was one of widening discrepancy between law
and practice and of creeping peculation, which, judging from the three
installments of confidential Grand Council archives published in *Wen-
hsien ts'ung-pien,* may have become nation-wide and semi-institutionalized,
at least between 1776 and 1799. It was the widespread peculation from
the Ch'ien-lung era onwards that transformed the benevolent despotism
of K'ang-hsi and Yung-cheng into a malevolent despotism that had so
much to do with the outbreak of the White Lotus and subsequent rebellions. Third, the exigency of the Taiping wars forced the post-1850 Ch'ing
government to resort to the sale of office on a scale seldom paralleled in
Chinese history—a factor which was regarded by many a post-Taiping
statesman and official as the taproot of all administrative evils. Fourth,
during and after the Taiping rebellion there was a tendency toward increasing political decentralization caused by the growth of the powers
of the provincial authorities and by the increasing inability of the provincial authorities to exert effective control over the local officials. Fifth,
for the first time in her long history, China was brought into the mael-
strom of modern world politics by the West, whose culture was in many
ways her equal and in some crucial ways her superior. While prior to the
Opium War the working of some of these factors had contributed to the
weakening of the Manchu empire, it was the convergence and interplay of all these factors after 1840 that eventually brought about the
downfall of the Ch'ing dynasty and the disintegration of traditional
Chinese institutions and Confucian culture.

3

The Manchus, for all their efforts to retain their own identity (even as they created the Chinese dynasty, Ch'ing), relied on identification with China to keep themselves afloat. They had to stay Manchu enough to enjoy the conquest, but Chinese enough to make and sustain it. What they sustained, up to about a century ago, and what sustained them was a China "at the center of the world. . . . No one had moved the center away; the conquerors simply moved into it." Centrality was an essential part of the sense of Chinese identity.

FROM

The Persistence of Tradition in Chinese Foreign Policy

MARK MANCALL

BOTH the Communist and the Nationalist Chinese are heirs to a set of assumptions concerning the nature of the international order which do not readily conform to the traditional European assumptions based on equally sovereign nation-states. China's assumptions were evolved over a 2,000-year period on the basis of the realities of East Asia. "Sinitic civilization," to use Toynbee's term, developed to a remarkable extent separate from the civilizations of Europe and the Near and Middle East. East Asia was cut off from the other areas of civilization by vast oceans, high mountains, and seemingly endless deserts. Protected from the outside by barriers, Chinese civilization spread to, or strongly influenced, those areas that were geographically accessible to the continental civilization: Korea, Japan, the Ryukyus, and Southeast Asia. More often than not, these areas voluntarily sought the influence of China, rather than having it forced upon them. In this self-contained East Asian world, China was the only power. To live in her shadow meant to accept many of the material attributes of her civilization: the Chinese writing system; the Chinese language, at least for official purposes; the Chinese calendar; Chinese taste and art forms. China, whose age and size and power made her the recognized center of her distinctive world, gave conscious voice

Mark Mancall, "The Persistence of Tradition in Chinese Foreign Policy," *The Annals of the American Academy of Political and Social Science*, No. 349 (September 1963), pp. 16–22. Reprinted by permission of the editors. Footnotes omitted.

to her primacy. The civilized world was *t'ien-hsia,* "all under Heaven," and the ruler of this world was China's emperor, *t'ien-tzu,* "the son of Heaven." China termed herself *Chung-kuo,* "the Middle Kingdom," "the Central country."

China's image of her cultural and power centrality in East Asia found expression, both ideologically and institutionally, in the world order. Ideologically, this order was an extension of the Confucian hierarchic and inegalitarian social order of China herself. If China was civilized, the rest of the world lived in descending states of barbarism the farther away they were from China's political and cultural frontiers. The barbarians could become civilized by accommodating themselves to China. Accommodation meant the acceptance of various facets of China's culture and the political recognition of China's power. Institutionally, China's centrality found expression in the tribute system, which reached the level of classical development in the Ming (1368–1644) and Ch'ing (1644–1911) dynasties. The validity of this Sinocentric East Asian world order was proved, for both the Chinese and the barbarians, by the fact that even the non-Chinese nomads of Inner Asia and Manchuria, finding themselves in power in China for about half of the last two millennia, used the Chinese tradition in international relations.

Although it is not possible in the context of this article to detail the entire nature of the complex Confucian world view, it is possible to isolate certain separate but closely related traditional Chinese assumptions concerning the nature of the world order. These assumptions differ significantly from Western assumptions, yesterday and today. Traditionally, these assumptions were accepted by those who participated in the tribute system, to a greater or lesser degree depending on the extent to which the non-Chinese participants had absorbed Chinese culture. Thus, the Koreans consciously accepted and acted on these assumptions right down to the end of the nineteenth century, while the Dutch, outside of East Asia, paid lip service to them in the seventeenth century in order to obtain the benefits of trade with China. Britain, in the nineteenth century, refused to accept these assumptions as the basis for intercourse with China and insisted on free trade and free access to the Chinese market. War resulted.

TRADITIONAL CHINESE ASSUMPTIONS

The traditional Chinese conception of the world order may be summarized, in abbreviated and somewhat oversimplified form, within the framework of the following five assumptions:

(1) The traditional world order is hierarchical, not egalitarian. The concept of the legal equality or the sovereignty of the individual political units in the world order did not exist. All political units arranged themselves hierarchically. There was a central recognized authority. Tra-

ditionally, that central authority was China. China's authority was institutionalized in the tribute system. All forms of international intercourse, including political, cultural, and economic relations, took place within the framework of the tribute system. This system was valuable for both the tributary (tribute-payer) and the tribute-receiver. The presentation of tribute enabled the tributary to trade with China through the exchange of tribute for gifts at the court and through the legalization of controlled trade along the frontiers. Politically, the tributary often received validation for his political power in his own environment from the Chinese emperor, in the form of patents of office and investiture. This was a valuable technique for the establishment of legitimacy by local native rulers.

China, the tribute-receiver, also benefited from the system in a variety of ways. The surrounding tributary barbarians recognized that, to participate in the benefits of China's civilization, they had to recognize the existence of China's power and, consequently, the inviolability of China's frontiers. When, in the course of the dynastic cycle, China was weak, the system would break down. China, at the same time, was also able to trade with the barbarians for items necessary to her economy without admitting her dependence for these items on trade with the barbarians. For instance, the Central Asian nomads were "permitted" to present horses in tribute and to trade horses for Chinese products at frontier markets as a gracious boon granted by the emperor. China, needing horses for her armies, actually though not theoretically depended on the nomads for this important item. In this way, the myth of China's self-sufficiency was preserved. In 1793 the Ch'ien-lung emperor could issue an edict to the King of England in which he insisted that, among other things, ". . . The Celestial Empire, ruling all within the four seas, simply concentrates on carrying out the affairs of Government properly, and does not value rare and precious things . . . we have never valued ingenious articles, nor do we have the slightest need of your Country's manufactures."

(2) China's centrality in the world order was a function of her civilization and virtue, particularly the virtue of China's ruler. The world order was as much an ethical as a political phenomenon. Harmony on the international scene, as on the domestic, was the product of the emperor's virtue. If he committed unvirtuous acts, the rivers would flood, the mountains shake, the people revolt. By extension, the world order would crumble while the barbarians invaded China's frontier. The "Mandate of Heaven" extended to international society through China's primacy in the tribute system.

(3) The world hierarchy was universal. There were no other hierarchies and no other sources of power on the international scene. Because of the absence of alternative powers, no concept of the "balance

of power" ever developed. *All* units within the system were subservient to China, and those political units which were geographically too distant to participate simply lived in a kind of limbo or international political vacuum. In modern parlance, one might say that all states were satellites of China. Within the satellites, a great deal of "self-determination" existed, but opposition to China was considered rebellion against the established order and the valid tradition, to be dealt with accordingly.

(4) National power was the reflection of national virtue. Power was, therefore, by definition more "moral" than in the West, because it derived from the possession of virtue. Consequently, there was no conflict between "right" and "might." To the traditional Chinese political thinker, "might" never made "right"; on the contrary "right made might." Right and might were, in fact, synonymous in China. Hence, the use of might was justified by its very existence, because, without right, there would have been no might in the first place.

(5) International society was the extension of internal society. There were no "nation-states," and concepts such as "international" and "interstate" are inappropriate to describe the situation. Clear boundaries of jurisdiction and power simply did not exist. What boundaries there were were cultural. The Great Wall demarcated the boundary between China's sedentary agricultural bureaucratic Confucian society and the barbarians' nomadic steppe societies. It was never a political or even a jurisdictional boundary. Nor was the ocean a boundary, for Japan, Korea, the Ryukyus, and the Southeast Asian kingdoms came to China across the seas within the framework of the tribute system, and, therefore, China's power, despite her continental orientation, extended culturally and often politically to maritime nations as well.

OPERATIONAL TECHNIQUES

In fact, the principle of hierarchy, which was operative in almost all Asian societies internally, governed relations even among states in situations where China was not a factor. Korea, for instance, often conducted its relations with Japan on a tribute pattern. Ladakh presented tribute to Tibet, and Cambodia might present tribute to a stronger Thailand. The Nguyen rulers of Vietnam might call themselves "emperors" at home, but, in communicating with China, they called themselves "kings," a clear example of the extension of hierarchy.

Furthermore, just as factionalism was condemned at home, so was it condemned abroad as well. Inside China, society was, theoretically, unitary. There was no official recognition of the distinction between state and party, either at court or in the bureaucracy. Where combinations might develop among the barbarians to challenge China's power primacy, it was conscious Chinese policy to "use the barbarians against the barbarians." For instance, a constant theme in Chinese foreign policy from

1858 on has been the use of Russia against the rest of the West, whether it meant the use of British fears of Russian penetration into Asia in the second half of the nineteenth century to obtain British co-operation in the maintenance of the Manchu dynasty in power or the use of the Soviet Union's nuclear umbrella to shield China from "American imperialism" in the middle of the twentieth century.

Traditionally, in other words, political techniques developed for control inside China could be used externally as well. Developments in the mid-nineteenth century provide a good example. The Manchu dynasty was weak in the face of a rising tide of rebellion which swept over South and Central China. It lacked sufficient military power internally to suppress the rebellion on its own. Consequently, relying on orthodox Confucian loyalties, it was able, as the symbol of Confucian orthodoxy and stability, to win or keep the loyalty of such Chinese leaders as Tseng Kuo-fan and Tso Tsung-t'ang who, though clearly recognizing that the Manchus were outlanders, nevertheless wholeheartedly supported the dynasty as the only alternative to chaos and an unknown future. Chaos and instability were anathema to the imperial Confucianists, and order and stability were highly prized conditions. In the same way, the Manchus were able to convince the British and other Westerners that the dynasty's continued power was the only hope for a stable China which would be open to commercial penetration. Thus, at several points, when the West could easily have toppled the dynasty, it hesitated to do so for fear that the consequent instability would damage commerce. In 1860, when the British and French occupied Peking, they carefully refrained from overthrowing the Manchu throne. In 1900, when the Allied army occupied Peking in the wake of the Boxer affair, the West carefully maintained the fiction that what had actually been a war between China and the West had only been a rebellion by the Boxers against the dynasty, which the West had helped to subdue. Without this fiction, the Western powers would, by the logic of their own arguments, have been forced to inflict a disastrous defeat on the dynasty, which would have resulted in its overthrow. In this fashion, China's rulers have often been able to maintain their positions at moments of weakness as well as at moments of strength, both internally and internationally.

Consequently, external stability—like internal stability—was not dependent on a balance of power between rival forces or competing nation-states. At moments of strength, the dynasty could maintain international stability by virtue of its ability to wield great physical and economic power. At moments of weakness, the dynasty could still command the Confucian loyalties of its cultural satellites and could use such techniques as "divide and rule" to maintain its position and the world hierarchy.

Chinese external policy was obviously based on China's assumptions concerning the world order. In other words, its primary objective, its axiomatic policy was the maintenance of the only conceivable order, the world hierarchy. There were no other primary values to conflict with this, no moral inhibitions to prevent the development of calculated policies, in Professor May's definition. Nor was there any conflict concerning the means to be used to obtain the primary policy objective. Disagreement might take place, as it often did, over the efficiency of one calculated policy or another. But the only inhibition placed on the development of a wide range of diplomatic—and military—weapons was physical. Consequently, China's policy-makers had a remarkable degree of flexibility in the formulation of immediate policies. China could go to great lengths to maintain her centrality, even to the extent of recognizing the superiority of a barbarian dynasty or ruler, such as the Manchus. In the end, of course, whether or not the barbarian was "Sinicized," he had to rule China, and the East Asian world order, on the basis of China's traditional hierarchical assumptions. It was simply inconceivable for anyone to challenge the superiority of China's ruler, whether that ruler was Chinese or barbarian.

The Sinitic world system faced its greatest challenge with the arrival in East Asia of Western powers who did not accept the assumptions on which the system itself was based. In the face of the Russians, who arrived in East Asia in the middle of the seventeenth century and immediately posed a challenge to the system, the Confucian world order demonstrated a remarkable resilience and capacity for compromise. The vigorous and capable K'ang-hsi emperor of the Manchu dynasty clearly recognized that the Russians had to be dealt with in such a way that the assumptions of the traditional order itself were not challenged. Consequently, a unique system of political and commercial institutions was developed for communications between the Manchu and Russian empires, consciously avoiding questioning basic assumptions. For instance, communications between Petersburg and Peking took place between court officials of secondary or tertiary rank, thus bypassing the issue of the czar's having to address the emperor as a superior. Russian trade caravans to Peking, though consciously recognized by both sides as strictly commercial enterprises devoid of politico-cultural content, could be entered in official Manchu court records as tribute caravans, if necessary. Gifts to court officials, which normally accompanied trade anyway, could be considered tribute even though the Russian caravan masters and merchants were never required to perform the tribute ceremonial of the kowtow. The kowtow was necessary for admission to the emperor's presence on formal court occasions, but a merchant did not necessarily have access to the emperor. This system worked remarkably well from 1728 to about 1858. The Manchu emperors could rest secure in the thought that the hierarchical world order remained unchallenged by the Russians, while the Russians were content with the thought that they had obtained their objective, trade, without having to participate directly in the onerous tribute system. The Manchus could accept the compromise out of fear, reasonable or not, of Russian power to disturb the stability of Central Asia, an area of prime importance to all dynasties in China.

THE CLASH OF SYSTEMS

The great and unresolved challenge to the system came from the Western maritime powers. Although at an earlier date, the Dutch were prepared to be enrolled in the tribute system to gain material advantages, the English, by the middle of the nineteenth century, were not. English pride and theories of international practice prevented any compromise. Profit and progress, commerce and civilization, were part of a European syndrome of self-confident capitalism in the middle of the nineteenth century. When the Canton system failed to satisfy the commercial hopes of the Manchester magnates, London demanded free and uncontrolled access to the Chinese market and the establishment of permanent British representatives at Peking to defend British interests, on the model of European diplomatic practice. Although opium was the immediate cause of the Opium War, it was in a more profound sense the conflict of two diametrically opposed concepts of the world system—East Asian hierarchy as opposed to European egalitarianism—which resulted in the first serious armed clashes between China and the West.

After 1842 China, now internally weak and externally facing enemies from Europe and America who did not accept the validity of the assumptions on which the East Asian world order rested, saw the breakdown of her traditional system. Former tributary states became European colonies. Foreign representatives were established in Peking on an equal footing with Chinese officials. European diplomatic institutions had to be adopted, and European international law was studied and used to combat the West. In short, European imperialism, which forced China to recognize the existence of an alternative international power that was, in fact, materially more powerful than China, broke down the autonomous Sinitic world order. By 1949 China possessed a complete set of Western diplomatic institutions.

The breakdown of the institutions of the traditional world system after 1842 took place far faster than did the erosion of the assumptions on which the Confucian internal and external social order was based. For instance, during the decades of the "self-strengthening" movement which followed China's humiliation between 1842 and 1860, Western arms were adopted and Western diplomatic institutions were adapted for China's use. Ambassadors were sent abroad, a prototype of a foreign office—the *Tsung-li yamen*—was established in Peking, and textbooks on Western international law and other subjects were translated into Chinese. But, significantly, all this activity in studying and adopting Western material and diplomatic techniques was justified on the basis of utility: it was all a means of defending China and of preserving Chinese civilization from the West. Furthermore, at the same time that China was forced to deal with the West on the West's terms, Korea remained anchored to China through the traditional tribute system, a fact which created no little confusion and dismay in Western chancelleries. . . .

4   *If "centrality was an essential part of the sense of Chinese identity," pressure against the center was a recurring phenomenon in Chinese history. When it occurred in the late nineteenth century, during and after the trauma of the Taiping Rebellion, it reflected the ruin of the Confucian empire that had exemplified and perpetuated the ethnocentric identity. Not only did it reflect the ruin, it helped to effect it.*

Regionalism in Nineteenth-Century China

FRANZ MICHAEL

R EGIONALISM has been one of the most important phenomena in Chinese imperial history. By "regionalism" is meant the emergence in key areas of China of military and political power centers that assumed some of the important functions of the state but still remained within its framework. The emergence of such regional power centers occurred in periods of crisis, when the authority of the dynasty's central government had been weakened and the dynasty's political decline invited the establishment of such regional governmental machines.

The nineteenth century was a time of such internal crisis: the Ch'ing dynasty, weakened by the decline of its administrative and military organization, was shaken by a number of large rebellions that threatened the survival of the dynasty. During this period of chaos and rebellion, regional armies were formed by outstanding gentry leaders—men like Tseng Kuo-fan, who established the pattern followed by others and who became the mentor and senior colleague of Li Hung-chang, one of the leading figures in the China of his time. These regional leaders organized their own military forces in their home regions, combined this locally-based military power with political organizations loyal to them, and drew their financial support from the regions they occupied. These regional organizations provided their leaders with bases of autonomous power.

Yet they did not challenge the final authority of the dynasty itself.

Franz Michael, "Regionalism in Nineteenth-Century China," introduction to Stanley Spector, *Li Hung-chang and the Huai Army* (University of Washington Press: Seattle, 1964), pp. xxi–xliii. Reprinted by permission of the publishers. Footnotes omitted.

The powers they exercised were indeed invasions into the central field of authority which a strong dynastic government would never permit, but the incapacity of the weakened Ch'ing government to carry out successfully its administrative and military responsibilities left a power void, which was then filled by these regional leaders. In assuming military, administrative, and financial authority, the regionalists still recognized the ideological authority of the dynastic center of the state based on the mandate of heaven. And for that reason their assumption of authority and their organization of regional bureaucratic machines remained within the framework of the dynastic state, even while undermining its authority and contributing to its eventual downfall.

What made possible the emergence of such regional organizations and what determined their nature? The answer lies in the bureaucratic nature of Chinese society; the relation between the Chinese society and state; the character of the educated elite, the gentry, and its functions in society and state; and in the central government's problem of maintaining control over its own local administration and preserving an appropriate balance between the power of the state and the autonomy of the sphere of the Confucian social order. Indeed, an examination of the phenomenon of regionalism, which emerged when the whole imperial system was out of balance, provides a clearer view of the complex system of balances and tensions that was maintained when the Confucian society and state were functioning successfully.

THE DUAL ROLE OF THE GENTRY

The emergence of regional organizations that cut into the power of the dynastic government was made possible by the dual role played by the educated elite of imperial China, the gentry, which provided the social leadership that managed the affairs of Chinese society and also formed the stratum from which the government selected its official staff and on which it had therefore to depend.

Whenever the central authority declined, regional political organizations could be formed and assume some functions of government because the stratum of educated elite from which the state staffed its organization remained intact; the members of this educated elite continued to act as social functionaries and were always ready to lead or to transfer their service to the newly emerging political organizations. It was the gentry's role in state and society that formed the link between social continuity and political reorganization.

The gentry's role in imperial society and state was based on their acknowledged superiority in the knowledge of the rules of human conduct and management of human affairs accepted in this society. Their authority was based on their education—an education through which they gained not only the skills needed for the management of people and affairs, skill in the writing of the official language, knowledge of the history and practice of government, and proficiency in the handling of affairs within the existing social order, but, most of all, an inculcation in the ethical precepts of Confucianism, which were the heart of the Chinese cultural tradition. The Confucian order, of which the gentry were the guardians and representatives, assigned to them functions of arbiter and of organizer, which they were assumed to carry out by applying in practice the ethical tenets of the Confucian teachings that made up the principles of operation of both the society and state. Through their knowledge of the accepted rules of human conduct, this educated elite had become a professional group that provided the managers of affairs indispensable for the functioning of the Confucian order. Their qualifications were individually gained through education in the Confucian classics, and recognized and guaranteed by the dynastic government through the examination system.

The relationship between the dynastic governments and the educated stratum, the Confucian gentry, originated in early imperial time when the Han rulers made their peace with the Confucian scholars and accepted their services for the state. In doing this the dynasty recognized the Confucian interpretation of the social order and gained at the same time the sanction for its government that Confucianism provided. In Sung time this relationship between the educated elite and the state became formalized through the full development of the examination system, which gave the state's confirmation of the gentry's academic qualification as the necessary prerequisite for official service. By Ch'ing time this system had reached further sophistication, and the gentry's leading position and privileges were entirely based on the academic degrees that verified the gentry's qualification. The qualification thus ascertained gave the gentry not only a monopoly of state service but also the state's assent to their autonomous role as public functionaries in society.

The government's acceptance of the gentry's role as public functionaries in society was a major factor that worked for the stability of the Chinese system. Chinese imperial history is famous for the length of its unbroken tradition of over 2,000 years. However, it was the social institutional tradition and its intellectual basis rather than the political order that provided the continuity of Chinese imperial history. The instability of the dynastic history with its cyclical crises and new beginnings stands in marked contrast to the relative stability of the social institutional order in imperial times. The survival of the Chinese tradition therefore depended on the strength of its social order.

The importance of the social order in the continuity of Chinese history was all the greater because the area of the activity of the dynastic state was far more limited than is usually recognized. The dynastic government concerned itself in the main with what it regarded as the decisive spheres of political authority—the areas of supreme importance for power and control. Military force was in principle a government prerogative; the people were forbidden by law to carry arms, and only the emperor's officers and officials had the right to lead troops. The dynastic government reserved to itself the right to impose and collect taxes, and the government had the monopoly of appointment of civil and military officials, who were solely responsible to the head of the government, the emperor. The government had also the lawmaking power, though its code was a criminal code only and therefore limited in its sphere of application. It was meant to support the Confucian moral code, which was basic for all human relations. These were the major areas in which the government tried to maintain a monopoly, and although in other spheres officials might become active, there was no attempt to monopolize; and much of the official activity shaded over and was connected with the autonomous power of the local leadership of the gentry.

The limited scope of state functions can also be readily deduced from the small size of the government's official staff. During Ch'ing time there were only some 40,000 civil and military officials—most of whom were in the capital—to manage, with the help of their secretaries and underlings, all those affairs that the government reserved for itself or tried to handle. This small number of officials is in sharp contrast to the large size of the whole group of degree-holding gentry, from which this staff was selected. In Ch'ing time some 1,000,000 to 1,500,000 gentry provided the social leadership that could carry on the affairs that the government did not handle.

The large majority of the gentry thus never became officials but carried on in their home districts and provinces a great variety of functions on which the well-being of society and the safety of the government depended. The services the gentry were expected to render ranged from arbitration, welfare activities, and the management or co-management of the vital public works to the education of the future gentry generation and the maintenance of the Confucian system itself. In the services they rendered, the gentry acted on their own and not under the orders of the government or under the discipline of the administrative organization. Their responsibility was not—like that of the officials—toward the emperor. To them, their education had given them an obligation to serve society, to "carry the burden of the world on their shoulders," and while their responsibility included a loyalty to the Confucian state as well as to the society, this loyalty was not necessarily focused on the ruling house if it had lost its "mandate."

Though not under government authority, the gentry services were, however, linked to the political divisions of the state. The members of the gentry carried on their functions within the jurisdictional areas of their home districts and provinces. The area of their gentry services was not that of any landed property of their own. The gentry's social responsibility was that of a professional group whose position and power depended on the certification of educational qualification by state examination degrees. These degrees were allocated to the districts and provinces —the political areas in which the gentry played a functional role. The social autonomy of the gentry was therefore placed in the framework of the political divisions of the state, a system that enhanced the importance of the gentry's role of social leadership and facilitated its transition to a role of political authority within the state structure.

Within these areas, the gentry handled a vast number of widely divergent responsibilities. They acted as arbitrators in local conflicts between individuals, families, villages, and even districts and provinces. They had to care for the poor and weak; they organized the rice kitchens and the charity granaries, and collected and administered the funds used to alleviate the difficulties of the poorest elements of the population. They organized and managed local public works: the building of roads, bridges, dikes for flood protection, and irrigation and drainage canals so vital for the agricultural economy. The arbitration, the charity, the public works could be small matters or very large ones. The large ones were of obvious importance, and the small ones were not isolated activities that occurred occasionally, but were a systematic handling of all the many problems that concerned the people of the area. Taken together the activities of the gentry determined the well-being and the peace and order of their areas.

For the society as a whole the gentry were thus a group of social functionaries who were professional managers who handled judicial, economic, welfare, and a host of other problems. The gentry were qualified for such work through their Confucian education, which gave them the knowledge of the moral code which was the operating system of regulations for the management of human affairs in the Confucian society. This code provided them with uniform standards for decisions in their large area of management of affairs in what had become a bureaucratic society.

STATE AND SOCIETY

The work of the officials in government and the activities of the gentry in society were, however, not sharply delineated and kept apart. In the important area of public works, for instance, there was a close link between official and gentry management and responsibilities. While smaller works were often undertaken by the gentry themselves, with or without formal official approval and participation, the larger works were initiated and frequently directed and financed by the government, but with the help of the gentry. Even when the officials took a most active part in organizing public works, they depended on the gentry for cooperation in bringing in the local population and frequently providing funds from the area concerned. For the Ch'ing period, it may be safe to say that practically all the public works undertaken were done with gentry participation, if not by the gentry on their own. This cooperation between government and gentry could be observed in many other fields. No local official could manage his district without the practical cooperation of the local gentry.

Since the gentry already managed important public functions in the districts and in the provinces, their responsibilities could be expanded if need and opportunity arose. Even those services which were in time of strong government a monopoly of the administration could be taken over by this local leadership if the government's internal decay and corruption paralyzed official action or made it ineffective. The power that slipped from the hands of the official administrators could be taken up by the local leaders, who, backed by local military force, could rebuild from local and regional roots the political organization and power which the government was not able to retain. For the gentry maintained, in times of such crisis, its status, prestige, and monopoly of training, which enabled some of its leading members to move up from their social base and assume a new official role in the newly formed regional governmental organizations. The very existence of this large educated elite of the gentry and its autonomous role of managing the vast areas of public affairs was therefore not only the basis of the survival of the traditional order in times of crisis but also a potential threat to the central government's control of the state administrative system and therefore an element of constant concern to the dynasty.

One may indeed wonder about this role of the gentry. Why had, even at the end of the imperial time, the Ch'ing dynasty, as highly sophisticated in its administrative system and methods as it was, limited its official staff and its administrative activities to the most essential aspects of government? Why did it rely so heavily on the gentry to manage local affairs under their own initiative? The Ch'ing government certainly had the power to prevent any real local autonomy of the common people and had initiated subadministrative systems of control, such as the *pao-chia* and *li-chia*, which were meant to prevent any such local autonomy. Why did the government not manage all public affairs through appointed officials or subofficials under its direct control? Why did it leave so much leeway, privilege, and responsibility to the gentry? The answer, we hold, lay essentially in the ideological authority of the gentry, which no emperor could take away from them.

Their Confucian learning gave the gentry not only the knowledge of the accepted code of human relations necessary for their professional activities but also the authority to interpret these rules in a society whose order was based on the Confucian tenets. The Confucian principles were based on an interpretation of the social order which, by its very nature, limited the jurisdictional activity of the state and left a large sphere of human relations to the working of a moral code in society which was to be applied by those who were believed to be versed in it. This whole tradition remained in the hands of the gentry, whose services to the state depended on the dynasty's acceptance of the Confucian system as a whole. The gentry themselves carried on and transmitted the Confucian traditions in their role as teachers outside state control. Any attempt to limit or undermine their functions as teachers and leaders of society would have touched at the hearts of the Confucian system.

This position gave the ruling stratum a special status in relation to the head of the government, the emperor, the holder of the heavenly mandate, who was in theory all powerful but who depended on the gentry to carry out his will. His problem was to maintain a central control over a bureaucracy which was only in part in his government administration and which, outside it, carried on the education in, and propagation of, a system of ethical values, beliefs, and ideas which remained outside imperial control and was believed to be a part of an absolute truth, to be accepted by the emperor as much as by its guardians, the educated elite, and by all the people who believed in it.

The dynastic government could only attempt to relate this intellectual sphere to its own system of authority. To do this, the government established its system of examinations through which the results of Confucian education were given formal recognition. This system of examinations not only gave government approval to the educated but in practice also enabled the government to have a say in the selection of the social leadership. During the Ch'ing dynasty, only those who had gained an examination degree were formally recognized as members of the privileged educated group. By setting quotas for the examinations, the government succeeded in limiting the gentry and in gaining some control over admission to this group.

The interests of the government and of the gentry largely coincided, but they could be at variance; and it was the government's concern to prevent this ruling stratum from organizing an opposition and becoming dangerous, as it was the gentry's concern to maintain its prerogatives and defend community and group interests against overbearing central power. Conflicts between the interests of the central government and the gentry, if kept within bounds, could provide a useful check on abuses by either side, but they could also lead to a stifling conformity or a breakdown of government.

THE CH'ING POLICY OF CONTROL AS A SELF-DEFEATING SYSTEM

There was no clear line of authority between the functions of officials and those of the gentry, and the official who represented the interests of the government of the state was at the same time a member of the gentry in his home area. The danger that the central government sought to avoid was an invasion of state power and assumption of official authority by members of the gentry and, most of all, a joining of forces between local officials and gentry in the establishment of centers of local bureaucratic power which the central government could no longer control. To prevent this threat, the imperial governments of successive dynasties devised a number of measures to divide and check the authority of the officials of their administration and to supervise and control the gentry. The measures became more sophisticated in time and reached a high degree of development under the Ch'ing dynasty. But then, as earlier, they did not prevent the eventual disintegration of central control, and in fact may have contributed to dynastic decline.

To check the power of the gentry and the bureaucracy, the Ch'ing dynasty, like earlier imperial governments, widely applied the system of playing one group against another and one official against another. An alien dynasty could rely on its own group as a special source of power, and the Manchus are a most revealing example of the way in which a foreign group could build its own authority into the Chinese administrative system.

More important still may have been the checks established within the officialdom itself. In Ch'ing times, one can discern two distinct types of official careers: service in the central government and in local and regional administrations. The inner corps of officials at the court and in the central government offices can be differentiated from the men who made their careers in the districts, prefectures, and provinces. The offices of the provincial and local administrators themselves were divided in a system in which no one had full authority and each official could be used to check another. The division and overlapping of authority among officials at the provincial level was obviously a major security measure. The governors, the financial commissioners, the judicial commissioners, the salt intendants, the educational commissioners, and the provincial commanders-in-chief of Ch'ing time were all responsible to higher central authority, but there was no clear definition of their respective spheres of function. They were dependent on cooperation, and yet were rivals. They were appointed by the central government, on which their career depended. In some cases they were to report on each other, and none of them, not even the governor-general, was in full control within a geographical area of jurisdiction. None was therefore able to organize his bureaucratic organization against the government, but also none was able to act quickly and show initiative to solve an urgent problem or to introduce new measures and changes for general improvement.

In the central government there was an equal lack of authority for any given position. Everything indeed depended on the emperor. It was a system which placed all premium on security and none on initiative. To prevent a link between officials and gentry, no official was permitted to serve in his home district or province, and each term of office was too short to allow for acquaintance and connection with the local social leadership. This measure was meant to keep gentry and officials apart but worked to the disadvantage of efficient government.

The main means for preserving the power of the imperial government, however, was the monopoly (or near monopoly) maintained in the three decisive areas of authority: appointment of officials, control of taxation, and control of the army. A strong imperial government would have full authority in these fields. Corrosion of government control in these areas was a sign of dynastic decline.

The Ch'ing government's loss of control resulted from a growing ineffectiveness of the whole bureaucratic machine, as had occurred before in the dynastic cycles. Such decline has been ascribed to corruption, so often mentioned in Chinese sources; and this factor, in the view of most historians, has been the main cause of the downfall of Chinese dynasties. But corruption itself is a phenomenon caused by some deeper factors; it is not an explanation in itself. Some corruption may exist in almost all government systems and existed probably in China at almost all times. It is only when corruption reaches such a degree that the whole administrative organization becomes ineffective that it leads to the breakdown of government. Why did this occur ever again in Chinese history and when was the crisis point reached? The answer may be that the system of control itself caused its own decline. The system of checks, division of authority, and the use of terror, at times against individuals and families, at others against whole groups to prevent independence or autonomy, was, in a sense, self-defeating. It discouraged all initiative, all resourceful action, and stifled the administrative machine to such a degree that only routine measures could be carried out and officials could not easily deal with emergencies. It handicapped all energetic, ambitious, and enterprising members of the whole administrative organization. There was little leeway for new ventures, and the only way to get ahead was by getting a greater share of the existing government revenue. To move up or even to hold their own, officials had to build up their connections and secure their positions and actions against the bad will and denunciations of competitors or rivals. The system itself therefore made necessary a regulated giving of gifts and contributions in an atmosphere of intrigue and influence-peddling which no one could escape. The very safety measures of the system led to its undoing.

The last resort of government authority was the army. Military victory was the basis for the establishment of new dynasties. A centrally controlled military force was the guarantee of their continuation in power. But the army was a part of the administrative organization, and it too was prone to corruption. When the officers pocketed the pay of their soldiers and the ranks were depleted by desertion, the central army became useless as a fighting force and even an additional cause of unrest.

THE CH'ING MILITARY AND ITS DECLINE

As a conquest dynasty, the Manchus started their rule with a mixture of military forces—their own banner troops and a Chinese professional army, the *lü-ying*. In the organization of these forces the stress on central control and security was brought to an extreme.

Already in Manchuria when the banner forces were established, they were organized in such a way that no military commander could have full authority. The banners were administrative as well as military units; each banner had its agricultural land assigned to it, but the land consisted of scattered plots intermingled with land belonging to other banners, so that no territorial unit was created. Each banner had a bureaucratic administration handled by an appointed staff. The commanders for military campaigns were appointed for each occasion, and each force was made up of small units from different banners.

After the conquest of China the banner troops became a special imperial guard, a sort of security force, garrisoned at the capital and in a few key strategic locations around the country; a part of the banners remained in Manchuria. Each garrison was made up of a mixture of units from different banners, served by their respective banner administrations. Even the Manchus' own security force was thus held down by administrative safeguards that could not but hamper its military effectiveness.

The *lü-ying* were scattered around the country in smaller garrisons, none large enough to resist the concentrated force of the nearest Manchu garrison. The *lü-ying* soldiers were professionals, dependent on their pay and usually natives of the region of their garrison. Their officers were members of the official bureaucracy, appointed to their positions and not permitted to serve in their home districts or provinces; they were rotated at frequent intervals and were dependent for their careers on the central government. No central command over the *lü-ying* forces existed; the emperor alone remained the supreme military authority. Brigade generals and provincial commanders-in-chief had command over several garrisons, but their power was limited by an intricate system of checks and balances.

Some units were under the command of governors and governors-general, and there was no clear division of authority or chain of command between the governors-general, governors, commanders-in-chief, and brigade generals. Even lower administrators had command over military forces for the defense of their administrative areas. The administration of the *lü-ying* was in the hands of the Ministry of Defense, one of the six administrative agencies.

Whenever a campaign was to be undertaken, the commander-in-chief had to be specially appointed, and his force was to be made up of a mixture of banner and *lü-ying* troops drawn from several garrisons. It can readily be seen how clumsy the administration and deployment of these military forces became, and how inevitably they would share the ills of the whole administrative organization.

The decline of the banners and *lü-ying* forces was already apparent in the eighteenth century and had become most serious by the middle of the nineteenth century. The banners were the first to deteriorate. Their forces labored under special handicap. The banner soldiers were prohibited from leaving their units to become farmers or to follow any other profession. They were to remain a privileged, salaried group, isolated from the general Chinese life. The pay of the garrisons was set at the beginning of the dynasty and remained the same. When the banner families increased, there were no additional funds to add a corresponding number of positions to the ranks, and the pay became insufficient. The pay had been fixed in relation to the prices of the middle of the seventeenth century, prices which had gone up four to ten times during the eighteenth and nineteenth centuries. What had been a comfortable salary in the beginning became an insufficient dole for a force whose morale was broken by lack of training and long years of inactivity. On several occasions a special sum was given by the emperor for distribution to the banner garrisons to alleviate their economic hardships. But when this money was spent—and it was spent rather quickly—nothing had changed. The Manchus had the choice either of permitting the banner population to enter professions and to merge with the Chinese population or of continuing to keep them as a group apart in a sort of privileged decay. They chose the latter course and hoped that in this way they would retain the loyalty of a group that had no way out. And indeed from the period of the Taiping Rebellion down to the Chinese Revolution of 1911, the Manchu garrisons, though no longer a serious military factor, remained loyal. Whole garrisons were wiped out, and, as the reports put it, "died loyally."

The decline of the *lü-ying* forces started somewhat later and was brought about by slightly different causes. Though individual examples of evil practices are described as early as the seventeenth century, the *lü-ying* retained their fighting value until the end of the eighteenth century and still played the major part in the campaigns under Ch'ien-lung. With the turn of the nineteenth century, however, the *lü-ying* shared in the general decline of the administration. Comments in many sources began to indicate the prevailing corruption and malpractice. The officers quite generally followed the practice of pocketing the pay of the soldiers, and those who were not handling such funds were bribed into complicity by large gifts. Indeed, the embezzlement of pay by the officers was a very close parallel to the embezzlement of tax money by the local administrators, except that one was taken on the way from the source to the government, the other on the way from the government to the recipient. Since the soldiers did not receive enough to live on, there were large-scale desertions from the forces. The actual strength of the units at the beginning of the nineteenth century has been estimated at one-half to one-sixth of the nominal units recorded on the books. These desertions were not hindered by the officers, who continued to pocket the money of soldiers no longer present. Those that remained in the garrisons had to look for other income, which they found as peddlers, small-scale traders, or as thieves and robbers. The soldiers' main compensation in lean times came during campaigns, when they looted and ravaged the areas in which they were supposed to fight. Since campaigns also meant that the officers would receive government funds for supplies, they became profitable economic enterprises for officers and men, and were drawn out as long as feasible at the expense of the government. Officers and headquarters got rich, and military appointments were highly valued and paid for.

In the famous corruption case of Ho Shen, who had become fabulously rich as the leading official under Ch'ien-lung, a major accusation was the corruption of the military organization which he had fostered and from which he had profited. The seriousness of the decline of this aspect of government was fully realized by the court, but little effective action could be taken. At several times an attempt was made to reduce the size of the *lü-ying* army and use the funds saved for better pay. Since the actual size of units was so much smaller than the nominal number of soldiers, such reduction would have cut into the amount of graft of the officers and administrators. These imperial orders were sabotaged in the military organization, and in the first half of the nineteenth century most of the *lü-ying* army became worse than useless.

With the weakening of the army the Chinese government lost its ability to maintain order and prevent the unrest that resulted from the discontent with maladministration. The decline of the imperial government's administration and its military force invited an extension of authority by nonofficial local leaders. The power abdicated by the imperial government was taken over by local officials and gentry, and the second phase of the cycle began with the build-up of local power.

Of the three elements that were the keys to power in the battle between central and local power—administrative appointment, taxation, and control of the army—the last was the decisive factor in such times of crisis and change. The establishment of a bureaucratic administration and a system of taxation was made possible by military control. Even early in its rule, the Ch'ing government accepted the forces of local leaders into its service as auxiliaries when rebellions occurred. As long as the regular central armies of the banners and the *lü-ying* were strong and reliable, these local organizations were no threat to central control, and their leaders could be either eliminated or paid off with rank and position in the administration. Whenever possible, such local forces were incorporated into the *lü-ying* army after the emergencies or local disturbances were over. The rest were officially "disbanded," a procedure that took them off the official records but did not necessarily remove them as political and military factors from the districts where they had been organized. With the decline of the administration and armies it was, however, no longer possible for the government to eliminate or incorporate local forces. The retreat of government activity increased the gentry's responsibility in local defense. Their local military activities were sometimes undertaken with the knowledge and approval of officials, but sometimes without such approval or even in open opposition to the officials, as for example, in defense of an area against high taxation or in resistance against government measures or government favoritism in the conflict between different communities. In the official reports there is an increase of examples of so-called "bad gentry," gentry leaders who for one reason or another led forces in opposition to the government.

Military organizational and command ability did not, however, require the administrative qualifications of the gentry. Local upstarts, so-called bullies, and "bandit leaders," could use the time of political chaos and popular despair and discontent to organize a military force and establish their own local authority. Local leadership was frequently provided by the heads of secret societies, which existed at all times during the last centuries of imperial history but grew more important during periods of political chaos and discontent, when they could become the organizational framework of military uprisings.

In reporting the development of local military organizations of the time, the officials judged the forces according to their relationship to the government. If they were approved of, they were counted as government forces; if not, they were "bad gentry," "bandits," or "rebels" according to the size and political purpose of the force. The actual story was much more complex, and the line between "good" and "bad" gentry, or between "bandit" and officially recognized local corps was rather fluid. A military leader could change sides two or three times, as for example Miao P'ei-lin, one of the best known military organizers in Anhwei province during the time of the Taiping and Nien rebellions. Much of the fighting was carried out on a local level, and the officials often remained neutral as long as possible. When they sided with one of the contestants, the other automatically became a bandit. In the official terminology the accepted military organizations were approved *t'uan-lien,* local corps; those in opposition were *fei,* or bandits. Sometimes there was even a distinction drawn between "good" and "bad" *t'uan,* just as a distinction was drawn between "good" and "bad" gentry.

Toward the middle of the nineteenth century, the conditions created by the decline of government and local unrest had reached crisis proportions. These were the conditions that could be exploited by ambitious leaders to organize the discontented and armed local people for a general uprising in rebellion against the government. The rebellions of that time, the Taiping, the Nien, and the Moslem rebellions, all originated from small-scale warfare among armed groups and from local battles, in which the government took sides only when a local disturbance became serious enough to pose a threat against its own authority.

The rank and file of these rebel forces were mostly peasants; for that reason these, like earlier rebellions in Chinese history, have sometimes been characterized as "peasant rebellions." True, peasants made up the manpower of the rebel armies—discontented peasants who had left their fields because conditions had become intolerable—but these were not peasants joining rebel armies to fight for peasants' rights. Becoming a soldier was a way out of misery and an opportunity for better things, and peasants also went into the armies that declining dynasties raised to defend themselves. But the leaders of the rebellious armies did not fight for a peasant revolution, and those among them who had been peasants left, like the rank and file, their land and their peasant life to profit from the conquest of empire. They wanted to move up into the bureaucratic elite, become emperor or official, and escape the misery of their previous life. This had been the tradition of rebellions. The heroes of Chinese history were not social revolutionaries but military commanders and high officials, heroic in their fighting and skillful in their politics. This kind of traditional rebellion was not an attempt to change the system, and when there was a promise of military success the gentry could join the rebellious force or offer their services to the victor to re-establish the political system on the same social base, or they might themselves organize the rebellious uprising.

THE DEFENSE OF THE SOCIAL ORDER

The situation in the nineteenth century, however, differed from the past in one crucial point. Of the three major rebellions of that time, the

Taiping Rebellion was the only one whose openly expressed purpose was the conquest of the empire and the establishment of an imperial government. The Taiping Rebellion differed from the others, and from earlier rebellions, in the role that a religious ideology played in its organization and the sanctioning of its leadership, and in the new political and social structure it attempted to establish. Its leaders wanted not only to overthrow and replace the imperial government but to establish a new religious ideological system as the foundation for the new state and the training of its new elite. In this sense the Taipings were revolutionary. They attacked not only the dynasty but also the ideology and with it the ruling stratum itself.

The Taipings might very well have succeeded in destroying the dynasty, but their attempt to overthrow the ruling elite required as its first condition for any chance of success the ability to build up a counter-elite of their own for their government and administration. Of great interest are the Taiping attempts to create such an elite. Two of their most important leaders, Yang Hsiu-ch'ing, the first main military organizer and actual head of the Taiping administration, and Hung Jen-kan, the cousin of the Heavenly King, who joined the rebellion in its last stage, attempted this and failed. The Taipings were destroyed partly because of their inability to create a government of their own based on a new bureaucratic elite which they never succeeded in producing.

The attack against the Confucian order forced the gentry to fight the Taipings in order to perserve the system itself. Tseng Kuo-fan, who became the defender of the Ch'ing government against the Taiping attack, appealed to his fellow gentry to come to the support of the Confucian system instead of calling on them to save the dynasty. Speaking of the Taiping ideological attack against tradition, he said:

How could that be a change that concerns only our Ch'ing dynasty? No, it is a serious change that concerns our entire moral tradition (*ming-chiao*) from its very beginnings, and makes our Confucius and our Mencius weep in the netherworld. How can anyone who can read and write remain quietly seated, hands in sleeves, without thinking of doing something about it?

The defeat of the Taipings came then not from the government forces but from the new regional armies that had been formed in the provinces the Taipings had overrun—mainly Hunan and Anhwei—the armies of Tseng Kuo-fan, Li Hung-chang, Tso Tsung-t'ang, and others. The first successful resistance against the Taiping forces had been carried on by local corps led by gentry. When the imperial government realized this, it encouraged the gentry to organize on a large scale what it expected would be such local corps. To tolerate and encourage such a development was not new. It had already been done during the Opium War a decade earlier. Now with the growing threat of the Taiping armies, the government not only permitted such organization to be carried on by gentry on the spot but encouraged some of its trusted officials to resign from government service to form the desired defensive force as gentry at home.

THE NEW REGIONALISM

Tseng Kuo-fan, the creator of the so-called Hunan army, which became the model for other provincial armies, had, however, a larger program in mind. Instead of establishing a number of local corps which could be valuable for local defense but too weak and small and too hard to move to be useful in campaigns against the large Taiping armies, Tseng Kuo-fan organized a regional army which could be used outside its home area as a force for regular military campaigns. In establishing such an army he made use of the existing local corps and combined them into a larger force. The organizational pattern of this regional army also followed the model of the local corps. Its commanders selected their own officers, and each officer in charge of a unit picked his own men and remained responsible for their pay and welfare. There was a personal loyalty between men and officers and between the officers and their commanders. The army units were under the personal authority of their officers and carried their names. The whole regional force was loyal to Tseng Kuo-fan, who controlled it. It was Tseng Kuo-fan who appointed and dismissed officers, thus forming and dissolving units at will. Officers' promotions depended on him, although they were still formally approved by the court on Tseng's proposal. The soldiers and the officers came from the province in which the army was formed—Hunan, the home province of Tseng Kuo-fan. Financial support came from the Hunan gentry, who also provided the officers of the force.

Tseng Kuo-fan soon realized, however, that to finance his army and its campaigns he needed larger resources than the contributions collected by the gentry. What he needed was regular appointment as an official governing the area so that he could control its tax. The dualism between regular administration and the new military organization was bound to lead to conflict and rivalry, which handicapped the effort of defense by the new army. The government resisted for a long time the acceptance of the inevitable, and only when its own armies were destroyed by the Taipings did it appoint Tseng Kuo-fan and later other regional army commanders such as Li Hung-chang and Tso Tsung-t'ang as governors of the provinces their armies defended. The Ch'ing government had to disregard its own rules on division of authority both in the administration and in the military system and on the maintenance of central control over the army, and had to permit a combination of loyal local forces into regional armies under commanders who established their own military and administrative organizations. It had to permit the violation and abrogation of all the principles of divided authority and central control on which its political system and security depended. The appointments of Tseng, Li, and others added to the military power of these regional commanders the power of civil administration in their own provinces. What they had done with their armies they now did with their administrative organizations: they selected and appointed their own men, thus creating their own bureaucratic organizations. In contrast to their military organizations, their administrative staffs were not selected primarily from their own provinces, an indication that it was personal and organizational loyalty rather than attachment to a geographic area on which the new bureaucratic units were founded. Regionalism, as we like to call this development, must therefore not be interpreted narrowly as a provincialism with a local patriotism hostile to outsiders. The leaders of these new bureaucratic organizations that grew within the imperial bureaucracy could be shifted from one province to another without losing control of their organizations, which they took with them, and without even losing their military power, since their armies remained loyal to them.

Even when the head of a regional organization and some of his staff and forces were transferred to the capital, this transfer did not mean a merger with the central government. Li Hung-chang, and later Yüan Shih-k'ai, still based their power on the personal loyalty of their organization and their control of funds and military forces, even when they had been transferred to Peking as governor-general of the capital province or high officials of the central government. Such moves did not transform their regional organizations into the basis of a new central government power.

Only after the revolution did Yüan Shih-k'ai attempt to rebuild a central government from his own organization, adding to his own military and administrative power the claim to central authority, which had become vacant since the dynasty had lost the heavenly mandate and which Yüan Shih-k'ai attempted to assert for himself in a mingling of traditional and modern sanctions of government. But he failed. At this time, of course, Confucianism, which had provided the unity between state and society and had maintained the concept of the state even in times of rebellion and regional decline, had lost all support. Without it and without the gentry, whose dual role had been based on it, the regional organizations deteriorated into warlordism. With the end of Confucianism, new guiding principles would be needed to reintegrate both state and society.

In its origins, however, nineteenth-century regionalism had, as in earlier times, been made possible by the traditional relationship of state and society. The new regional leadership had emerged from the local gentry, who extended their area of function to include what had been the prerogative of the government—the defense of their home districts and provinces and, indeed, of the whole society. The new administrative organizations that were established maintained close contact with the local gentry, from whom they continued to derive their support. The regional leaders owed their power to the control of their own armed forces, their own administrative staff, and their own funds. But the government had to add its official blessing and recognition through the formality of appointing these leaders and members of their staffs to provincial or other office within the official hierarchy. The regional machine remained therefore a part of the official bureaucracy, undermining its central control. This development tended to dissolve central authority and create new regional nuclei of power, as dangerous to the dynasty as open rebellion.

When the emergency was over and the main danger seemed to have passed, the imperial government attempted to reduce or break the new autonomous power of the new leaders. But the regional power, once established, eventually held its own. The organizations of Tseng Kuo-fan, Li Hung-chang, and other regional leaders of the nineteenth century marked the beginning of the disintegration of dynastic power that finally led to the collapse of the dynasty and to the system of warlordism that replaced it.

When in the nineteenth century the power of the Ch'ing dynasty declined because of the corruption of the administration and the disintegration of the central armies followed by rebellions, it was the gentry leadership that rebuilt local government through military and administrative organizations under its control. Once more, when the political structure was at the point of collapse, the gentry leaders acted to preserve the continuum of the social order. And in this they succeeded at the time.

The new gentry leadership remained loyal to the Ch'ing dynasty because the Taiping uprising had been directed not merely against the dynasty but against the social system itself. Once victory over the Taipings was secured, the new leaders did not dissolve their political and military organizations in spite of the imperial government's attempt to reduce or break their autonomous power. There was no real T'ung-chih Restoration, since the regional power, once established, carried on; and the central government failed to regain that crucial part of its military, administrative, and financial authority that it had lost. The problem of the political decline was not resolved. And before it could be resolved through a new centralization of dynastic power under a new mandate, the intellectual crisis of the Confucian beliefs brought on by the impact of the West undermined the social order itself, which was made more vulnerable by the disintegration of its political institutions. Whether under other political conditions this system itself could have been transformed to survive in the world of the twentieth century, whether for instance reforms like those of K'ang Yu-wei might have had a chance for success, is a matter of speculation that cannot concern us here.

The crisis of the decline of the gentry itself, however, came only after the early crisis in which the gentry preserved the system. In this earlier crisis the elements of decline and continuity of traditional state and society were still at work. The special role of an educated stratum, the gentry, in state and society; the reliance of the Ch'ing government on the services of the gentry in the official bureaucracy; the complex of stratagems developed to maintain central control over the bureaucracy and to neutralize the gentry; the breakdown of this system of control in inefficiency and corruption; the build-up of local and regional military power; and the role of the educated in preserving social and intellectual continuity—these appear as the main factors in the Ch'ing dynastic crisis of the middle nineteenth century, factors that we believe to be of importance, with variations, for earlier periods as well.

Li Hung-chang's career characterizes the history of this crisis. Following the example of Tseng Kuo-fan, the founder and organizer of the first regional army of the time, and under Tseng's patronage, Li Hung-chang organized his own regional force and created his own administrative organization, which remained the basis of his power within the system of the Ch'ing dynasty. But he also represented a development that went beyond the traditional regional leadership. The history of Li's career took its special course because it occurred at the end of imperial times, when institutional problems of traditional Chinese history became merged with new elements brought in by the impact of the West. Li's establishment of a base at Shanghai and his use of the financial resources of the new economic development were an application of traditional methods of organization and control to the new world of trade and industry introduced to China through the treaty ports. Li's application of the traditional gentry-official system for managing the Chinese agricultural economy to the new aspects of the economy remained characteristic of the system of political control that continued to stifle private enterprise and prevented the Chinese revolution from running its full course.

5

Modern Chinese regionalism, or provincialism (in the political sense of the word—equivalent to or subsumed under the category of regionalism), menaced the integrity of political China and of the traditional sense of identity. The dissipation of central order into provincialism, politically, was intimately linked with the dissolution of ecumenical Confucianism. The latter had been cosmopolitan in its own way; now it became provincial—in the cultural sense of the word. And a Chinese national identity superseded it, a new identity, with associations of a new cosmopolitanism.

The Province, the Nation, and the World: The Problem of Chinese Identity

JOSEPH R. LEVENSON

ONCE, in the 1950's, I attended a conference on "Europa, Erbe und Aufgabe." "Europa" meant "West Europa," the inheritance was Hellenism and Christianity, the task (assumed with surprising aplomb, in a happy act of oblivion) was the preservation of sweetness and light through this David's-band in the middle distance, between the giants, the philistine materialists, America and Russia. There were other surprises. China received a passing (or failing) mention. It was paired, not with the Soviet Union, but with the United States: areas outside Europe which had been subject to the influence of Europe.

It was a nice conceit, rather like indexing, "J. S. Bach: composed the accompaniment to Gounod's 'Ave Maria'" (one can find it in "The Well-Tempered Clavichord"). And no one need be ill-tempered, for his country or his "field," because of a bit of deprecation—especially when it suggests a bit of truth. The United States and China (to trade on a

Joseph R. Levenson, "The Province, the Nation, and the World: The Problem of Chinese Identity," in Albert Feuerwerker, Rhoads Murphey, and Mary C. Wright, *Approaches to Modern Chinese History* (University of California Press: Berkeley and Los Angeles, 1967), pp. 268–288. Reprinted by permission of The Regents of the University of California.

famous title) may have been pasted together too casually in Mainz, but
Europe did pose to them both, through all of American history and the
latest part of China's, the problem of "Provincialism."

For generations, Americans have pondered the theme of innocence
and experience. Christopher Newman was Henry James' *The American*.
A nation of new men: perhaps it meant that America had it better, no
ruined towers—or was it the callow land, gauche and timidly genteel,
provincial? Yet, whatever it was doing, taking dictation or sending lessons
back, America shared in a Western world. If America was provinces, its
capital, in Europe, was really its own. But nineteenth-century China,
which had plenty of ruined pagodas (or vanished, beyond ruin), was still
a world itself. It had its own provincials within it while Confucian
sophisticates ruled. It was when this world faded and a nation began to
emerge that the old sophistication began to fail. Cosmopolitan in the
Chinese imperial world, Confucianists struck a provincial note in the
wider world of the nations. And consistently, provincialism as a literal,
political fact dragged at the nationalists of the early twentieth century,
post-Confucianists with a wide range, who figuratively, culturally, were
changing the implications of "provincial."

Yet, when it came to establishing a Communist China, heir to the
nationalist revolution and (some think) more essentially national in its
fervor than ideological, a feeling for provinces was invited, not discouraged. Invited—in a way: the Communists were turning back the
past, repelling it, not turning back to it. Modern history had not gone
for nothing. They were exorcising the anti-national potential of the
provinces. It was an act of killing the blooms (or certifying the deaths)
of provincial selves, then not blowing them away, but pressing them into
a national album. What blighted them was the cosmopolitan spirit—the
same spirit (others think) that stamped the Chinese Communists as
national all right, but national in an internationalist ideological sense.

PROVINCIALISM (LITERAL) AND RESISTANCE
TO NATIONALISM

How nationalism became prominent in China is a story by itself. But
if nationalism be taken as given, embroilment with provincialism will
have to be there, too. French Revolutionaries, classic nationalists of that
modern world which was now receiving China, had insisted that
provinces be transcended, particularities smoothed away, to serve the sense
of nation. Chinese history since the Opium War had seen the issue in
many forms. There were the myriad examples of interest, sympathy, even
consciousness cut off, and seen to be cut off, well below the level of any
national integration. There were the observations, at home and abroad,
that foreign conquest of the whole China would be easier to achieve
while the inhabitants failed to see it as a whole. There was the running

debate, in the context of shared nationalism, about the technical question of *administrative* provincialism, decentralization. There were the streams of provincial sentiment, rising out of propinquity and expressed in separate organizations and areas of action, which flowed into the movement for revolutionary national union, even while they bedeviled it with divisive threats of faction. There was the "objectively" nationalist character of anti-Ch'ing provincialism in the last few years of the dynasty (or one could turn this around, to explain the chaos of the Republic, with its growing national feeling while the center could not hold)—Manchu centralizers (the conservative provincialists' targets), Manchu "usurpers" (the radical nationalists' targets), and Manchu purveyors of provincial plums to foreigners (the targets of both) were the same Manchus. There was the insinuating nationalist corruption of the atavistic rhetoric of provincial xenophobia, and of provincial warlord slogans of political self-assertion.

So much for the political implications of provincialism, its capacity for inhibiting nationalism, aborting it, indirectly abetting it, or submitting to its solvent influence. But if these were all, no especially modern theme would have been sounded in Chinese history. The Chinese Empire, too —*t'ien-hsia*, the world of all-under-Heaven—knew tensions between the provinces and center, and the wholeness of China was certainly asserted. Yet it was not in the name of nationalism, but of Confucian universality. Why were such nineteenth-century officials as Tseng Kuo-fan and Chang Chih-tung loyal to the dynasty after the Taiping Rebellion? Why did they not seize the chance, on late-T'ang lines, to be regional satraps? It was the Confucianism of a man like Tseng that committed him to Empire, not region, even his own (really almost his own) beloved Hunan. For Confucianism was "high culture," above local ground. Tseng's literati language, the classical written style, had no provincial life; it was the language of no province, only of a past. This is part of what was meant when iconoclasts of the twentieth century called it, and wished it, dead.

Ironically, this was the language which had made the spoken forms *mere* speech, provincial, since none of them was the sole language of *t'ien-hsia*, the property of some men in all provinces. What all men in each province spoke was dialect, even the "mandarin" speech of Ch'ing Peking, supreme as speech—but speech was not supreme. Everywhere in the world dialect is a vehicle of restricted views on the world, compared to national languages, the media, translatable and translating, for world expression. And yet, by this criterion, in the cosmopolitan, revolutionary twentieth century, this same Chinese literary language, a very model of the more-than-provincial on its own historic ground, was arraigned as provincial: inadequate for world expression, when the world was not its own.

PROVINCIALISM (FIGURATIVE) AND NATIONALIST RESENTMENT

It was an aura, then, of cultural revolution which distinguished nationalists from Confucian universalists (whether as radicals the nationalists scored tradition, or as conservatives they showed in themselves the marks of its corrosion). They were still an elite, like the Confucianists —no distinction there—for the nationalism had to be preached first by men who knew the world, at least more of the world than "provincials" would ever know. Knowing this, they knew that provincial differences within China, compared to the foreign clash with China in general, paled in significance. And goaded by provincial unawareness, they were hortatory and lofty, to make the provincials *see* the nation which the elite could not but see. Where provincials would drone along the accustomed ways, nationalists would break with custom—by pondering foreign ways —to liberate creativity, to create a liberated nation. Like Nehru on Le Corbusier's Chandigarh ("The site chosen is free from the existing encumbrances of old towns and old traditions. Let it be the first large expression of our creative genius flowering on our newly earned freedom."), like Emerson repudiating "provincial culture" as "excessively deferential toward the past . . .," they made a connection between creativity and shaking free of tradition—or of provincialism.

This is provincialism in the figurative sense. If the Chinese past had congealed, resisting free and fresh intellectual probing, then China itself was provincial, together with the stale literati who organized the past, and whose cosmopolitan standing was now in the past itself. At least they should have been provincial and obsolete, and would be, when the avant-garde that saw it could expose it to the nation, and make the nation conscious. What new men saw was the "anachronization" of language that expressed traditional values. First it became inadequate, then sham —used to conceal a worldly interest, not just to explain the world. When Lu Hsün published what he saw between the lines of *jen, i,* and other classical terms, he was not quite ready to say that these grams of instant Confucianism no longer spoke to him; they did speak, and spoke deceitfully. Confucianists, that is, were not quite yet provincials, resting quietly, quaintly using vocabulary whose tone had slipped from universal range to local color. One does not fight a safely retired provincial, but smiles at him. Lu Hsün was not smiling.

The fully provincial is not only partial but really *passé.* Szechuan newspapers, for a year or two after 1919, gave a fine example of the provincializing process. They used the colloquial *pai-hua,* the language symbol of new thought and a post-Confucian world, and then abandoned it: "more space and less literary value than the literary language." And this took place in a context of Szechuan's retrogression from alignment with the nation. Thus, to go back to the literati's language, which was sophisticated, cosmopolitan, in the old world, was a provincial act, both literally and figuratively, in the new.

The modern historian Ku Chieh-kang, using a Chinese province literally as his reference point, shows what the metaphor "provincialism" implies. Discussing the work of two nineteenth-century Cantonese historians, he described their book as written "from the standpoint of that region—nevertheless, they show rather a lot of intelligent judgment." The expectation of limited views in "the provinces," the scientific historian's condescension, could hardly be more obvious. (Thus Matthew Arnold, wishing to "see life clearly and see it whole," dismissed the view of the Protestant sects as partial—and provincial.) Ku, like other post-Confucianists, saw China whole, and they prescribed for the nation's ills not Chinese medicine, but cosmopolitan science. The Confucian classics had etched out a Chinese "world" identity, above provincial identities in the past. But a Chinese *national* identity (which rendered the classics a purely national historical possession) involved a new "world" intellectual appeal —transcendence of nation to build a nation which itself transcended provinces.

The narrower the horizons, the more homogeneous the society; as Redfield noted in folk societies, by and large the country, "the provinces," shows local uniformity and regional diversity. But nationalism is the product of cities, and modern industrial cities, full of the *dépaysés*, reverse the pattern: it is local diversity—division of labor and a varied range of experience—with more and more international uniformity. Hence the paradox of the technological revolution, making nations more and more alike ("continents into provinces and countries," thought Yen Fu), while passions rise for national independence. Chinese nationalists' rejection of provincialism—in which they included, or to which they reduced, Confucian cosmopolitanism—was a fateful modern gesture; it launched China into modern cosmopolitanism, and into all the doubts, the search for roots, which the highly technological modern world is heir to.

THE COSMOPOLITAN WASTE LAND

The modern world is the culture of cities, with their connotation of rootlessness, the severing of bonds (in both the "good" and the "bad" sense: "*Stadtluft macht frei*" / "New York's a lonely town"). Another "bad" sense—Tagore: "Calcutta, Bombay, Hong Kong and other cities are more or less alike, wearing big masks which represent no country in particular." Another "good" sense—H. G. Wells: "Yet don't you think this very fact is an indication that we are reaching out for a new world-wide human order which refuses to be localized?" This recalls Michelet, who saw "the local spirit . . . disappearing every day . . . man's own power will uproot him from the earth . . . to the idea of the universal fatherland, to the city of Providence." But William Blake: "To Generalize

is to be an Idiot, to particularize is the Alone Distinction of Merit";
and J. M. Synge, for the west of Ireland, deprecating "the modern
literature of towns," clinging to the "springtime of the local life," before
"the straw has turned into bricks"; and the composer Vaughan-Williams,
ready for international audiences but not cosmopolitan art: "As our body
politic becomes more unified, so do the duties of the individual members
of that body become more, not less, defined and differentiated." This is
organic theory, vitalism; and what is the city but artifice compared to
the life of nature ("conquered," for Michelet, by his dear but dry abstractions, "society and liberty"), the organic life of the country, the
provinces? But what if the provinces really are provincial, in the sense of
Hume and Henry James: "provincial" meaning "barbarous and ignorant"
(the Scottish preachers), "common and inelegant" (the Cambridge
ladies)? What if the regional man's ignorance of the world is not what
Allen Tate admires, "an intense and creative ignorance," "the only
effective check upon the standardizing forces of the outside world . . . "?
Whether the cosmopolitan city is the spoiler or creator, the anti-cosmopolitan note of duty, "the duties of the individual," is the note of
desperation.

For time passes and "provincial" and "anachronistic" tend to coincide.
Out from the center means backwards in time. Venice and Florence,
"provincialized" by the unification of Italy (like the famous Greek cities
under Roman centralization), became largely cities of museums, and
museums as cities. "I was reminded of Nice or Biarritz in the time of
Napoleon III," wrote Lévi-Strauss of the "Tristes Tropiques," provincial
Brazil. Except for the occasional anti-nationalist, avowedly "provincial,"
only a rustic, a natural provincial, would be caught wearing the queue in
China after the Ch'ing. The urban years of the Chinese Communist
Party were the years of its unequivocally modern bias; it was the nineteen-
thirties, in back country, that the indigenous and the old (as in a measure
of medical provincialism) recovered a certain standing with the Party. No
wonder Trotsky, intransigently urban and explicitly cosmopolitan, arraigned the Party leadership for reducing revolution to "provincial peasant
revolts"—provincial not merely in the categories of political geography,
but in a deeper sense than that.

NATIONAL THEATER

Trotsky was wrong about the political prospects of the Party in the
provinces. Culturally, too, the Communists, with their revolutionary
nationalist and internationalist commitments, did not succumb to provincialism, whether temporal or spatial. They went neither "backwards in
time" to the high culture of the Empire, nor "out from the center" to
folk traditions. Their cosmopolitanism, both as an agent to kill provincialism and as a resource to fill its place, remained inviolate. In their early

city days, as in Shanghai in the nineteen-twenties, they knew they ran afoul of provincial sentiment; the "rootless" class approach to combination was impeded by provincial guilds, which were trying by natural ties to humanize the vast nowhere city. And later, in the country, though provincials became their protégés after Liberation, the waste land was not re-sown, provincial traditions were not revived to any pre-nationalist, pre-cosmopolitan, vibrant historical reality. Peasants became actors, the Party was director, the revival was theater.

For traditions, authentic in the past on local ground, may survive in the mind, reenacted with all the kaleidoscopic variety and the ultimate detachment which an actor's roles (as distinct from his own *persona*) imply. One grows into oneself, but the actor has to contrive a role, and contriving means consciousness. Awareness of Eden was expulsion from Eden. Even if an actor's only role is to be himself—even if the repertoire, the kaleidoscope, is only the director's—consciousness is there: self-consciousness, the blight on the natural local idiom, the provincial's awareness that now he is "provincial," discovered by central casting for a city impresario. Is it only the true provincial who can, and can only, "be himself," without affectation: the boon, and the flaw, of a truly rooted identity? But the only provincials left are unauthentic, when their ways are being observed for conversion into "theater." When the bars are down and men are observed, their being observed affects them. We know the modern psychology of provincial and national dress; from the same cosmopolitan viewpoint that makes national dress "provincial," they both are called, significantly, "costume," and their wearers compelled to consciousness. It is as if they were characters in a historical novel of the anachronistic kind, where the issues, the sensibilities, are the author's, so that the "exactness" of the environment is a product of dead research, not living empathy, and the characters are a *cast* of characters, clad not in their own clothes but in costume.

Another type of consciousness: Ku Hung-ming, late Ch'ing and early Republican (in chronology, not in sentiment!), took pleasure in showing Europeans his knowledge of their culture so that no one should imagine that his Chinese affirmations were the fruits of a mere provincialism. But in the eyes of Chinese nationalists, Ku's last stand for the old cosmopolitanism made him precisely quaint and provincial. Unyielding apologist for practices like foot-binding—such a scandal to the moderns—he seemed to be striking attitudes all his life, playing a role, assuming theatrical poses. It was a special type of provincialism, divorced from spontaneity and becoming a performance, in the fullness of consciousness.

Consciousness, fatal to provincial authenticity, is essential to cosmopolitanism. All the world's a stage. It is appropriate, in the cosmopolitan world, that Marx and Freud, two of the most impressive contributors to the modern temper, suggest conversion to consciousness as the typical

modern theme. Even the modern irrationalists, celebrants of the uncon-
scious like Knut Hamsun or D. H. Lawrence, mean to bring it to conscious attention. They are primitivistic, not primitive. The Soil Grows,
the Serpent Plumes for thee, *hypocrite lecteur*, provincialistic cosmopolitan. Just as for the Marxist the perennial class-struggle should issue forth
in class-consciousness; just as for the Freudian the perennial subconscious
should be dredged up to consciousness; so for the cosmopolitan in general
(who may be wedded to nationality, which is also the product of consciousness—Renan called it, "a daily plebiscite"), the "natural" ways of
the provinces are collected into a pick-and-choose amalgam. Things which
have "just grown" from organic local roots—many things from many roots
—are codified and selected in acts of conscious scrutiny.

Here, then, I wish to convey the idea of Chinese revolutionaries creating their own "theater." In another study I interpreted their action—
against the world to join the world, against their past to keep it theirs, but
past—as a long striving to make their museums themselves; it was to
escape being exhibits, antiques preserved for foreign delectation. It
amounted to this: let foreigners not be cosmopolitan *at Chinese expense*
(as Japanese who prefer Brecht to kabuki—"for foreigners"—hold that the
Western taste which the national must resist is the Western *schwärmerei*
about the national traditional arts). "Gratitude" for the interest of foreigners in one's own past achievements would amount to accepting provincial status in the current cosmopolitan world, not vindicating the
sufficiency, the sophistication, of one's own.

Perhaps that is one of the reasons why the work of Lin Shu, the prolific adapter of European novels into literary Chinese early in the
twentieth century, left radical nationalists with a queasy feeling. The cosmopolitan aspect of the enterprise, the interest in Dickens and Dumas
and the rest, was not the trouble; the provincialism was. It wasn't the
feat but the humility: Lin was fond of the use of *hsiao* ("filial piety")
in his titles, e.g., *Hsiao-nü Nai-erh chuan*, for *The Old Curiosity Shop*,
with its superhumanly filial "Little Nell." Was Lin (who opposed the
vernacular movement) just tactfully easing the traditional sort of Chinese
reader into a foreign literature? Or was he defending ancient Chinese
virtues by pointing out the *cachet* that came from enshrinement in foreign books? This would be the note of provincialism that vitiated the
cosmopolitan effort.

And so autonomous Chinese "theater" and autonomous Chinese "museum" came in together. The only way to keep from being patronized for
one's "ancient wisdom" or "local color"—the only way to avoid feeding
the cosmopolitan appetites of others—was to patronize one's own, on
one's own, in a spirit as modern and non-provincial as that of the West
which would make China provincial. Hence, "theater," the mode in

which provincial traditions, under Chinese Communist aegis, came to be rehabilitated. Such traditions, we know, had once been considered by early nationalists as inhibitors of national consciousness. But if they could be squeezed from the historical stage, they could be restored to just—"the stage." At last they could be regarded, in sophisticated spirit, as a diversified repertoire to which the nation gave attention, not as divisive single spectacles to which the provinces gave themselves. The provinces made an aggregation, and the attitude towards idiosyncrasy was not impatience any more but acceptance, even celebration, as in the loving revival (and *collection,* in every sense of the word) of provincial traditions in opera, lore, and legend. Communists might trip the Shensi light fantastic, the *yang-ko,* partly to get themselves into Shensi—and partly to get Shensi into China. Shantung should know and lay equal claim to what Szechuan had created. All provincials should share all provincialisms, patronize each provincial performance, and so diffuse the provincial spirit—the best way to depress it.

If we have time for a snack between the acts, let us turn, for another analogy, to cuisine. Provincial cuisines may be the delectation of the cosmopolitan. For these to have been created in the first place, there had to be limits, ingredients and combinations which were not locally known. But the cosmopolitan knows them all and may use them all, prizing the parts for making a perfect whole, and breaking down the wholeness which the creative limits formerly defined. A Jewish style of life, for example, may be more endangered when everyone eats bagels than when Jews eat hot cross buns. Such was the anti-provincial, cosmopolitan vision of the nationalist Michelet (if only he could have known!), who looked for the French provinces to flavor the national character while they yielded to the higher designs of nation, and then in the fullness of time, world state. To consciousness and homogenization, as characteristics of modern times, one should add specialization, the end of self-sufficiency. In the national collective, provincial characteristics are available—simple contributions (how one can patronize the simple!) to a compound.

The "provincialism" of provinces, taken one by one, lies in their relative simplicity. They lend themselves—Chinese provinces certainly did, historically—to stereotyped identities, which are death to ambiguity. Writers with a sophisticated modern sensibility (Proust, or James, for whom "American innocence," an innocence of guile and ambiguity, was provincialism itself) thrive on ambiguity, rejecting single, simple lines in the coloring of characters. Just so, the nation is a sophisticated concept: not only is it farther along toward abstraction than the local, rooted province, but it seems, as an amalgam, inherently more ambiguous. The sum of many stereotypes—honest Shensi, greedy Kiangsi . . . —is not so easy to stereotype. The collector of many traditions is not so bound to tradition. And provincial traditions at last, as contributions to a repertoire of roles, not a congeries of identities, would no longer make a range of natural styles, dividing the nation or aborting the nation's birth.

How, then, could Communists preserve Confucius, whom once they had to attack? They put him in the museum (cf. Henry Ford, a new man for a new world, and his Dearborn "old America"). And how could Communists redeem provincials, whom once they had to deplore? They put them in the theater—less a provincial theater (victory of the old) than Old Vic in the capital. And the provinces go to pot, the common pot. The original anti-provincial aims were not gainsaid, but accomplished.

Accordingly, Chinese Communist economic indulgence of local expression, like cultural indulgence, has been really nationalist and centralizing. There is a difference between decentralization as a technical prescription and decentralization as a pre-nationalist "fact of nature." "Centralized decentralization" (ordained from the center, in the interests of the totality) is analogous to nationalist provincialism, whereby "provincial culture" may be patronized for central and modern, not provincial and pre-modern reasons. The question of degree of centralization, which fluctuates, is only a technical question; the whole is always the end concern.

"We no longer look on the past as a son looks on his father, from whom he may learn something, but as a grown man looks on a child. . . ." (Valéry, on modern civilization—"a machine . . . [which] will not tolerate less than world-wide rule.") From Confucianism to communism is a history like that, from reverence to condescension, and condescension sets the tone for the epithet, "provincial." This is the tone of the Chinese Communists' curious elitism, with its Heepish humility before "the people"—condescension, really, as the very term, "the people," "the (*little*) people," implies. "The people," in their several provincialisms, have created roles (*in the past*), and therefore they can be honored. But the Party, in the true spirit of elites, assembles and directs the repertoire, and the peasants, with their contributions from fine local cultures, are put on the stage. This is a fair specimen of modern "psychic tourism," joy in the "authentic" while the authenticity fades under the stare. But it is a Chinese stare at last, the revolutionary independence of making one's own theater (like one's own museum)—taking from the West not just certain values (in revolution against the "feudal-Confucian" past), but (in revolution against a "bourgeois-imperialist" presence) the license to condescend.

COMMUNIST PROVINCIALISM: CLASS AND NATION

The authenticity fades, the provincial becomes a part—a part of the nation, a part in theatrical repertoire. Is the actor, everywhere in the world, in danger of losing his own *persona*, Ortega y Gasset's "irrevocable 'I,' " menaced by the "mass man . . . mounted on a few poor abstractions . . ."? Is local ground paradise lost in the cosmopolitan present? "To us today" (the words of Richard McKeon), "the sense of tradition is not strong, not so much because we have no tradition but because we have mixed so many traditions." There are those who feel that art has lost its sting, since (given modern technology, the ground of cosmopolitan diffusion) we see or hear it, all different kinds of it, all the time. And so it is with provincialisms, collected and run by on the stage. What had cultural bite in the concentrated province becomes bland when gathered up in the nationalist's aggregate: the price of sophistication. This is what is meant by the sophisticate's envy of the simple (provincial) man, Yeats' ideal audience ("a simple Connemara man"), an audience he despaired of. Yeats, his personal culture ranging as far as the Upanishads and the Nō, was apparently far removed from the mass culture he hated, the culture he wished to spare the "Connemara man." But he was just as modern as the mass blight, "Calcutta, Bombay, Hong Kong," in their big impersonal masks. Yeats, like Tagore with his cosmopolitan culture, was as far from a lost Bengal or Connemara as any faceless victim of standardized mass society.

One of the things that has stripped provincial roots (and spread a non-provincial culture, in the variants "mass" and "sophisticated") is the universality won by science. Science used to be much more stylized, colored by local cultures, than today. Now it is cosmopolitan, "objectively": in modern times, nothing is more provincial than stylized science. (Psychiatry has been relatively slow to break away from national schools and styles: a way of saying that its standing as science is still not fully secure.) It is sophisticated to mourn the loss of stylization in art (the loss that makes the waste land) and to insist upon it in science. A "subjective" cosmopolitanism invades the provinces, as sophisticates, hopefully and blightingly, seek "the real thing" for their rootless miscellanies. But "the real thing" existed, the province was authentic, when sciences and arts were provincial together. When science was cosmopolitanized, reunion impended, at a level above the provinces, a level where (for the arts) the satisfaction of cosmopolitan taste brings, like a shadow, unappeasable regrets.

Is this a version of "Civilization (sophistication) and Its Discontents" —Freud and the nemesis of progress? Then it would not be by chance (comrades) that Communist China, unequivocally "progressive," should de-nature its local traditions by preserving them in the museum-theater way.

That is, the Communists were not reactionary, even when they seemed to be. Their provincialist excursions were neither primordially anti-nationalist (see above), nor in line with integral nationalism (see below). Provincial traditions, when collected into a national package, could be accommodated to communism because they added up, not to regional consciousness, which could splinter the nation, but to class consciousness. This is tantamount to saying, in response to another conundrum—is it really other?—that peasant passions could be properly channeled to Chinese nationalist communism in spite of the primal Marxist coolness to peasantries. The province is connected with "the people," since in Confucian China it was the mandarin literati, in or out of office, who had a trans-provincial identity. Not only their central-bureaucratic "world" standing but their normative high culture (and the language that enshrined it —a cosmopolitan language quite distinct from the local, living dialects, which were *heard* but not *read*) raised them above the barriers of provinces.

Literati had prized local connections and were ready enough, of course, to raise their local standing. But it was their "worldly" ties and identity that gave them the best lever. Intellectually, as Huang Tsung-hsi insisted in his early Ch'ing *Ming-ju hsüeh-an*, schools of thought might be tied to special localities. But these distinctions, these particular claims, often proudly asserted, for the significance of provinces, were felt to be claims to leadership in universal Confucian significance. Provincial *shu-yüan* (Confucian academies) inspired local pride, but the pride was for localities as centers of illumination for the whole intellectual world. It was not just pride in the province, but a fundamental assertion that the province—the *literati's* province—was not "provincial." It was a different case entirely with the sub-intellectual local popular forms. Indeed, the literati's well-developed sense of lofty eminence expressed itself in scorn for the merely local. When the Ch'ing scholar Chang Hsüeh-ch'eng criticized the Sung scholar Ou-yang Hsiu for niggling about choice of words, he called it "three-house village scholarship" (a rough equivalent of "provincial"). And if the Confucianists felt themselves so serenely above the provincial—both the literally provincial outsider, *sans* classical education and doomed to be of one time and one place, and the metaphorically provincial insider bruised in a polemic among the learned— then the Communists, in turning the tables on the "feudalist" literati, granting the low "provincials" a title to "People's China," were only stating the logic of revolution.

In the implications of local history objectively considered, one can see the grounds for a Marxist concern with provinces. As a field, local history tends to be social history, with an emphasis on way of life and impersonal trends within it; since the stage is remote and small, individual persons, even local notables, while they may "reflect" history, seem to have too narrow a scope to "make" it. What distinguishes "objective" local history (and Marxist scientism assumes objectivity) from "subjective" local history is that the latter implies what the Communist feel for the province helps to undo: a personal feeling for roots, a loving sense of place, vitality, and vividness instead of the scientist's abstractions. And what distinguishes "objective" local history from amateur "local antiquities" is that, in the latter, individuals, local notables, may well be the subject of discourse. But local (provincial) history, out of range of "the capital" with its levers of power on the grand scale, for the wide arena, is more in the anonymous vein, history of "the people"; and anonymity, with its veiled intimations of determinism, may suggest, to the suggestible, class analysis and dialectical materialism.

When attended to in a Marxist spirit, the contours of provincial life, the offerings of provincial culture, convey (as Lukacs puts it) the "concrete significance of time and place": they are the stuff of that Communist ideal, historical reality (or simply, in the aesthetic realm, *realism*). It has nothing to do with direct concern for the province, and everything to do with indirect concern for the class-conscious nation. Since intellectuals, with their famous lack of concreteness and their cosmopolitan view, wash off the smell of locality, they contrive "superstructure." It is this which releases "substructure," the materialist's realm of reality, to provinces.

But the provinces do not keep it for themselves; they make a nation, an aggregation, which claims the sum of provincial popular values. When high art and culture become international, as the province of cosmopolitans, the only popular art is national. And popular art (again, Lukacs) is anti-capitalist, in the sense that the proper art of advanced capitalist society, with its social division of labor, is a coterie art divorced from popular life. Then "the people" equal a nation—and an international class. That is why the Communists, assuming this, seem both anti-cosmopolitan and cosmopolitan. They counter the cosmopolitan with the provincial, in the interests of the nation—a leveling nation, with that egalitarian passion which led, in the classic example, from the "Marseillaise" to the "Internationale." Their provincialism being so ambiguous, it is hardly surprising that the same is true of their anti-cosmopolitanism. The anti-provincial provincialists are cosmopolitan anti-cosmopolites.

COMMUNIST PROVINCIALISM: CLASS AND WORLD

The benign attitude toward provincial identity, a Chinese nationalist version of provincialism, is the key to communism as a nationalist version of internationalism. For communism is by no means just a cover for Chinese nationalism, any more than the nationalism is just a cover (instead of a consumer) for provincialism.

As a Communist-nationalist version of provincialism, far removed from a pre-nationalist one, we must distinguish it from an integral-nationalist version. The Chinese provinces are not savored for some mystic one-ness of organic irreducibility. Here the Chinese Communist attitude differs from that of the nationalist provincialism of the proto-fascist Action Française or the Nazis, with their "Ich bin vom Saar . . . Ich bin vom Schwarzwald" choruses of Nuremberg Rally mystagogy. The Nazis conceived of a "Germanism" brooding in all the organic localities, which were archaistically praised. The spirit of the past was called from the vasty deep, in romantic Wagnerian old Nurembergs. But Chinese Communist "provincialism" (like Chinese Communist "Confucianism") conceived of making the provinces past by collecting bequests for the synthesizing nation. In romantic integral nationalism on Nazi lines, the locality is microcosm containing the nation; for Chinese Communists the nation is macrocosm, composed of local elements.

And when an integral nationalist like Barrès or Maurras sounded paeans to the provinces, he was appreciating their limiting (hence, their nationalist) potential as a counter to internationalism, which he attributed to class-conscious radicals. In this right-wing nationalism, nation confronted class, and the appeal to roots (peasant and provincial) was an appeal against an urban, cosmopolitan abstraction. This was just as modern an outlook as the Marxist: far from a conservative internationalism like Metternich's (". . . Europe a pris pour moi la valeur d'une patrie"), and far from a conservative sub-nationalism, where provincial identity was self-sufficient and a natural endowment, with no need of deep angling to bring it up to consciousness. In wartime Vichy, with its Barrèsian, Maurrasian background, Pétain welcomed peasant groups parading (charading) in provincial costume. The provincialism was just as synthetic as the Chinese Communists': the two kinds of nationalists surely have much in common, as modern contrivers of consciousness. But if they belong together in the same world, they belong at opposite poles.

For while the Chinese Communists (and the Soviets), like integral nationalists, struck attitudes against "rootless cosmopolitans," the Communist attitude was hardly supposed to stifle class-consciousness—it assumed class-consciousness. "The people" (for the Chinese Communists), the provincials, were posed not only against "feudalists" (the Confucian-literati establishment, the supra-provincials in the *t'ien-hsia*), but against "bourgeois," and these would-be cosmopolitans in the new post-*t'ien-hsia* world. In the political sphere, this theme was adumbrated in the Opium War, when the conviction arose, to be revived by the Communists, that the Cantonese provincials had really defeated the British, only to see the officials and merchants of Canton city connive at yielding to the foreign will. And in the cultural sphere in Communist China, "bourgeois cosmopolitans" were indicted for holding, for example, that literature is independent of society. Society was taken to mean the real (not platonically), the phenomenal, the material conditions of life, "the concrete significance of time and place": the surroundings where writers are "at home." That is why Feng Hsüeh-feng was purged as a rightist in 1957—for advocating internationalization of "national form" (which was, usually on the folklore model, "people's").

Yet, if the Party was condemning cosmopolitanism not in order to stifle class-consciousness but to enhance it (thus winning abroad the title of "provincial" for the culture it supported), it was really opening the way for a sort of cosmopolitanism—as long as the class which absorbed it was not an enemy but a friend. What were "the people" whom the Communists found in the provinces, beneath the cosmopolitan culture (in *t'ien-hsia*, Confucian-world, terms) of yesterday's "feudalists" and the cosmopolitan culture (in *shih-chieh*, modern world, terms) of today's bourgeoisie? For some purposes "the people" were *min-tsu*, an organic community of integral nationality; not a cosmopolitan conception. An organism, while more than a cell, is less than an aggregation. It made, particularly in Kuomintang usage, for a conception of national essence—transcending individuals, but an individual itself, a folk, in its resistance to cosmopolitanism. For the Communists, however, "the people" were generally not *min-tsu* but *jen-min*, not organic, collective life but a collectivist abstraction—and not single and self-contained, but cosmopolitan.

As *jen-min*, provincials have supra-national not sub-national associations. "The people," located first at their most particular in the local earth of the provinces, then move into the abstract as the trans-national, trans-cultural, universal ground of a more-than-Chinese vision of the world. Province equals folk; nation equals the folk of province and province; folk equals "the people" of the world. Perhaps the claques for Cuban bongo-drummers were not convened in Peking just as a diplomatic tactic after all.

In short, Mao's peasant, one of his Hunan "folk" or of any other province, is quite distinct from the "Connemara man": Mao's constituency is a world-wide category, not the stubborn flesh and blood (though a poetic conceit) of a single provincial place. The industrialization which cosmopolitanizes the world is Mao's cause, Yeats' curse. Mao's provincial folk, as nationalized as the railroads, and the underpinning of international class society, are a futuristic fancy, not a phantom of nostalgia.

No wonder Liu Shao-ch'i could pay an even-handed tribute to "Nationalism and Internationalism." Nationalism, hostilities at an end with one seemingly natural foe, provincialism, could plausibly be at peace with another, internationalism—especially since provincialism, conceived in class, not classical terms, as aggregate and distillate informed the other two.

RECAPITULATION

The Ch'ing period was one of transition from *t'ien-hsia* to *kuo-chia*, empire and world to nation. Chinese nationalism involved a scaling up from a collection of provinces, a scaling down from a world. The Confucian *t'ien-hsia* had been its own cosmos, and the owners of the high culture embedded in classical language, transcending provincial speech, were culturally never provincial, though they had provincial ties. Such ties were part of, not rival to, ecumenical Confucianism, trans-provincial or *worldly* and cosmopolitan. These ties formed part of the personal-relationship ambiance of Confucianism, with its amateur's resistance to the impersonal-Legalist, specialist-cog variety of culture.

Industrialization, no Confucian value, has been conducive to uniformity in various ways—turning people into cogs (the critics say), erasing distinctions of provinces and obliterating the human, local ties. But it makes for diversity, too: the diversity of the many vocational types that come in with specialization. And specialization makes new elites, of professionals, not amateurs on the Confucian model. It is the professional field, not the fields of Flanders or Hunan, that more and more provides the "local" or particular identity.

Early Chinese nationalists, late Ch'ing and Republican, who were created by the rise of industrial nations and were seeking that kind of power for their own, strained against provincial ties politically, and scorned the self-sufficiency of literati-China, intellectually, as smothering and narrow. The Ch'ing's, the Empire's cosmopolitans became the Republic's the nation's provincials. And the Ch'ing's provincials, the rustics whose culture was too "low" to release them from local ground, were moving toward a radical reassessment. In sum (in part) modern Chinese history is this: a history of movement from the politics of Confucian faction (deriving at times from provincial fellow-feeling, but in a world commanded, overall, by a common Confucian fellowship) to the politics of a new world, an international politics conceived in terms of class. The province, the nation, and the world, in sequence and combination, have all entered the Chinese view—provincial, nationalist, cosmopolitan—of "China, Erbe und Aufgabe," "China, its inheritance and task."

PART TWO
The Sense of the Past

6

The next three selections deal with ". . . Confucianism, with its amateur's resistance to the impersonal-Legalist, specialist-cog variety of culture." The Ming period (1368–1644), especially in the "Wu culture" of the lower Yangtze valley, saw the cultural apotheosis of the confident gentleman amateurs, at a humanistic summit of refinement. This was the official high culture—officials' high culture—that accorded so ill with modern specialization, with "new elites, of professionals, not amateurs on the Confucian model." To such genteel amateurs, science, "progress," business, and utility (vocational education) were uncongenial. Tradition demeaned them all, for they all were subversive of tradition. And traditionalism, a sense of the past, breathed through the Ming culture, suffused the Ch'ing, and set it up for revolution when the Western world—the modern, expansive, scientific West—came crashing through the walls.

FROM

The Lore of the Chinese Lute: An Essay in Ch'in Ideology

ROBERT H. VAN GULIK

IT is much to be regretted that it has become a habit of western writers, when describing the history of China, to pass over the Ming dynasty in a few words, or at best, with a few pages. They dwell on the political decay that set in with the predominance of the eunuchs in Palace circles and, speaking of the cultural aspect of the period, they say that no new artistic impulses of importance are noticeable, that in all branches of art and literature nothing was accomplished beyond copying old models. And with regard to scientific pursuits, they repeat the judgement given by the scholars of the Ch'ing dynasty, pronouncing Ming scholarship shallow and uncritical.

Now, that Ch'ing scholars did little to show the glory of the Ming

Robert H. van Gulik, *The Lore of the Chinese Lute: An Essay in Ch'in Ideology,* rev. ed. (Tokyo: Sophia University, 1969), pp. 164–168. Reprinted by permission of the publishers. Footnote omitted.

dynasty is quite understandable. The hand of the Manchu conqueror rested heavily on the Chinese intellect, and to grow enthusiastic over the merits of the former dynasty was courting disaster. Less excusable is the negligent attitude of western scholars. For they have free access to the vast mass of original Ming materials that is preserved. That they did not use this opportunity, shows that until very recently among western sinologues there existed a strong tendency to study only the approved sections of Chinese literature, books that were found in the Ch'ing catalogues. But in order to see the culture of the Ming period as it really was, we must entirely ignore Ch'ing materials; they can only blur our view. We must turn to the original Ming materials, which, fortunately, still exist in abundance. Ming editions of the works of almost every Ming literatus of any importance have been preserved. Ming porcelain still tells its own tale, and genuine Ming paintings are by no means rare.

Surveying these materials I come to the conclusion that from a cultural point of view, the Ming period was one of the most glorious epochs in Chinese history. It was the period that saw a culmination of pure Chinese culture, the period that shows the most complete expression of Chinese ideals. The foreign influences that entered China during the T'ang and subsequent dynasties had been digested: in the Ming period a complete amalgamation is effected. During this period the Chinese spirit blossomed most luxuriantly; it was during the Ch'ing dynasty that the withering set in. When a tree is in full blossom, its gorgeous beauty amazes the observer; little does he care what the branches and the trunk look like. With the coming of autumn, the blossoms fall down, then the leaves, and the observer sees the tree in a more realistic way: he sees that here branches are broken, there a stem ends in an abrupt gnarl. The observer will know more, but enjoy less. This image may give an idea of the fundamental differences between the general spirit of Ming and Ch'ing cultures. Ming scholars wrote enthusiastic eulogies on a passage in the Classics that struck them as eminently wise; Ch'ing scholars pointed out that the punctuation of one sentence was erroneous. Ming literati reprinted the poetry of the T'ang and preceding periods in magnificent editions, with graceful characters on large-sized paper. Ch'ing scholars reprinted this same poetry in cheap looking editions, with small, angular characters, but with the text really improved.

During the Ming period the daily life of the scholar-official neared something like perfection. The literati of that time, mostly of an eclectic turn of mind, understood the secret of life, which consists of judiciously mixing beauty with comfort, and high ideals with purely practical views. This way of living is mirrored in the literature of the period. Numerous books are written on the refined pleasures of the cultured scholar. They describe in minute detail the art of tea drinking, the art of flower arrangement, of laying out gardens, of building rockeries, of playing chess and complicated wine games, of practising arrow throwing, ball games, and a multitude of other subjects that later were neglected, or fell entirely into oblivion.

It is only natural, therefore, that it was during the Ming period, too, that lute and lute music displayed their full and most sublime unfolding. In cultural centers all over the country great lute masters arose, and numerous handbooks were published. Their composers did not aim at retracing old music. Although they loved to dwell on the beauty of by-gone days, this was a sentiment, a mood, but little conducive to intensive study. They composed very original and most attractive new tunes, to which they assigned the old approved titles. This music is new, but how rich in tone, what subtle effects, what fullness of musical expression! Granted that the Ming lute players were mediocre students of musical history (with some brilliant exceptions like the Prince Tsai-yü), it can not be denied that they were gifted musicians.

In the circles of the literati, cultivating leisurely enjoyment and abstract contemplation, the various conceptions connected with the lute were more or less systematized, and pressed into formulae. Since many of the literati engaged in Taoist disciplines for prolonging life, and interested themselves in the search for the elixir of life and similar pursuits, the magical character of the lute was stressed more and more. Now the system of *ch'in* ideology reaches its full development, and the significance of the lute is definitely fixed.

During the Ch'ing dynasty the life of the literati loses much of its glamour. Especially in the earlier part of the Ch'ing period, literary pursuits are postponed to military prowess: the most skilful brush is powerless when confronted with the swords and bows of the Manchu bannermen. Later, it is true, literary ideals reasserted themselves; but the vigour and élan of the Ming period were never regained. South China was less affected. Up to the present it is still in South China that remnants of Ming culture must be looked for. Also it was the southern provinces that produced most of the great lute masters of the Ch'ing period.

When the Manchu supremacy had become more firmly established, the rulers could devote more attention to literary matters. Then Ch'ing scholarship develops, and acquires its many distinguishing features: a sharp critical spirit, extensive antiquarian research, the compiling of enormous works of literary reference, etc. Now serious attempts are made to reconstruct the old music. Old musical scores are collected, various systems of notation investigated, and musical theory is re-examined.

Many useful books about the lute and its music are written, but important additions to the repertoire are few. Mostly do the lute masters confine themselves to publishing the tunes of the Ming and preceding

dynasties in revised forms. The system of *ch'in* ideology is not worked
out further, often even completely disregarded. At best, the statements scattered over the various Ming handbooks are reprinted. In most handbooks
the teachings on the significance of the lute are left out, and replaced by
lengthy discussions on musical theory. A good example of such a dry
handbook is the *Tzŭ-yüan-t'ang* handbook. During the Ch'ing period
also the social standard of the lute experts dropped considerably.
While during the Ming and preceding periods famous lute performers
were as a rule great literati or high officials, in the Ch'ing period they
were mostly more or less professional musicians, who taught the lute
for a living. One shall look in vain in biographical works of the period
for the names of the publishers of the best handbooks.

The twentieth century brings the establishment of the Republic, and a
revaluation of all values. . . .

7

FROM

Fantastics and Eccentrics in Chinese Painting

JAMES CAHILL

THE place to be in the mid-eighteenth century, if one were a poet
or a painter or simply a devotee of elegant living, was Yangchow.
In this city on the Yangtze River, the lower terminus of the Grand
Canal, salt merchants made huge fortunes and spent them on pleasure. A
new social mobility allowed them to associate more easily than before
with men of the gentry and scholar class. The result was a new, rich, and
enthusiastic group of patrons for the scholarly arts—poetry, calligraphy,
painting. Painters were attracted to Yangchow by this market for their

James Cahill, *Fantastics and Eccentrics in Chinese Painting* (The
Asia Society: New York, 1967), pp. 92, 96. Reprinted by permission
of the publishers. Footnote omitted.

works, by the brilliant company, and by the aesthetic and other enjoy-
ments to be had in the lantern-lit pleasure boats that plied the canals at
night, bearing entertainers of all kinds.

One of the artists who came to Yangchow, arriving around 1723, was
Huang Shen (b. 1687, d. after 1768). Later he was to be included among
the "Eight Eccentrics of Yangchow" (*Yang-chou pa-kuai*). He started,
however, as a conservative, popular artist, specializing in figures, including
genre subjects, but also proficient in flowers and insects as well as landscapes. All these he had learned from his master, a minor painter of
Fukien Province, his birthplace. In Yangchow he met such scholar-
painters as the famous Cheng Hsieh (also one of the Eight Eccentrics)
and picked up some of their taste and style. In eighteenth century Yangchow a conscientious professional artist was in a curious predicament: in
order to be taken seriously he was frequently forced to emulate the
amateurs, publicly disowning, in effect, his technical training. Huang
adapted well, changing from a relatively careful, descriptive style to one
that featured an individual kind of playful calligraphy. Cheng Hsieh
praised his pictures of "wild precipices and tangled trees." . . .

The others of the Eight Eccentrics were mostly scholar-artists, and
painters of far more limited scope. Cheng Hsieh (1693–1765) painted
bamboo and orchids, Li Fang-ying (1696–1754) and Wang Shih-shen
(1686–1759) specialized in branches of blossoming plum and other
flower and plant subjects. All of them lived by their painting, in some
part, while retaining in principle their amateur status. A fastidious anti-
commercialism had long been the orthodox attitude for the scholar-artist.
Now the deviousness of the age made possible a curious reversal; selling
one's paintings could be passed off as simply a new kind of eccentricity.
Cheng Hsieh went so far as to post prices on his door, adding: "If you
present cold, hard cash, then my heart swells with joy and everything I
write or paint is excellent. . . . Honied talk of old friendships and past
companions is only the autumn wind blowing past my ear." Life in an
affluent society cost money, and no alternate means of getting enough of
it presented itself. None of the Eight Eccentrics who attempted a career
as an administrator in the bureaucracy made a real success of it. Li
Fang-ying served in several posts, including one as District Magistrate in
Anhui Province, but in the end had to sell his paintings to support himself in his last years. He never seems to have compromised by doing pur-
posely decorative or attractive pictures; his compositions are often lop-
sided, his brushwork rough, with a (largely deliberate) look of clumsiness.
Fortunately, this was just what many of the Yangchow patrons of art
admired and wanted. But one may wonder whether this celebration of
eccentricity did not foster in the artists a self-consciousness that is reflected in much of their work. Erratic behavior in art, when it comes to be

not only accepted but positively popular, is of course always in danger of slipping into the aesthetic posturing of a Dali. . . .

8

FROM

A Rejected Portrait by Lo P'ing: Pictorial Footnote to Waley's *Yüan Mei*

JAMES CAHILL

THE Chinese scholar-painters have always maintained that the painting reveals the man; let us look briefly into the known facts about Lo P'ing, to see what the man will reveal about the picture. He was born in 1733, at Yangchow in Kiangsu Province, and died in 1799. The whole of his life, excepting the time spent on a few trips, was spent in or around his birthplace. Yangchow was then a flourishing merchant city, a centre of the salt trade; it was also one of the main intellectual centers of the Chiang-nan region, that small area which was the locus of most of the vital movements in later Chinese art. The fourth of five sons, Lo P'ing was orphaned while a child, and was probably supported by his older brothers while he continued his studies. By the age of ten or eleven, he was attending literary gatherings held at the home of the mayor of the city, Ma Yüeh-kuan, where he was admired as a brilliant youth by the famous scholars assembled there. Among them were at least three painters—Wang Shih-shen, Chêng Hsieh, and Chin Nung—who were later to be numbered, with Lo P'ing himself, in the "Eight Strange Masters of Yangchow" (*Yang-chou pa-kuai*).

James Cahill, "A Rejected Portrait by Lo P'ing: Pictorial Footnote to Waley's *Yüan Mei*," *Asia Major*, New Series, VII, Parts 1–2, pp. 35–36, 38–39. Reprinted by permission of the editors. Footnotes omitted.

When he was in his early twenties, he became a disciple of the famous poet, calligrapher and painter, Chin Nung. Chin was then about seventy years old, and died around 1763, so that Lo P'ing's close association with him lasted not much more than seven years. Nevertheless, Chin Nung considered him to be his leading pupil and artistic heir.

It is a strange and somewhat paradoxical circumstance, symptomatic of the artistic climate of the age, that one of the most amateurish of amateur painters should have been the teacher of one who was eventually to earn his living with his brush, becoming (in a special sense) a professional. The truth is that Lo P'ing, as a painter of considerable technical facility, was largely self-taught. What he learned from his teacher, apart from some tricks of style which show up in his work, was the taste and attitude of the scholar-amateur. The literati society in which Lo P'ing moved had no use for the careful, tame work of the true professionals; and we may not find it hard to see why when we look at the pictures, which still exist by the thousands. In order to succeed among the literati in the vocation of painting, then, one had to join them in treating it as an avocation. One had to avoid the appearance of skill (another aspect of the paradox: Lo P'ing learning to be awkward from Chin Nung). One insisted upon preserving a certain independence, a reluctance to be dominated by the wishes of the prospective recipient of the picture. One conformed to a fiction by which artist and patron exchanged gifts, with no vulgar payment defiling their relationship. This attitude had relaxed a bit by the time of Lo P'ing: others of the Yangchow school, including his teacher Chin Nung and Chêng Hsieh, had been more open about selling their calligraphy and paintings, and even attached fixed prices to their works— a practice which would have horrified earlier scholar-painters. Lo P'ing probably did the same; his classical learning, and his ability as calligrapher and poet, allowed him to retain his scholar-amateur status nonetheless. Finally, one had to cultivate a touch of eccentricity, if one had not already acquired it naturally. Lo P'ing, for example, went about in old clothes, and claimed to be able to see ghosts in broad daylight. . . .

He was both prolific and versatile as a painter, and depicted a wider variety of subjects than most Chinese artists. He did pictures of flowering plum, orchids, and bamboo; of figures, including portraits and Buddhist images; and of animals. These were all subjects for which Chin Nung had been famous, and in which Lo P'ing followed him—grotesque portraits, for example, had been a Chin Nung speciality. In addition, he did pleasant, although generally minor, landscapes, fairly close in style to those of another Yangchow artist, Hua Yen (1682–1765). But his greatest popularity in Yangchow was the result of one of those occasional caprices which convert a little-known figure, who happens to do something odd which catches the public fancy, into a well-known one. He became Yangchow's favourite painter of ghosts. . . .

. . . Lo P'ing's ghosts are unmistakably people dressed in sheets; they seem to have been done in the same spirit as a leaf in one of his best-known albums, which illustrates a story about a man who "really saw" dragons. The dragons in that picture, although they are drawn with admirable liveliness, are more funny than awesome. It is not the painting of a man who has seen dragons, or expects to see them, but of one to whom the idea of seeing dragons is entertaining. The same is true of his ghosts.

A decline in serious concern over larger questions of the supernatural may sometimes stimulate a not very profound interest in trivial ones, as people become bored with disbelief, and find it exciting to credit, or pretend to credit, ghosts and dragons, sea serpents and flying saucers. In England the age of the Gothic novel, forerunner of the modern ghost story, its apparitions inspiring more *frisson* than fear, was perhaps a natural product of the Age of Reason. Yüan Mei, as Waley says, "lived in an age when belief was crumbling," and gave his contemporaries agreeable goose-pimples with tales of ghosts.

Once we are aware of the implications of this fondness for ghosts which bound Yüan Mei and Lo P'ing together, we can broaden our view to recognize a stronger bond in the attitude which underlay their fondness: an inclination to treat lightly what had once been taken seriously. Theirs are the works of men who suspect that the great achievements of poetry and painting were all achieved long ago, so that nothing can any longer be done with the same straightforwardness and conviction as it had commanded when it was done for the first time. Their aim was no doubt sincere, but the fresh, direct approach to the world lay far behind, out of reach. Lo P'ing, like many other later Chinese artists, regularly overlays his works with stylistic references to earlier modes of painting, and could safely assume in his audience a sophistication which insured that his subtleties would not be lost on them. Some such reference might well have found its way into the final state of our portrait, if it had ever been finished. The element of playfulness in Yüan Mei's writings is familiar to readers of Waley's translations, as the frequent occurrence of literary and historical allusions is to readers of the original writings. Both are certainly present in the "playfully written" inscription on the portrait, where they effectively serve to lighten the tone, and deflect the point, of what Yüan had to communicate. Converted into an occasion for learned allusions and facetious philosophizing, the potential cause of a contretemps lost its sting. The two men sat back to regard the event with a certain aesthetic admiration, having added another charming paragraph to the anecdotal history of the literati culture of Yangchow.

Lo P'ing's portrait of Yüan Mei, then, not only presents us with the artist and his sitter (in different ways), but also reveals a good deal about their intellectual environment. The great productive periods of Chinese civilization lay in the past, and the creative force which had inspired those periods was largely dissipated. What remained, however, was not inconsiderable. A taste, first of all, for the most delicate refinements of feeling. A perhaps excessive familiarity with what the past had produced, which encouraged poet and painter to indulge in complex plays upon earlier styles and motifs, even upon ideas and beliefs. A level of personal cultivation and civilized intercourse which permitted one temperamental artist to reject the work of another with such wit and elegance that the friendship between them was not disrupted. . . .

9

This early Ch'ing world of virtuosi and connoisseurs, then, was a world bound to the past, and a world bound to become past. Amateur preciosity (even professionalism might be an amateur's conceit, or amateurism a professional's disguise) was conventional. Even eccentricity was a conventional expectation. Orthodoxy ruled. The Manchus liked it that way, and the Chinese literati came to feel at home with Manchus, as long as the latter flattered the Chinese sense of identity and never flouted the Confucian sense of the past. Granting these desiderata to the literati, the Ch'ing were able to strengthen the throne against them. In so strengthening the throne's authority they strengthened orthodoxy, the authority of the past itself.

FROM

The Life and Thought of Chang Hsüeh-ch'eng (1738–1801)

DAVID SHEPHERD NIVISON

THE Manchu conquest of China had taken place in 1644, slightly less than a century before Chang's birth. In his lifetime the bitterness it had caused among the defeated Chinese gentry had subsided. But in the middle seventeenth century this bitterness had been intense. Many of the literati had been driven in despair to suicide. Repeated attempts were made to continue a hopeless military resistance. The writings of scholars driven into retirement show their reaction to events: political protest in Huang Tsung-hsi's (1610–95) *Mingi-i Tai-fang Lu;* injured national feeling in the historical thought of Wang Fu-chih (1619–92). It is generally agreed that the frustration of the Chinese literati, who at this time were suffering pangs of conscience for having allowed the barbarians to conquer China, had a profound effect on the development of Neo-Confucian thought in the seventeenth century. The Manchus gradually mollified the literati, but not the more sub-

David Shepherd Nivison, *The Life and Thought of Chang Hsüeh-ch'eng* (1738–1801) (Stanford University Press: Stanford, 1966), pp. 3–10, 17–19. Reprinted by permission of the publishers. © 1966 by the Board of Trustees of the Leland Stanford Junior University. Footnotes omitted.

merged classes, who continued to express their anti-Manchu feeling in the secret societies. Chinese, though always kept subordinate to Manchus, were given more and more important government positions; and the rulers, as patrons of Chinese culture, succeeded in shedding their identity as a barbarian group. By the eighteenth century it was possible for the government to grant posthumous honors to leaders of the resistance. Although he came from an area where the loyalist resistance had been especially strong, Chang appears to have accepted the reigning dynasty without reserve.

How had the Manchus managed this? For a half-dozen centuries before the Manchus seized power in the Chinese state, the authority and majesty of the throne had been gradually increasing, and the position of the officials gradually weakening. Many elements had contributed to this development. During the Ming (1368–1644), the imperial court had grown apart from the official class. To carry out its commands, it had a staff of eunuchs, a class of beings traditionally despised by the Confucian bureaucrat. Officials exercising the age-honored prerogative of remonstrance could be summarily executed, consigned to special prisons, or flogged, perhaps fatally, in court. Sometimes such treatment was earned by a hundred or more at once; for in the Ming, the official class retained its spirit. As the end of the dynasty neared, factional strife within the bureaucracy increased, especially between those who accommodated themselves to the power of the eunuchs and those who did not. Peasant rebellions completed the picture of a Chinese political order sick with dissension.

And so when the Manchus came, although they came in fact as conquerors, they were able to assume the role of reformers, within the Chinese world order, of Chinese ills. They did not submit to Chinese culture; they championed it. Within that culture they stressed the themes that supported harmonious submission to authority, painting a picture of late-Ming factionalism as totally depraved and urging the good official to make no common cause with others, to tend to his business, and to trust his prince in the decisions of government. At the same time, the fact of conquest remained. In a sense the Manchus succeeded to the role, in relation to the Chinese bureaucracy, of the late Ming eunuchs. They were a separate group, and their strength depended on their separateness and upon the imperial power that supported them. And so the Manchus combined their acceptance of Chinese culture with an insistence on their own separateness on the one hand and with a constant suspicion of Chinese loyalty and subservience on the other. A galling symbol of this subservience, the wearing of the Manchu queue, was imposed on all Chinese; and the military establishment remained a virtual Manchu monopoly until the T'ai-p'ing Rebellion in the mid-nineteenth century.

As time went on the Manchus ceased, inevitably, to be conquerors, ceased even to be warriors. They forgot their own language, and their prince came to be simply the legitimate Chinese sovereign. As this development progressed, the separateness of what was after all a tiny minority became dangerous. It would be fatal for the Manchus, whose power was coming increasingly to be rooted in their position in the political structure, to be isolated and identified as an alien group. In the eighteenth century, Manchu policy responded to this danger in various ways. The majesty, authority, and power of the emperor was built up as never before and guarded, by the Yung-cheng and Ch'ien-lung Emperors, with new jealousy. The court's patronage of Chinese arts and letters, begun in the seventeenth century, continued with greater flourish. A series of grandiose imperial projects of compilation involved the interest and participation of scholars, and thereby encouraged the scholar to think of official position as an opportunity for scholarly achievement rather than one for political action.

At the same time, official ideology urged submissiveness and respect for the throne upon the scholar-official class. Over and over again, the last years of the Ming were cited to show what could happen to the state if factionalism were to spread. The Yung-cheng Emperor's essay "On Factions" was ordered to be read regularly in government schools. This official ideology was first of all intended to reinforce imperial authority, but it had another aspect, as the edicts of the Ch'ien-lung Emperor show clearly. At times, the Emperor feared, there was a tendency for Chinese and Manchus to group around different court officials, or for the Chinese officials, who tended to be those who gained their positions by passing the examinations, to cover up for one another while being too ready to criticize their Manchu colleagues.

The Emperor's anxieties seem in fact a bit overblown. The Manchus were perhaps a separate group; throughout his life, Chang Hsüeh-ch'eng seems to have had none among his acquaintances. But the problem of Manchu-Chinese relations was not on his mind at all, and I suspect this was true of the great majority of the scholar-official class. Nonetheless the ideological and cultural climate encouraged by the court influenced him profoundly. Both in attitude and in philosophical theory he shows great respect for the state (after all, Emperor Kao-tsung, who reigned until almost the end of Chang's life, had ascended the throne before Chang was born). Imperial patronage of letters was an important factor in Chang's life, and he himself said that these imperial projects set the direction of intellectual interest for all of China. The imperial malediction on factions has a more than curious parallel, as we shall see, in Chang's own philosophy of history and learning.

The Manchu regime undoubtedly had some cause for anxiety. Popular resistance to the Manchus was part of a latent anti-foreign sentiment that has been part of Chinese culture since before the Yüan. The Manchu house was extremely sensitive to seditious remarks about its national origin, and up to the middle of the eighteenth century there had been a series of cases in which the government attempted to extirpate the writings of men who were considered to have offended this way. After 1774, a literary "inquisition" became general. But if the Manchus could not eradicate anti-foreignism, they seem to have diverted it and then to have ridden with it, by allying themselves with Confucian orthodoxy and against any influence—non-Chinese or other—which might challenge that orthodoxy. Thus, inquisition was combined with the grandest of the great imperial projects, the compilation of the Imperial Manuscript Library, *Ssu-k'u Ch'üan-shu and* its catalogs, a thoroughly Confucian summation of Chinese civilization. Chang Hsüeh-ch'eng himself seems to have accepted the inquisition as a proper safeguard against disrespect for legitimate authority. Concurrently, external influence was minimized. European trade was restricted to Canton. Christianity was suppressed. The risings of the secret societies, the Mohammedans, and other non-Chinese ethnic groups constituted a challenge to a Chinese, Confucian state by elements outside and alien to it. And although the state in the eighteenth century engaged in a broad campaign of expansion in Central Asia and the south, the attitude of the Chinese was defensive and more and more introspective. In the seventeenth century, some writers were at least aware of Western civilization. But in the eighteenth, people such as Chang seem to have been completely oblivious to the non-Chinese world.

The most important problems of the time were social and economic. With the growth of urban areas in Neo-Confucian China, the social base of the literate class had gradually expanded. A new popular literature of fiction and drama grew in importance; there was a new demand for the polite literature of occasional poetry, epitaphs, and biography, in which convention dictated not only modes of expression but content as well. Though popular literature was not respectable, it was nonetheless written —normally anonymously—by scholars for money; scholars received money, too, for much of their polite writing. This development was significant: it illustrated the fact that the literati were frequently hard pressed and were becoming far too numerous to be absorbed into the civil service.

For most, the avenue to appointment in the civil service was the Chinese examination system. During the entire last millennium of imperial China, the examinations played a very large part in a literary man's life, molding his education from early youth. But in the Ming and increasingly in the Ch'ing Dynasty, there was intense social and economic pressure placed upon the educated man to pass and qualify, if not for official position then at least for some intellectual means of support— such as teaching the sons of other literati how to write examination essays. One had the opportunity to take the examinations every three years. The provincial examination, the first really important test, was in the autumn. A successful examinee became a *chü-jen,* a "person sent up" to take the metropolitan examination in Peking early the following spring; success in this higher test made one a *chin-shih,* a "scholar admitted" to the Emperor's presence, where a final testing and grading took place. Only a tiny percentage reached the top, and many spent most of their lives either preparing for the examinations or repeatedly taking them. Chang himself succeeded only in middle age. The examinations did not require a detailed knowledge of administration and law, as one might have expected, but skill in writing on classical subjects in precise literary forms, the most important of these being the *pa-ku*—the eight-legged essay. Some young men, unable to be sensible, rebelled inwardly at this grotesque institution, though most—as did Chang—in the end resigned themselves to it. In the eighteenth century, however, even if one passed, one was not assured of a career. Appointment, except for those at the top of the list, was seldom immediate, and one might easily wait a decade, as did Chang's father.

As competition for appointments increased, public morality declined. Bribery became an inevitable part of the routine business of acquiring, exercising, and retaining office. And the difficulty was compounded by a dangerous ambiguity. What is a bribe? Confucian harmony calls for smooth relations among officials and between officials and people. Is the giving and receiving of presents wrong? The Emperor himself set the example, by expecting his officials to send him regular gifts (*kung,* "tribute") as an expression of their gratitude for the handsome additional stipend he granted them to enable them, ironically enough, to resist bribes.

Official corruption became more and more serious in the last half of the century. It may have been that the dominant Manchus, who as officials were in a position to apply great pressure to their Chinese subordinates, were becoming more luxury-loving; in any event in the last quarter of the century a Manchu, Ho-shen (1750–99), dominated both the civil service and the aged Emperor Kao-tsung. He created a network of political alliances throughout the empire and used his position to amass wealth rivaling that of the imperial house. During this time there were a number of celebrated prosecutions for large-scale embezzlement brought against officials who were said to be Ho's henchmen; one of the most dramatic of these was the arrest and execution of the governor and lieutenant governor of Shantung in 1782. Ho-shen's execution in 1799 did not repair the damage done. Corruption, together with the great cost of military campaigns at home and abroad, left the state at the end of the century with enormous deficits; the increasingly avaricious behavior of the officials, together with the increase of the population against the limits of subsistence, made recurrent rebellions more frequent and more serious. . . .

. . . The political climate of the eighteenth century was not that of the first half-century of the Manchu dynasty. The regime's ideological self-justification, difficult to accept at first, was by the eighteenth century a real intellectual fact, solidly founded in Confucian doctrine. The Manchus came as reformers of a Chinese polity sickened by dissension and appealed to the strong Neo-Confucian ideal of a harmonious social and political order. When there is good order in the world the *tao* is not a matter of argument; it is left (as the seventeenth-century writer Fei Mi said it should be) to the rulers. Such an order is in every way unified. It is not split into political factions or into bickering schools of thought. In it there is "unity between high and low," as the Yung-cheng Emperor wished.

In such an order, ruling men and guarding truth are not two separate roles. Li Kuang-ti (1642–1718), a high official close to the Kang-hsi Emperor, had said just this to his imperial master. In antiquity, Li argued, the *tao* and government had been united in the persons of sage-rulers; later, with Confucius and Chu Hsi, Heaven entrusted the *tao* to sages outside the state; but now, the present sovereign has indeed shown himself to be a sage. "Surely, Heaven is about to recommence the succession of Yao and Shun, and the authoritative line of the *tao* and government will again be united." This was not mere flattery; in effect Li was making a philosophical point: in the present imperial power the principles of knowledge and action, government and learning, were again one. Even the "search for truth in actual facts" had its political twist in support of authority. We find the Ch'ien-lung Emperor lecturing his censors instead of being lectured by them, as he would have been in an age in which men of learning restrained the throne. The Emperor cautioned them not to make charges of a general nature, but to keep their criticisms of conditions as specific as possible and to support them with evidence. For to do otherwise is to behave like Ming officials, who attacked each other with "empty words" and criticized the court merely to seek fame. The ideological atmosphere built up by the Manchu establishment must surely have had as pervasive an effect intellectually as any into conflict with the officials. . . .

10

"The ideological atmosphere built up by the Manchu establishment" was conservative to a degree. No wonder the Manchus could accommodate themselves to the Confucian Chinese gentry. The latter, in the main, qualified for gentry status through their learning, an indoctrination in conservatism. In addition, they had the natural conservatism of men with vested interests, which had been won for them or confirmed for them by that very indoctrination. Only when the vested social interests were threatened—by the general Western threat to the whole Chinese world—did the sense of the past yield to the sense of urgency and intellectual life turn away from its orientation to the past.

FROM

The Chinese Gentry: Studies on Their Role in Nineteenth-Century Chinese Society

CHUNG-LI CHANG

THE position of *shen-shih* or gentry was gained through the acquisition of a title, grade, degree, or official rank which automatically made the holder a member of the *shen-shih* group. The titles, grades, and degrees were meant to indicate the holders' educational standing. Official rank was generally conferred only upon people who had such proof of their educational standing.

The educational grades and degrees were obtained by passing the government examinations, which was the formal way of proving educational qualification. Those who became gentry through examination may therefore be called the "regular" group.

Educational titles could, however, be purchased. While those who bought such titles were usually literate and had some education, they

Chung-li Chang, *The Chinese Gentry: Studies on Their Role in Nineteenth-Century Chinese Society* (University of Washington Press: Seattle, 1955), pp. 3–6, 37, 43, 49–56, 62–66, 68, 197–198, 202–209. Reprinted with omissions by permission of the publishers. Footnotes omitted.

were not required to give any proof of educational qualifications. Such members of the gentry may be called the "irregular" group.

. . . In their educational standard and social position these gentry members who had achieved their position through examination were superior to those who had purchased their titles. This distinction was stressed by the "regulars" to protect their vested interest in their hard-won positions against the competition of the "irregular" group. There are indications that the central government used this rivalry as one means of controlling the gentry and balanced one group against the other so as to keep them both in hand. . . .

This "irregular" way of attaining gentry status could also lead to official rank and position. Those who purchased academic titles could then purchase official rank or position. Indeed, the academic title and the official rank or position were often purchased together. The "irregular" route led only to the lower offices, but such official rank, even though "irregularly" obtained, raised the holder's position as a member of the gentry. . . .

Among the gentry were also those who gained their position by acquiring military titles, grades, degrees, or official ranks. There existed in the examination system a special section of military examinations leading to the academic grades and degrees of military *sheng-yüan* (*wu-sheng-yüan*), military *chü-jen* (*wu-chü-jen*), and military *chin-shih* (*wu-chin-shih*). The holders of higher military degrees could become military officers. Men of military education could also buy the academic title of *chien-sheng* and from there move on to military office. The majority of the officers of the Chinese government army, however, rose from the ranks. They had not been gentry first, but the official rank thus obtained gave them gentry status. These military men from the ranks, who were a much smaller and less influential group within the gentry, were an exception to the general rule of educational qualification, since they had gained their gentry status without having first obtained an academic title, grade, or degree. . . .

The gentry were . . . a privileged group before the law.

They also had very important economic privileges. Special arrangements in tax payment and labor service conscription were provided for them, and stipends and other subsidies were granted for their educational advancement.

The taxes were of two kinds: *i*, official labor service, and *fu*, property tax paid in money or kind. From the first of these the gentry were exempted. Their dignity, their cultural refinement, and their life of study did not permit them to engage in manual labor. The training which qualified them for leadership exempted them from labor. Their property, on the other hand, was not exempted from tax, although the gentry used their influence to reduce their payments. . . .

The gentry's position gave them many advantages. Their privileges provided them with special exemptions and special immunities which were legally recognized and socially accepted. In actual practice, however, the gentry, relying upon their position, often extended their power beyond its formal limits.

Their exploitation of their position is evident in the field of taxation as many gentry members were able to evade payment or even to direct some of the revenue into their own pockets. The gentry landowners were supposed to pay the same amount of land tax and grain tribute as the commoner landowners. In practice, uneven payment of taxes was quite common. . . .

Refusal of tax payment and participation in tax collection were not the only ways in which the gentry could gain economic advantages. There were many other ways in which the gentry could share in the profits of the administration. Some gentry members tried to share in the profits of officials holding offices in the river works and salt administration or presiding over some rich localities where corruption was known to exist. In one edict the Emperor said that he had heard that officials, *chü-jen, kung-sheng, sheng-yüan,* and *chien-sheng,* and personal secretaries to officials, while passing by the river works project in Chiang-nan, requested and received financial assistance from officials in charge there. He alleged that such practices must have also occurred in the river works in Honan and Shantung and in the salt administration in various provinces and ordered severe punishment for such malpractices in the future.

Such malpractices among the gentry were sometimes furthered through the coöperation of the clerks and runners and sometimes through the coöperation of the officials themselves. In one locality, for instance, the gentry and the clerks collaborated in extorting payment from commoners. In another case involving a controversy between some gentry landowners and peasants, the officials were called unfair in their adjudication of the case.

The collaboration between gentry and officials for their mutual profit was furthered by frequent visits and the exchange of gifts. Such practices were frowned upon by the imperial government which disapproved of too much intimacy between the gentry and the local officials.

The gentry also were often successful in infringing upon the judicial authority of the government. Regulations indicate that the government tried to stop such practices. One regulation forbade the gentry to possess instruments of punishment or torture, but actual cases show that violations occurred. Some gentry members, relying on their position, visited the yamen frequently and interfered in local administration. They monopolized law suits and were accused of oppressing the village people. Such practices were said to be common and the Emperor repeatedly stressed their prohibition. Governor Ting Jih-ch'ang's directives to *hsien* magistrates on different occasions again indicate the active interference of gentry members in law suits. In one case, the gentry member convicted of interfering in law suits was a *sheng-yüan;* in a second case, a *chien-sheng* and a *sheng-yüan;* and in a third case, a holder of the title of *tu-ssu* or "first captain."

There were innumerable other ways in which the gentry could take advantage of their privileged position. To mention but a few more, along the Kwangtung coast beach lands extended by natural causes were claimed by the gentry as private property. Temples were sometimes controlled by gentry who used them as their personal property. On other occasions, land belonging to temples was confiscated through gentry effort, the rent being reserved for gentry benefit. Gambling was often backed by gentry who could obtain fees from gamblers. One report describes a struggle between incumbent officials and local gentry over the collection of fees from gambling clubs.

The gentry's participation in the management of local affairs also gave them opportunities for economic gains. For example, there were malpractices in the management of the "ever-normal" granaries. The purpose of the granaries was to lend grain in the spring and collect grain in the autumn so that the people would receive help, while the grain stored thus had a yearly turnover and did not decay. However, it was often not the poor but the gentry and local bullies who received the benefit of the loans.

Thus, in actual practice, the dominant position of the gentry group afforded its members many opportunities for economic gains and other advantages which extended far beyond their formal privileges.

The gentry as a social group with a leading position and special privileges performed certain social functions. They concerned themselves with the promotion of the welfare and the protection of the interests of their respective home areas. They represented the interests of their areas vis-à-vis the government officials. They undertook many tasks such as welfare activities, arbitration, public works, and at times the organization of local military corps or the collection of taxes. Their cultural leadership encompassed all the values of Confucian society but was also materially expressed in such actions as the preservation of village temples, schools, and examination halls. . . .

There are also indications that gentry members tended to move to the administrative centers and that rising in gentry status was often associated with moving to a more important town or city. . . .

Many of the tasks carried out by the gentry were of use to the government. They were tasks which might otherwise have been handled by officials. However, the official staff was too small and the funds inadequate to carry out all the necessary tasks, particularly in the field of local government. Moreover, the officials were handicapped by their short terms of office and their unfamiliarity with local conditions. Government regulations limited the time of official service at any one post and provided also that no official should hold office in his home area. These measures, which had the purpose of preventing officials from establishing local connections and power, also had the effect of hampering their efficiency. In the words of an official, "Officials will be transferred, unlike the gentry who stay at the place and are intimately associated with it. The officials are walled off, unlike the gentry who are close to see and hear."

Of the officials the district magistrates were closest to the life of the people at large. The district magistrate was the sole administrator of a district which could have a population of several hundred thousand people. His difficulty in governing so many people was greatly increased by the brevity of his term of office. . . .

Official action, especially in the districts, was therefore extremely limited, and actions by the gentry often took the place of administrative actions by the government. Such gentry actions may be called "quasi-official" since the gentry were acting in lieu of the government but not as an agency of the government. The gentry remained a social group and acted on a voluntary basis.

The gentry sometimes acted under the command of officials and in assistance to official actions. In other cases the officials initiated actions for the gentry to carry out but left the latter considerable freedom in their execution. In still other cases the gentry initiated actions for which it gained the approval of the official and sometimes actual official support, financially or otherwise. Often, however, the gentry simply went ahead with activities which the officials silently accepted or reluctantly tolerated. The coöperation between the officials and the gentry varied according to the task to be performed and also according to the situation of the moment. In times of crisis when the officials' ability to handle their duties was weakened and the problems to be settled increased, the sphere of gentry action naturally expanded. In the words of Hu Lin-i, one of the outstanding governors of the Taiping period, "Since the beginning of the insurrections, officials could do nothing successfully on local affairs without the help of the gentry."

The gentry acted as intermediaries between the government officials and the local people. As indicated earlier, they often advised the officials on the conduct of local affairs, and there were some gentry members whose advice and assistance were repeatedly sought by the local officials. But in representing the interests of their areas, the gentry sometimes came into conflict with the officials. . . .

In some instances, the gentry used their influence with the government to impose their wishes on local officials. In others, it was the gentry's position as local leaders which was their source of strength. . . .

A great deal of the practical management of local affairs was in the hands of the gentry. Numerous examples in local gazetteers show their very frequent activities in such public works as the repairing of roads, the building of bridges, the dredging of rivers, the construction of dikes, and the promotion of irrigation projects. . . .

Gentry members were also responsible for the construction and management of granaries in many localities. Decisions on granary policies could affect prices of agricultural products and could save the poor in times of need. Although the managers of granaries were generally appointed by the magistrates from among the local gentry, records reveal that these managers were usually recommended to the magistrates by influential gentry members of their localities.

The gentry also had a great share in local welfare matters. Sometimes officials took the initiative. In such cases the gentry were invited into the magistrates' office for consultation and were often appointed as managers of relief bureaus. In other cases, officials merely approved the organization of relief works, public cemeteries, foundling homes and other such undertakings, while the funds and management came from the gentry. . . .

Although gentry members generally had no judicial power in a strict sense, they settled many disputes by acting as arbitrators. . . .

The gentry also functioned as guardians of the traditional moral teachings. This was one of the main aspects of their role in Chinese society. In their whole life the gentry expressed the Chinese cultural tradition. This tradition and the gentry's concept of a true Confucian society, whether it deviated from or conformed with the official line of thought, cannot be dealt with here, but examples will be given to show the outward expression of the way in which they fulfilled this cultural function.

The gentry were actively engaged in teaching and illustrating the moral principles. Materially, they contributed heavily to the establishment of private colleges. It was claimed by contemporary and modern writers that it was in these colleges that the highest scholarly work was carried on. The government schools were supervised by the educational officials who were more concerned with discipline and examinations. The presidents of the private colleges were members of the "regular" upper gentry. *Sheng-yüan* who wanted to become serious scholars often sought admission to these institutions.

The gentry also contributed funds and lands, the proceeds of which were employed to subsidize students. They contributed to the repairing of the Confucian temples, the shrines for virtuous people, and so on.

The gentry, as could be expected, generally were ardent supporters of the examination system from which so many of them derived their power and prestige. Thus, we find the gentry actively engaged in the repairing of government schools. . . .

The construction and repair of examination halls for local examinations was also generally regarded as the responsibility of the gentry. . . . In general, all aimed at the continuation of the existing social order and the position of the gentry.

The gentry were also the compilers of the local gazetteers. One editor explained the purpose of such gazetteers as follows: "For a district to have a gazetteer is the same as for a country to have annals. The gazetteer will narrate past events, and the knowledge of past events will enable one to predict the future. . . . The superior men in studying it will understand the developments [of worldly affairs], and the common people in obeying the tradition recorded can maintain their work." . . .

During the early part of the nineteenth century, when China was in a relatively peaceful state, the government retained the control of military and police power and of taxation. During the crisis in the middle of the century, however, the gentry rapidly invaded these fields of action.

With the deterioration of the government forces, gentry members became military leaders of their own local and regional military organizations. . . .

Gentry members were also instrumental in the construction and repair of fortresses or earthwalls for local defense in many localities. . . .

. . . The gentry had to be constantly occupied with preparing for and taking examinations, devoting themselves to an "examination life." This practice, developed to its utmost refinement by the Ch'ing dynasty, was obviously not accidental.

Although the avowed purpose of the examination system was to select able men for offices, this purpose could have been accomplished with fewer examinations. Moreover, the content of the examinations had no relation to this theoretical aim. In the early part of the Ch'ing dynasty, there were still some questions dealing with administrative matters and with political philosophy. These parts of the examinations were eliminated in the second half of the dynastic period and the examinations became completely formal in content. Yet the gentry worked hard for these examinations since this was the only way to gain and keep their privileged positions. It has also been shown that the examination system did not provide an equal opportunity for everyone. Still for those who took the examinations, there was a worthwhile chance.

The question still remains as to what purpose was served by the constant occupation of a whole social group with formalized studies. What the examination system meant to the imperial government has been best expressed by an emperor of the T'ang dynasty who at the sight of his new successful candidates jubilantly exclaimed, "The heroes of the world have fallen within the range of my arrow shot!" He knew well that through the examination system he had brought under control the free-ranging thought of the leading social group. The Ch'ing dynasty went further. The constant drilling in traditional Confucian moral principles and the writing of formalized essays kept the minds of the gentry so occupied that they had little time for independent thought and study. Ch'in Shih-huang-ti had tried to control the scholars by forbidding them to read the classics, but the Ch'ing government tried to control them by making them read the classics. Their thought was channelled into the lines of official ideology in which the aspects of authority and discipline in the Confucian tradition were emphasized. The principles of loyalty and service, which were fundamental parts of this doctrine, were stressed not only in the examinations themselves but also in the schools, which were related to the examination system. . . .

Thus the schools and the whole examination system aimed at forcing the gentry and those who were striving to become gentry into an "examination life" and channeling their thoughts into the lines of official ideology which emphasized the principles of loyalty and service. The indoctrinated gentry were then to inculcate these principles upon the masses. The goal was a peaceful world satisfied with the Manchu rule and the existing social structure.

The examination system described above had its roots deep in the past. Dynasty after dynasty used it as a means of controlling society and maintaining a despotic rule. It constantly developed in detail up until Ch'ing times when we find the gentry and would-be gentry devoting their lives to the preparation for examinations. Through this scheme the court aimed at channeling the thought of the members of the upper group, indoctrinating them with the official line of Confucianism, and securing their loyalty and service. This system operated well in the early part of the Ch'ing dynasty, but in the nineteenth century it began to break down. The overformalization of essay writing and the overemphasis on calligraphy and poetical composition led the students to neglect the study of the Confucian classics. The trend was more and more toward empty forms without content or meaning. This change in the examination system affected the nature of the gentry. The ideological basis of the system was neglected, and the original aim of indoctrination in Confucian principles was no longer being well served. The government was losing its qualitative control over the gentry, just as it was losing its quantitative control through the breakdown of quota and purchase regulation.

By the close of the Ch'ing dynasty, the examination system was doomed to end. The changing international situation after 1840, and the changing economic conditions and social structure revealed the inadaptability of the

old examination system to a new life. The ignorance of the people and
the weakness of the state were fully exposed by the series of uprisings
within the country and the contacts with the West. . . .

Although the examination system was not actually abolished until
close to the end of the dynasty, its weakness was gradually felt since the
opening of the five ports in 1842 and the establishment of a new type of
school by Western missionaries. The first government move toward
Western learning, however, came after the Tientsin Treaty in 1860 when
the need of translators arose. In 1860 we find the first edict accepting
the principle of the study of foreign language. In 1862 the first foreign
language school was established in the capital, and early in 1863 another
was established in Shanghai through the request of Li Hung-chang who
reasoned as follows:

In China, those who understand foreign language are only some [private]
translators. All matters relating to negotiations [with foreigners] in bureaus
and troops are handled by locating these translators to transmit the message,
and they then do great harm to the foreign affairs aspect [of the government].
. . . The key to this important governmental function is thus entrusted to
their hands, causing misunderstanding between the parties and inability to
discern truth or falsity.

The leading statesmen, Tseng Kuo-fan, Hu Lin-i, Li Hung-chang, and
Tso Tsung-t'ang in the provinces, and Prince Kung and Grand Coun-
cillor Wen-hsiang in the capital, were among the first to see the importance of Western learning. They promoted the arsenal, translation
bureaus, language schools, and the sending of students abroad, and en-
deavored to adopt various Western technological achievements. But before 1884, the year in which the battle against the French at Ma-chiang,
Fukien, occurred, the majority of the officials still opposed the study of
Western learning. Ch'en K'ang-ch'i wrote in that year that the language
school had foreign instructors to teach astronomy, shipbuilding, machine-
making, and so forth. According to Ch'en, the Grand Secretariat at first
proposed that officials below 5th and 6th rank from the Grand Secretariat,
the various boards, and the Han-lin Acadamy be selected to study there.
But Censor Chang Sheng-tsao memorialized that astronomy should be
studied by *t'ien-wen-sheng*, students of astronomy, and engineering by
those in the Board of Works, and said that officials and scholars should
not learn such skills under barbarians. The subordinates of the various
departments and the Academy also considered such a shift as shameful.
Up to the time of Ch'en's writing, no officials had joined.

Even in the T'ung-chih period (1862–1874), a few far-sighted statesmen had expressed ideas on modernization, but no one had yet dared to
make open proposals on changing the examination system. Such a drastic
proposal was made, however, in Kuang-hsü 1 (1875), but it was received

with very little sympathy even among the progressive officials. Thus Wang Hsien-ch'ien, later a critic of the examination system, wrote that as Kiangsi provincial examiner he also had shown his disapproval of such a change at that time. He defended his earlier position by saying that, at that time, trade and the navy seemed to him the most important things to be considered.

The unpopularity of Western learning was also shown by the lack of interest in the publications of the translation bureau attached to the Chiangnan Arsenal. In the thirty years preceding the Sino-Japanese War, only about 13,000 copies of books on Western technology, translated by the bureau, were sold, an average of only about 400 copies sold each year.

As described also by Liang Ch'i-ch'ao and others, after 1884 the attitude toward foreign studies changed a little, but opposition was still strong. It was the Sino-Japanese War of 1895 that greatly stimulated the acceptance of Western learning.

Wang Hsien-ch'ien said, "Between Kuang-hsü *ting-yu* [1897] and *wu-hsü* [1898], the decline of eight-legged essay writing has reached its utmost. Many have discussed changing the examination system. I also do not favor [the examination system] and write this essay." Wang's essay reflects a general change in the attitude of men of the time. They no longer held the opinion that China could adapt herself to the new situation merely by acquiring Western-style battleships and weapons and machines. The defeat of 1895 demonstrated to these men the administrative weakness of the system, a weakness which resulted from the use of the old examination system to select personnel. Indeed, the old examination system merely drove the literate population to useless and endless efforts and could not survive in a changed situation.

The first real attempt to change the old examination system came in 1898 when an imperial edict ordered the abolishment of the part of the examination on formalized essay writing on the Four Books. In the same year an edict, based on a memorial written by Chang Chih-tung and Ch'en Pao-chen, ordered the abolishment of the section on poetry writing as well as the emphasis on calligraphy. However, the old system was restored shortly afterwards upon the failure of the reform movement led by K'ang Yu-wei, and the content of the examinations was not changed again until after the Boxer Rebellion of 1900.

Thus, the government's first response to the growing demand for a change in the examination system was to shift the traditional emphasis on formalized essay writing, poetry writing, and calligraphy to discussions of current national and international affairs. The edict of Kuang-hsü 24/6/1 (1898) rearranged the three parts of the provincial and metropolitan examination so that the first part dealt with Chinese history and current political issues, and the second part with foreign political and technological knowledge. The third part still dealt with the classics. This subject which had formerly had sole importance was reduced to the least important position.

Schools which gave new courses on Western learning but still retained Chinese classics as the main subject were promoted, beginning in 1901. However, their progress was slow because of the continuing existence of the examination system, even though it was modified in content. The incompatibility of the existence of the examination system with the process of promoting schools was discussed by several leading statesmen after the Boxer Rebellion. Several memorials requested the gradual reduction of the examination quota with the aim of eventually abolishing the examination system. One joint memorial of 1903 by Chang Po-hsi, Yung-ch'ing, and Chang Chih-tung stated:

Since the issuance of the edict to promote new schools, it has already been more than two years. But up to the present time there are not many new schools in the various provinces. The cause is the difficulty in obtaining funds. Public funds are limited. Therefore, contribution from among the people is completely relied upon. . . . But with the examination system not changed and the quota not reduced, people will hesitate. . . . Those who enter the new schools can rely on the examination system and would not only not devote themselves to study but also would not obey discipline.

The regulation governing schools, *Tsou-ting hsüeh-t'ang chang-ch'eng,* was issued on Kuang-shü 29/11/26 (1903). It marked the beginning of a new era in the Chinese education system by establishing for the first time a complete school system. The policy of the government was now firmly set that schools were to be emphasized while the examination system was eventually to be concluded. For the time being, the suggestion of gradual reduction of examination quotas was adopted. The demand for new schools was greatly increased by the Russo-Japanese War of 1904, since many Chinese attributed the victory of Japan to the development of new schools. Finally, Yüan Shih-k'ai and others memorialized and argued strongly on the inappropriateness of the continued existence of the old examination system and requested its immediate abolition to facilitate the establishing of new schools. The memorial contains the following statement:

The reduction of examination quotas, with the expectation that they will be abolished after three examination years, so that after ten years the selection of scholars will all be done in the schools, has truly been proclaimed to the world. . . . Your officials, in observing the worldly situation and watching the progressing trend, feel that the present critical condition is even more serious than it was formerly. Immediate wholehearted effort is imperative. But with the old examination system not discontinued for one day, the scholars all have the thought of success through luck, thus reducing their aspirations toward industrious and fruitful studies. The people are all watching, and schools established through private efforts have been very few. . . . Even if the examination system were immediately discontinued, for wide establishment of schools [throughout the country], more than ten years will be needed before talent can thrive. If a delay of ten years is permitted for the discontinuance of the examination system, . . . it will be more than twenty years before the use of talents is available. With strong neighbors surrounding and waiting, how could they wait for us?

Finally, on Kuang-hsü 31/8/4 (1905), an historic edict was issued marking the end of the old examination system:

Instructions to Grand Secretariat: Regarding the memorial of Yüan Shih-k'ai and others requesting the discontinuance of the examination system in order to promote schools and reporting on the plans concerning it, in the period of the Three Dynasties and earlier, the selection of scholars was all through schools and talented men were thriving, which is really the honored way of China in promoting the virtuous and cultivating talents. Also the results of the richness and strength of Eastern and Western countries are all based on schools. At present the situation is critical and the storing of talent is urgent. The court, in considering that recent examinations often fall into empty subjects, has on various occasions issued edicts ordering governors-general and governors of various provinces to establish schools widely in the hope that the people of the country will all approach toward concrete learning to be ready for service. The intention is indeed deep and profound. Formerly, upon the memorial of the educational minister, the provincial and metropolitan examination quotas were permitted to be gradually reduced and abolished within three examination periods. Now according to memorials of the governor-general and others, if the examination system is allowed to continue, the people will hesitate, and in order to promote the establishment of schools, the examination system must be first discontinued. What is presented is not without foresight. It is hereby ordered that beginning from the *ping-yu* examination year (1906), all provincial and metropolitan examinations will be discontinued. The *sui* and *k'o* examinations [to admit *sheng-yüan*] in the various provinces will also be then discontinued. The former *chü-jen, kung-sheng,* and *sheng-yüan* will be given an appropriate outlet and other items shall all be dealt with as requested. In essence the [modern] school system is the same as the system of schools in ancient times. In its encouragement of talent, it is also not different from the examination system. Regulations on various occasions have considered the refining of conduct and reading of classics as the base, while the various branches of natural sciences are all of practical use. The officials and gentry should thus make known these aims and rise, after hearing this, to establish more schools and popularize education. The state will then obtain the benefit in cultivating talent and the localities will also share the honor. After the issuance of this edict, the educational minister should speedily publish and distribute various textbooks to ascertain the direction and broaden the cultivation of talent. The respective governors-general and governors are also held responsible for devoting their full attention to the making of over-all plans and for giving strict instructions to the *fu, t'ing, chou,* and *hsien* magistrates to establish grade schools speedily all over the cities and countryside and to select instructors carefully and broaden the people's knowledge. Each should seriously engage in the work and constantly keep watch. Shun slovenly attitudes that will lead to malpractices. It is definitely expected that virtue will be advanced and knowledge improved and that *t'i* [body] and *yung* [use] will both be provided. Let all meet the utmost intention of the court in promoting learning and cultivating talent.

Thus, the Manchu court, even though reluctantly, had to yield to the trend of the time and make this historic move. The actual development of the school system was yet to come, but the way was now cleared with the abolition of the examination system.

In short, the examination system had operated well when it fulfilled its basic purpose of channeling thought. But in the nineteenth century it suffered an inner breakdown and proved inadaptable to the new needs brought about by the impact of the West. The Ch'ing examination system could no longer serve as a prop to a changed society. . . .

11

In the area of sense of the past lies one of the great areas of modern change in Chinese sensibility. Traditionalism had been the Confucian way, a universal principle of civilization in the abstract. The Chinese gentry through Ch'ing had a profoundly conservative temper, and it schooled itself (and legitimized itself) with a conservative philosophy. For the past was the repository of universal truths. "But in the nineteenth century . . . inner breakdown . . . the impact of the West. . . ." Various kinds of iconoclasts, feeling a sense of urgency, disowned past authorities and the authority of the past.

Conservatism, however, was not merely challenged, it was revived and reassessed as a symbiotic relative of radicalism, truly modern in tone even when atavistic in content. Twentieth-century Confucianism was not traditional; it was traditionalistic. It was not a serene philosophy but a state of troubled mind. One looked to the past not really for universal wisdom, the touchstone of civilization in general, but for the basis of Chinese civilization, the "national essence." This search for the old was something new, a search for the particular Chinese treasure, imperiled now, it seemed, by Chinese revolutionaries of foreign inspiration.

From Revolution to Restoration: The Transformation of Kuomintang Ideology

MARY C. WRIGHT

THE accession to power of the Kuomintang in 1927–1928 marked the end of the era in which revolutionary strains had been dominant in the party's program and the beginning of one of the most interesting and instructive of the many efforts in history to make a revolution the heir of ancient tradition. The Kuomintang effort was noteworthy

Mary C. Wright, "From Revolution to Restoration: The Transformation of Kuomintang Ideology," *Far Eastern Quarterly*, XIV, No. 4 (August 1955), pp. 515–532. Reprinted by permission of the editors. Footnotes omitted.

for four reasons: (1) the rapidity with which its course was reversed; (2) the magnitude of the gulf between the Confucian political and social system which the Kuomintang sought to restore and the national and social revolution which the party had lately led to victory; (3) the full and uninhibited adherence of Chiang Kai-shek and other leaders not only to the values of the traditional society but to the specific institutions in which these had been embodied; and (4) a well-documented, persistent and self-conscious effort on the part of these leaders to win the competition with the Communists by detailed application in the mid-twentieth century of precisely the means which the Imperial Chinese Government had applied against the Taiping Rebellion in the mid-nineteenth.

As the new rulers of China, Kuomintang leaders searched China's past for ways of dealing with economic decline, social dissolution, political incapacity and armed uprisings; and they seized upon the T'ung-chih Restoration of the 1860's as a model. While the Kuomintang in its revolutionary days had regarded itself as the heir of the great Taiping Rebellion, the Kuomintang in power identified itself with the Imperial Government and its apparently successful Restoration.

In brief, the T'ung-chih Restoration had saved the Ch'ing dynasty and the traditional social order in the face of domestic and foreign threats apparently greater than those with which the Kuomintang was confronted. In 1860 a weak monarch had been in flight in Jehol while foreign troops roamed the streets of his capital and burned his Summer Palace. The Taiping forces with their capital at Nanking had been in control of the richest and most populous areas of the country and straddled its economic life lines. The Nien rebels were enlarging their sphere of activity and there were Moslem uprisings in both the Northwest and the Southwest. In these circumstances it had been widely assumed that total collapse was in sight. And yet within a matter of months a new government had come to power in the capital, and provincial leaders and local gentry had rallied around the alien monarchy as the defender of the Confucian society. In the following years, the tide of Western encroachment had been stayed, new instruments for the handling of foreign affairs had been created, the rebellions had been put down and rather remarkable headway had been made toward rehabilitation of the agricultural economy, reassertion of local control, revival and modernization of the armed forces, and restoration of the Confucian system of cheap and effective civil government through an intricately balanced bureaucracy of able and thoroughly indoctrinated officials over a passive and thoroughly indoctrinated populace. In appraising this achievement, Chinese statesmen and historians of the time used the ancient term *chung-hsing* 中興 — "revival" or "restoration."

Chiang Kai-shek and his colleagues attributed the achievements of the T'ung-chih Restoration to the stern moral character and insight into the working of the Confucian social process which had characterized the heroes of the age, notably Prince Kung, Tseng Kuo-fan, Tso Tsung-t'ang and Hu Lin-i. They saw that the Restoration had involved not politics alone but the whole of Chinese life; not only the suppression of rebellion, the selection and control of officials and the training of armies, but also the norms of behavior in ordinary social life, personal relations outside as well as within the family, the role of women, the relation between the generations, the choice of jobs, the demand for goods, the forms of recreation. Kuomintang leaders saw in the T'ung-chih Restoration Confucian ideas in a form which appeared relevant to twentieth century problems of domestic tranquillity and international security. They did not see that the T'ung-chih Restoration, for all its brilliance, had in the end failed precisely because the requirements for maintaining the Confucian social order and the requirements for ensuring China's survival in the modern world had proved quite fundamentally opposed.

The issue of Confucianism as a social principle and of the T'ung-chih Restoration as a guide to its revival were squarely joined in the Kuomintang-Communist struggle for the control of China's destiny. According to the co-founder of the Chinese Communist Party Ch'en Tu-hsiu: ". . . the question of Confucianism relates not only to the Constitution; it is the basic question of our people's actual life and ethical thought. The essence of Confucianism is that the 'principles of social usage' (*li*) are the basis of our country's ethics and politics. Their preservation or destruction is a question which our country must soon resolve, and it should be resolved before questions of the form of state or of the constitution." The Communists studied the lessons of the T'ung-chih Restoration almost as carefully as did the Nationalists, and dubbed it "a counter-revolution achieved with foreign support." In the Communist view, the Kuomintang exaltation of the Restoration and the virtual canonization of Tseng Kuo-fan were fraudulent and futile efforts to anesthetize youth, the fabrication of a legend out of whole cloth by fascist theoreticians.

As they made their bid for power, the Communists called the conflict in the interpretation of Tseng's character and career one of the battle-fronts in the struggle between the "democracy-demanding Chinese people and the property-owning classes." They insisted that Sun Yat-sen, like all true revolutionaries of the early Kuomintang, had repudiated Tseng and had considered himself the younger brother of the Taiping leader Hung Hsiu-ch'uan.

In contrast to Communist doctrinal consistency in implacable opposition to Confucianism in general and to the T'ung-chih Restoration in particular, dominant Kuomintang views shifted and varied in the years preceding the party's accession to power, for the issues of a Confucian society vs. a modern society, of restoration vs. revolution, had not been sharply posed until the years of heightened intellectual and social ferment after 1916. Among early Kuomintang leaders, including Sun Yat-sen and Chang T'ai-yen, the issue of nationalism had been primary and the establishment of the republican capital at Nanking a vindication of the Ming Dynasty rather than of the Taiping Rebellion. Indeed Chang's views seem to have differed from those of his monarchist political opponents largely on the question of the nationality of the chief of state. And while Sun himself was sharply critical of those who saw nothing but the nationality issue, he did not consider the revolution of 1911 a break in the main course of Chinese history but as a continuation of five thousand years of glory.

As late as 1915, when Yüan Shih-k'ai assumed autocratic powers, the Kuomintang's own argument against the pretender to the Confucian monarchy and the "stabilizing" figure of the age rested on essentially Confucian grounds. The leader of the uncompromising armed opposition to Yüan, "Martyr of the Revolution Ts'ai Sung-p'o" (Ts'ai O) himself selected maxims from the works of the heroes of the Restoration, Tseng Kuo-fan and Hu Lin-i, and issued them to his revolutionary forces as basic indoctrination material. In his preface Ts'ai wrote that where values and morale were concerned, discussion of the present was less useful than transmission of the teachings of antiquity; that while antiquity was sometimes too remote to be directly relevant, Tseng and Hu had lived only a half-century ago, so that what they had to say was of urgent importance today.

After 1915, however, Chinese history moved rapidly and in the years following the May 4th movement of 1919 a Communist-Nationalist coalition centered at Canton gained strength. In 1924 the first congress of the reorganized Kuomintang issued a radical declaration which provided the basis of a common program with the Communists. Borodin was at the height of his influence and the young Chiang Kai-shek, recently returned from the Soviet Union, was commander of the revolutionary Whampoa Military Academy with Chou En-lai as director of the political department. It was in these extraordinary circumstances that Chiang selected for the Academy's textbook his own enlarged version of Ts'ai O's selections from the maxims of Tseng Kuo-fan and Hu Lin-i and it was to this step that Chiang's later success was subsequently attributed.

In his preface Chiang wrote that the reason for the success of the Restoration and the failure of the Taiping Rebellion was not difference in ability, for in ability the Taiping heroes Hung Hsiu-ch'uan, Shih Ta-k'ai and Li Hsiu-ch'eng were the equals of the Restoration heroes Tseng Kuo-fan, Hu Lin-i and Tso Tsung-t'ang. In Chiang's view, Tseng had been the leader of the age because he acclaimed virtue and embodied proper personal conduct. It was because of this that Chiang took Tseng for his master.

Chiang continued that he himself had been studying the works of

Tseng and Hu for some time, and had earlier decided to "postpone" writing the history of the Taiping Rebellion he had once intended as a guide to his comrades, and to compile instead a selection of the works of Tseng and Hu as their guide. For convenience he was using Ts'ai O's compilation as a basis, but he had made certain additions, particularly with reference to mental discipline, and had included selections from the works of Tso Tsung-t'ang as well. And Chiang concluded: "Alack! The words of Tseng, Hu and Tso are the voice of true experience in governing men, the things I wish to say but cannot put into words . . . I wish to present a copy to each of my comrades in the Academy so that in future there will be a foundation for the command of the army and the government of the country."

In 1924 Chiang Kai-shek's view of the army of the revolution as the stabilizer of Chinese society along Restoration lines contrasted sharply with most of the published statements of the Party's position. There were a few like Tai Chi-t'ao who were already urging the use of the party organization "to restore the spirit of our ancestors and thus cause the country to flourish." But Chiang's own position was still ambivalent. In 1924 at Whampoa he lectured on Tseng and stability but he also lectured on revolution. There was nothing about the Confucian order in his manifesto to the nation of August 1926. In 1933–1934 he lectured only on stability and the Confucian code of behavior. In 1924, while Chiang extolled Tseng, his references to the Taiping Rebellion were polite. In 1932 he spat upon it. And in 1933–1934 at Lu-shan Chiang took his stand not only against the Communists and the Taiping Rebellion but against all the rebellions in Chinese history, going back to the Red Eyebrows and the Yellow Turbans. His cause was one with the cause of Hu Lin-i, he proclaimed, because: "If we do not exterminate the red bandits, we cannot preserve the old morals and ancient wisdom handed down from our ancestors. . . ."

The full turn in the Kuomintang position took place between 1924 and 1928, and Chiang was always ahead of the party. The proclamations of the first two congresses of the Kuomintang were revolutionary documents. In the first (1924), the enemies of the party were specified as the constitutional clique, the federal autonomy clique, the compromisers, and the groups dominated by business men. The manifesto of the second congress (1926) was similar but more sharply anti-imperialist in the Marxist sense. The enemies of the party were the warlords, the bureaucrats, the compradors and the local bosses. With the third congress in 1929 the picture changed and the enemies of the party became the "agents of red imperialism." Radicals now either reformed their outlook or left the party, while many of those purged in earlier years returned to the fold.

Even at the high-tide of the northern expedition there were already those who called Chiang Kai-shek today's Tseng, who compared T'ang Sheng-chih 唐生智 to Hu Lin-i. When the Communist Propaganda Corps called on Generalissimo Chiang, its leader was struck by the fact that the phrases, the procedure, the whole atmosphere already suggested the traditional rulers of China. The Communist view of the alternatives before the Kuomintang late in 1926 was illustrated in a poster hung at the Peasants' Association in a small town near Nan-ch'ang. On one side was a Confucian Temple, on the other the "World Park," featuring Marx, Lenin and a vacant third position. In the center a man in Chinese Nationalist uniform was carrying the portrait of Sun Yat-sen toward the Confucian Temple. The legend read: "Sun ought to be in the world park but Tai (Chi-t'ao) wants him in the Confucian Temple."

Public and avowed veneration for Confucius was resumed in 1928. As late as 1927 a mob had dragged a straw effigy of Confucius through the streets of Changsha and beat and burned it, and the National Government itself had on February 15 ordered the abolition of official Confucian rites and turned the funds over to public education on the grounds that "The principles of Confucius were despotic. For more than twenty centuries they have served to oppress the people and to enslave thought. . . . As to the cult of Confucius, it is superstitious and out of place in the modern world . . . China is now a Republic. These vestiges of absolutism should be effaced from the memory of citizens." The vestiges were not effaced for long. On November 6, 1928 Chiang Kai-shek was urging his officers to spend their leisure in the study of the Four Books. In 1931 Confucius' birthday became a national holiday. Nationalist troops were ordered to give special protection to all local Confucian temples. Recognition increased by degrees, culminating in the recanonization of Confucius in 1934 when Yeh Ch'u-ts'ang was sent as the official delegate of the National Government to take part in the ceremonies at the Confucian Temple at Ch'ü-fu.

The Kuomintang never ceased talking about revolution. It merely redefined the term in a precisely opposite sense. As Ch'en Li-fu said in 1935, the "new" to which the revolution must lead was new in the sense that the Chou dynasty was new, new in the sense of slow adjustment and renewal of ancient and unchanging principles. The official party history declared that Taiping thought was contrary to the spirit of Chinese culture, of which the Kuomintang was the true revolutionary carrier. The party elder Chang Chi told the party's Central Training Corps in 1943 that the rejection of the sage kings and loyal ministers of the past which had characterized the early period of the revolution had been an error of youth, one which the party had long since corrected. In these circumstances, T'ao Hsi-sheng wrote, as well he might, that the historic origins of the Kuomintang were subtle and confused, for the party was "the heir of both the Taiping Rebellion and of Tseng Kuo-fan." By 1953 the confusion had disappeared and reversal in the meaning of revolution was complete. According to T'ao: "Revolutionaries are scholars who take the *ching-shih* (statesmanship) studies of the late Ming and early Ch'ing as their basis, but who have also imbibed Western thought."

The change in the orientation of the Kuomintang was marked by a growing cult of Tseng Kuo-fan. In 1922 it had been difficult to believe that Tseng had been dead only fifty years, so much had Chinese life apparently changed. By 1932 he seemed very much alive again, as his works were reissued in large volume and discussions of his life and its meaning filled the new books and magazines. Again and again Tseng was described as the leading meritorious official of the Restoration of the Ch'ing house and the pillar of the Restoration; the greatest man in modern Chinese history because he preserved not only the Ch'ing house but China; the greatest statesman of the Restoration, even greater as a thinker; a man of grand vision who renovated the old society.

After 1928, *The Maxims of Tseng and Hu* became virtually part of the Kuomintang Party canon. New compilations and new editions of Ts'ai O's original compilation poured from the presses. Orders to study the maxims became a routine part of lectures by Party leaders to army officers. Ts'ai himself was increasingly identified with the Restoration and he became a "model for youth" because he combined Tseng's "capacity" (*tu*), Tso's ability and Chiang Chung-yüan's courage.

This apotheosis of Tseng, and of Chiang Kai-shek as a greater Tseng, was not unprotested but the critics had little effect. Repeatedly in times of crisis Chiang called on the nation to rise taking Tseng as its model. Tseng was everything: the symbol of "spiritual mobilization" in the war against Japan, the consummate military commander, the embodiment of party discipline, the arbiter of the academic world, the proof incarnate that every man might through diligence and moral firmness rise to the heights.

The choice of the Restoration as a model was logical enough once the Kuomintang leaders had ceased to consider the party a spearhead of revolution and come to regard it as an instrument for restoring order. With their new outlook, they declared that the new period of revolutionary construction required qualities opposite to those needed in the preceding period of revolutionary destruction. The revolution could now go forward only if the party purged itself in one sweep of the evil tendencies left over from its earlier history and concentrated on reestablishing the fixed and secure relationships of the Confucian order. And the main and obvious feature of the Restoration was that these Confucian relationships had been re-established in the face of a revolutionary threat, and that order had thereby been restored.

The new Confucians of the Kuomintang were men of action, not philosophers. Chiang Kai-shek might quote the whole of the "great harmony" passage of the *Li chi* to the People's Political Conference, and other leaders might refer in passing to any appropriate classical dictum, but Kuomintang leaders did not attempt to expound the Confucianism of the party in theoretical terms. They pulled from Confucianism, on an *ad hoc* basis, whatever seemed likely to promote internal order. Reasonably enough, their chief emphasis, like that of the Restoration leaders, was on the principles of social usage (*li*) and the associated virtues of *i, lien* and *ch'ih*.

There is little point in attempting a systematic analysis of exactly what the Kuomintang meant by *li, i, lien* and *ch'ih*. They were discussed incessantly in party literature, but never very precisely or reflectively. Chiang Kai-shek instructed party workers that *li*—the principles of social usage—meant precise and meticulous behavior in accordance with the unchanging principles of nature, society and the state. He told army officers that *li* and the associated virtues of *i, lien,* and *ch'ih* were the only sources of order, discipline, vision and courage in the army, the best defense against the loss of loyalty which, as Tseng Kuo-fan had pointed out, was the great cause of all rebellions. He told the general public not what these virtues were in positive terms, but what their absence entailed: in the absence of *li,* there was inattention to order, discipline and rules; in the absence of *i,* there was lack of good faith and neglect of duty; in the absence of *lien* there was confusion between right and wrong, between public and private; in the absence of *ch'ih* there was imperceptiveness and irresolution.

If to the shadowy negative connotations which Chiang gave to these four terms we add Ch'en Li-fu's positive connotations, we are further than ever from a definition. According to Ch'en, when *li* is present the standards of civilized and barbaric are clear; with *i,* the distinctions of true and false are clear; with *lien,* the distinctions of taking and receiving are clear; with *ch'ih,* the criteria of good and evil are clear.

While the philosophic meaning of this version of the doctrine of the rites is confused and scarcely worth discussion, its political and social meaning is clear enough, and worth careful attention. The thing that is really being discussed all the time is the means of insuring social stability and popular discipline. In the view of the Kuomintang ideologists, Confucianism was the most effective and cheapest means ever devised by man for this purpose. They saw that the Confucian order had held together because certain canons of behavior had been hammered in by precept and example so effectively that deviation was nearly impossible. In their view the content of these canons mattered less than reviving the habit of behaving in accordance with fixed and unquestioned rules. This it was hoped would end the opposition to Kuomintang control. That the disciplinary effectiveness of the canon was dependent on its whole content and its whole context seems never to have occurred to them.

What has sometimes been called Chiang Kai-shek's idealism stemmed from this belief that indoctrination and habit are more effective than physical force in social control. In the mid-1930's, as economic crises and Japanese threats mounted, he stated that if the classic virtues of *li, i, lien,* and *ch'ih* had been more assiduously cultivated in recent years, China would not then be facing either domestic or foreign difficulties. As his armies fell back before the advancing Japanese in 1939, he blamed neglect of the doctrine of the rites and urged salvation of the nation through renewed emphasis on loyalty and filial piety. And when, in 1950, his armies had retreated to Formosa, he attributed the Communist victory primarily to Kuomintang loss of morale. He replaced the morally discredited Central Executive Committee with a new Central Reform Committee with the charge: "We must inherit our five thousand year old culture and make it a guide in human progress."

Chiang's insistence that the decisive element in human affairs, and in the flourishing and decay of civilizations, is the moral purpose of men, is good Confucian doctrine and more particularly good Restoration doctrine. But in Chiang's conception of this moral purpose and of the legacy from which it springs there is an important new element. For Chiang the Confucian way of life has lost its traditional rational and universal qualities and it has become imbued with a romantic nationalism. It has supreme value because it is Chinese, the source of *our* great past, the promise of *our* great future. There are not one but two anomalies in the statement that the task of the revolution is "to revive our Chinese culture, to restore our people's ancient virtues, to proclaim our Chinese national soul."

Out of all these five thousand years of which the Generalissimo talked, it was the T'ung-chih Restoration which held his attention. As he took command of the anti-Communist forces in the critical battles in Hupeh in 1932 his thoughts turned to Hu Lin-i, whom he eventually came to consider as even greater than Tseng Kuo-fan. The Communists, he reflected, were nothing like so formidable a foe as the Taipings had been. He meditated about the way in which Hu had pacified the area, turned defeat into victory and overcome his environment. If Hu's principles could be mastered they could become "the ultimate guiding principles for our suppression of the Communists today."

While in theory the new Kuomintang policy was modelled on Restoration policy in all fields, in practice the Kuomintang emphasized Restoration lessons with respect to local control, military leadership and strategy, and revival of the Confucian ideology. Restoration principles in other fields—notably economics—were almost entirely ignored. It is true that Chiang quoted with unreserved approval Hu Lin-i's version of the classic principle: "If civil government is weakened, then the people's livelihood has nothing on which to depend. Even though you kill a thousand bandits a day, you will not remedy the general situation." But Chiang also instructed party workers that it was an error to quote the classics to the effect that adequate food and clothing were prerequisite to virtue. On the contrary, Chiang stated, the people must first be virtuous; only then will they have the moral strength to obtain food and clothing.

For the Kuomintang, agriculture was the basis of the state in theory, but the Kuomintang documentation lacks the Restoration emphasis on water control, public works, reduction of the land tax, and control of currency and speculation in the interest of the agrarian economy. And evidently Kuomintang leaders did not agree with Restoration leaders that the Confucian virtues flourish only in an agrarian society, that industry and commerce are profoundly disruptive of the traditional way of life. For as the "Confucian" governor of Kwangtung put it in a stormy interview with Hu Shih: "In building production, we may use foreign machines, foreign sciences, even foreign engineers. But for building men we must have roots; and these roots must be sought within China's ancient culture."

By contrast with its relative neglect of Restoration precedents in economic policy, the Kuomintang gave close attention to certain aspects of Restoration local control. In 1930 in Kiangsi, where the Red armies had their bases, it seemed to the Kuomintang that control could best be reasserted by applying Tseng Kuo-fan's three basic principles: strict law enforcement, revival of the *pao-chia* system and organization of the gentry. This was "the best model in history for learning how to exterminate Communists."

Chiang and other leaders reiterated these principles and repeatedly tried to put them into effect. Logically enough, they tried to build up the position of the gentry. Old privileges were restored and new ones added in the hope that the gentry might once again play its traditional role of maintaining local order and indoctrinating the peasantry. In 1939 Chiang Kai-shek wired all regional and local government and party officials to remind the gentry throughout the country that, in the words of the *Lun-yü,* when the wind moves, the grass bends; that the gentry could educate beyond where government orders could reach; that the country could be saved only if they recovered their "true national spirit" and remembered that "for several thousand years our country has considered loyalty and filial piety as the basis of the state."

Revival of the *pao-chia* system of collective responsibility and the related militia system was as important in the Kuomintang program of local control as was reinstatement of the gentry. Ch'ing statements on the *pao-chia* were carefully studied and reissued for the guidance of army officers and local officials, with particular attention to the plan of "strengthening the walls and clearing out the countryside" which was first developed for the suppression of the White Lotus Rebellion. The compilations reissued by the Kuomintang emphasized such points as: "The villages of the *chou* and *hsien* are like the leaves and branches of a tree; if the leaves and branches are damaged, the root and trunk have nothing to shelter them." For this reason, "To defend cities is not as good as to defend villages." In the defense of villages, the *pao-chia* and the militia must function together, the one preventing traitors from operating within the area, the other warding off outside attack. In this, "the poor serve with their strength, the rich contribute money, and separate families are banded together in large groups." This last, the party noted, is the very essence of the system.

The Kuomintang evidently accepted the Ch'ing arguments without reservation, and ordered the full re-institution of the *pao-chia* system against which they as revolutionaries had once railed, with particular attention to its use in Communist-infested areas.

The Kuomintang gave less emphasis to good local government in connection with local control than the Restoration leaders gave to this subject. In the Kuomintang sources, there is relatively little attention to the slowness of justice, the interference of the clerks and other abuses which Restoration leaders considered major causes of local dissatisfaction and revolt. While the Kuomintang in theory considered the quality of officials to be a matter of major importance, the Restoration emphasis on the quality of local officials was lacking. Moreover since the actual machinery through which these men of ability were supposed to be elected, trained and controlled had long since collapsed, Kuomintang discussions of the subject often lacked practical point.

The second field in which the Kuomintang modelled itself closely on the Restoration was military leadership and strategy. From the time when Chiang first used Ts'ai O's book as a text at the Whampoa Military Academy in 1924, Nationalist army officers were lectured to about the principles to be learned from studying the careers of Restoration leaders. As Ts'ai O put it, and others have repeated, the Restoration experience shows that the essential qualities of a good commander are: (1) a sense of public duty and in consequence of this a respect for the troops; (2) fearlessness in the face of death; and (3) indifference to fame. Ts'ai noted that while Westerners valued genius in military men, Tseng and Hu emphasized the good heart and thereby transformed an era of catastrophic rebellion into an era of immortal glory.

If the officers of the Nationalist army have fallen short of this goal, it has not been for want of instruction.

Restoration precedents also dominated Kuomintang thinking about strategy. While the campaigns against the Taiping furnished the chief lessons, those against the Nienfei were not neglected. In analyzing the various campaigns, the Kuomintang consistently drew the lessons from the Ch'ing side. The Party was not interested in learning how the Nienfei might have avoided being trapped, but in mastering the relentless *hua-ho ch'uan-ti* hemming-in strategy by which the Ch'ing trapped the rebels. In 1930 Chiang Kai-shek ordered the compilation of all the proclamations and reports—even the troop songs—of the Ch'ing campaign against the Nienfei, for the specific purpose of using similar methods against the Communists. In 1948, researchers in the Ministry of National Defense were still hopefully studying this problem. Interestingly enough, the conclusion was drawn that the secret of Ch'ing success lay less in superior fire-power than in the attention which Tseng Kuo-fan and others devoted to the appointment of good local officials and to the discipline of troops so that popular support of the Government would be assured.

The Kuomintang effort to use Restoration models in local control and in military affairs obviously required an intensified campaign to revive the Confucian ideology. To the Kuomintang the question of education was the most critical of all, for according to the training manual for party political workers: "During several decades of revolutionary war, the old culture has collapsed in most areas, and a new culture has not yet been created."

The Kuomintang indoctrination program took many forms: reprinting of the works of Tseng Kuo-fan and their assignment in the schools; publicity to all Confucian ceremonies; a flood of books and articles on the traditional virtues; manifestoes by selected professors on the preservation of the Chinese heritage; and a government-ordered "read the classics" movement, promulgated from the "cradle of the Nationalist revolution, Canton." Liberal comment might be scathing, but Hu Shih was expelled from Kwangtung for lecturing against this movement and threatened with loss of his civil rights. To counter the left-wing pamphlets and the learned Marxist treatises which offered new solutions for the country's ills, special popular editions of traditional works were released in the most disturbed areas, and books in conflict with the doctrine of the rites (*li-chiao*) were banned.

With the movement to revive the classics went its corollary—a movement to discourage education in the modern humanities and social sciences. With Chinese studies as the basis, it was argued, only science and technology need be borrowed from the West. This was of course not a new idea. As T. F. Tsiang pointed out, it was a reversion to the policy of the T'ung-chih Restoration and history had proved that the Restoration formula was unworkable.

Kuomintang leaders thought otherwise. In their view, history had *not* discredited the T'ung-chih Restoration. In Chiang Kai-shek's view, a little science might be useful, but Chinese education, like Chinese civilization, had a special basic character, and this could best be preserved through studies of Tseng Kuo-fan and Hu Lin-i.

The whole of the neo-Restoration of the Kuomintang was a dismal failure; a far sadder spectacle than the T'ung-chih Restoration which it tried to copy. Local control was not reasserted. Army morale was not restored. There was never really any effort to revive the Confucian economy. And above all there was no general resurgence of Confucian values and mores. All this is scarcely surprising. The principles which the Kuomintang tried to use had long since been tried under far more hopeful circumstances and found wanting.

Yet this Restorationism of the Kuomintang cannot be dismissed as a joke. For all its foolishness, it was the ideology of the only political movement which ever had a chance of successfully competing with the Communists, and the character of the competition was gravely affected by the persistence of the doctrine of the rites. While the Kuomintang was not a monolith, criticism on this point of the primacy of the doctrine of the rites and of the lessons to be learned from the T'ung-chih Restoration came largely from the party's opponents. On this point there was little protest either from the splinter parties associated with the Kuomintang, or from the partially independent regional military leaders.

Within the Kuomintang itself there were fissures but not on this point. Li Tsung-jen, leader of the Free China opposition to Chiang Kai-shek, declared from New York in 1950: "After Chiang Kai-shek, it was thought any change was for the better. But after one year of trial, the people found that whereas Chiang Kai-shek was only interested in money and in depriving people of their material well being, the Communists aim at depriving them of their soul." But Li, like Chiang, went on to reassert the hard core of the Confucian social doctrine: "For over 4000 years the Chinese people were knitted together by a moral code, apart from a common written language, the same blood strain and a cultural heritage. The code of morals expounded by Confucius and the rest of our sages is the only reason Chinese exist as a people and as a country. This code of morals distinguishes Chinese from other people by defining the correct relationship between parents and children, husband and wife, brother and sister, teacher and student, friend and friend." As Vice-president and then Acting President of the Chinese National Government, Li offered a program of opposition to Chiang for failing to fulfill the responsibilities of a Confucian head of state, but of even greater opposition to the Communists for their denial of the very aims of the Confucian state. Li might easily be Prince Kung writing on the principles of social usage as the basis of the state.

Formerly the Communists were not the only outspoken critics of the neo-restorationism of the Kuomintang. As has been indicated above, the leading liberals of the twenties and thirties noted the successive waves of reaction and voiced their views with vigor. Long ago Hu Shih warned the new Confucians that they were doing what the leaders of the T'ung-chih Restoration had done, and he urged them to study the reasons for the Restoration's failure and to take warning. In Hu's view at that time, the leaders of the Restoration had failed because in their attempt to preserve the Chinese basis while selectively adapting from the West, they tried to preserve too much. They could not bring themselves to relinquish what had to be relinquished. Hu pointed out that again and again in the history of the twentieth century, whenever it appeared that the decision had at last been taken to initiate long-overdue reforms, a conservative clique had always re-emerged and had succeeded in blocking change on the ground that the precious "Chinese heritage" was being threatened. For Hu, their arguments were spurious: "They buy airplanes and artillery; naturally they can select the newest 1935 automobile; they merely want to use 2500 year old classics to teach men to be men."

Hu was arguing against superficial modernization, urging fundamental modernization, and he thought that the Restoration, to which it had become so fashionable to refer, taught a lesson opposite to that currently drawn; for Hu the T'ung-chih Restoration taught that limited, controlled, conservative modernization was simply impossible. And yet fundamentally, the difference between Hu and those whom he criticized was a matter of degree. He was willing to relinquish more than they, but by no means everything. He was optimistic; he considered that Chinese tradition was so strong and vigorous that radical adjustments could be made without danger of its loss.

It is nearly meaningless to say of a twentieth century Chinese thinker or politician that he is striving to select from the Chinese past the principles of enduring value and to adapt them to meet the problems of the modern world, for in various ways that is what they all have done with the exception of the leadership of the Communist party. For all the others, the hold of the traditional has been too powerful for the most ardent modernizer to escape, and the demands of the modern too compelling for the most confirmed traditionalist to ignore. The core of all intellectual and political controversy in China's turbulent twentieth century has been the restatement of Chang Chih-tung's formula: *Chung-hsüeh wei-t'i; hsi-hsüeh wei-yung* (Chinese studies as the basis; Western studies for practical use).

Faced with this dilemma, intellectual and political leaders of three decades professed optimism about the possibility of a viable compromise. They argued hotly, but their arguments could be reduced to disagreement about the elements of the two civilizations which it was desirable and feasible to blend. A man might attack his opponent as a compromiser, as limited to the Restoration mentality, but his own solution nearly always proved in the end another version of *chung-hsüeh wei-t'i; hsi-hsüeh wei-yung*.

During the past twenty years this lingering optimism, this hope that with new proportions this formula might somehow work has nearly disappeared in the face of a polarization of Chinese opinion. Those who have wanted a strong, modern China, even at the cost of the "Chinese basis" have drifted toward the Communists, who have been the only consistent advocates of fundamental social change. Those who have believed that there was something of enduring value in the Confucian tradition have had no practicable alternative to the neo-restorationism of the Kuomintang.

In these circumstances interpretations have been extreme. The Restoration has been taken to prove either that the traditional society it sought to restore was an evil and ugly thing, or that that society was a splendid thing which must govern China's future. Fung Yu-lan is one of the few who have recently urged "sympathetic understanding" of traditional China without urging that it be revived: "In saying this I have no intention of supporting it as a working social system in present day China. In order to live in the modern world in a position worthy of her past China must be industrialized. Where there is industrialization there is no place for the traditional family system and the traditional social structure."

But Fung is now with the Communists. From Formosa it is still said that the spirit of Chinese culture is everlasting, that it is at work today on the mainland and within the Communist party; that Communism was accepted because of certain superficial similarities to Confucianism; that sooner or later the mainland population will recognize that they are two opposed systems and will reject Communism and modernization in favor of the Confucian social order. The controversy is not over, and as long as men dispute the relation of China's future to China's past they will probably continue to dispute the true meaning of the T'ung-chih Restoration.

PART THREE
The Sense of Urgency

12

If the Kuomintang, the self-styled "Nationalists" (but not the only nationalists) of twentieth-century China, turned from revolution to admiration of old-style "restoration," why did they do so? Class warfare appalled them when they rose to the top; and men at the bottom, stirring, had set off a sort of class warfare in the old days, prior to that cherished "restoration." Though the Nationalists themselves had risen from the ashes of the Ch'ing, it was nineteenth-century peasants, with a desperate sense of urgency and the rudiments of class consciousness, who had begun to light the flame.

FROM

Strangers at the Gate:
Social Disorder in South China,
1839–1861

FREDERIC WAKEMAN, JR.

CLASS AND CLAN

> In his village, Chiang Pen-chen founded a *Sheng-p'ing* public office, and built a shrine to the righteous braves in order to appease their noble spirits and inspire the people.—*P'an-yü Hsien-chih,* 19:9-a

THE society of nineteenth-century Kwangtung was an intricate complex of interlocking associations: militia groups, hong, secret societies, gentry committees, pirate bands, "public offices," and—above all—lineage groups. It was the last of these, manifested as the clan (*tsu*), which seemed to distinguish South China from the rest of the empire. This was not because clans did not exist elsewhere; but in Kwangtung these huge, exogamous lineages were a primary and ubiquitous form of mass organization. For one, they were the province's largest landowners. Their

Frederic Wakeman, Jr., *Strangers at the Gate: Social Disorder in South China, 1839–1861* (University of California Press: Berkeley and Los Angeles, 1966), pp. 109–125. Reprinted by permission of The Regents of the University of California. Footnotes omitted.

"clan fields" (*chi-t'ien* or *ch'ang-tien*) provided an income which was used by the clan elders to pay students' stipends, degree-holders' subsidies, examination expenses, relief for the poor or disabled, and care for the ill. Sometimes the rents were simply divided among the individual families within the clan. Just as often, those same families would plough their shares back into the purchase of more clan fields. The increment was staggering. In one Kuang-chou delta town of five thousand families, for example, there were 130 clan temples supported by rents totaling 900,000 dollars a year.

Such rich and influential sibs were each a "focus of economic and political power" in Kwangtung. Clansmen who basked in the reflected glory of prestigious gentry leaders, or who welcomed the clan as a set of allies in case of local conflict, were naturally reluctant to leave its protective embrace. The lands themselves symbolized this unity, this source of collective power and prestige. At the same time, however,

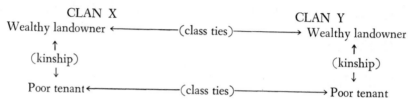

FIGURE 1. Kin-class axes within the lineage group.

other forces—also represented by clan fields—helped drive the lineage apart. The clan or *tsu* did not represent a set of either idyllic or static relationships. The very rents that paid for subsidies were often collected from poorer kinsmen, tenants of their own clan. These peasants could, and did, harbor deep resentments against the clan leaders who enforced high rents or usury. Sometimes clan rules recognized this by forbidding the rental of *chi-t'ien* to kinsmen. But in regions where clan and village were one and the same, this kind of rule could not be enforced. Thus, there were constant forces pushing and pulling against each other, sometimes dissolving and sometimes uniting the clan. These forces can be represented in a number of ways. The starkest would assume that two axes existed within the lineage group, one representing class and the other kinship. Landowners and tenants each shared potential, if not actual, class interests with their counterparts in other clans. At the same time, however, this horizontal solidarity was mollified by the vertical ties of kinship. Thus, the clans helped stabilize the countryside by mitigating class conflict. Unfortunately, one of the most powerful techniques of lineage unification—clan wars—also disrupted rural Kwangtung.

In 1766, the Ch'ien-lung Emperor became quite concerned over the large number of clan wars then being fought in Kwangtung.

The ritual land attached to the ancestral halls in the eastern part of Kwangtung frequently caused armed feuds [between clans]. . . . If the land is used lawfully to consolidate and harmonize [kinship relations] . . . it is not a bad practice at all. But if [it induces people] to rely on the numerical strength or financial power of their clans to oppress their fellow villagers, or even worse, to assemble mobs and fight with weapons . . . [such a practice] surely should not be allowed to spread. This wicked custom is especially prevalent in Fukien and Kwangtung provinces.

The Emperor then ordered that an investigation be carried out. What followed showed that some clans controlled many, many mou of *chi-t'ien*. The rents from these were collected each year in turn by one of the *chia* (family) within the clan. This family then paid whatever taxes were due and loaned out the rest on interest. Wealth begot wealth, and soon the countryside was divided into very rich and very poor *tsu*. The former easily oppressed the latter. But if two clans of equal strength and wealth were to quarrel over land or water rights, only warfare could decide the outcome. A battle was planned. Each clan assembled in its ancestral hall. The kinsmen were promised that the wounded would be paid rewards, the dead enshrined with honor, the bereaved guaranteed a lifetime stipend. If one of the enemy were to die, and the murder were to come to the attention of the local magistrate, then one of the clansmen who was wanted for another crime would volunteer to act as a "forfeit." By turning himself in, he satisfied the magistrate and ensured a steady future income for his family from clan funds.

In sharp contrast, clan wars in a province like Kiangsi never involved gentry participation. It was the peasants themselves who secretly decided when to fight, and who chose leaders from among themselves. Only after the battle did they turn to clan notables for legal protection. Naturally, the wealthier members of the sib disapproved of all this and frequently tried to judge the peasant ringleaders themselves. But when the elders gathered in their own ancestral hall, they were apt to face a peasant mob of their kinsmen who would try to prevent the trial from taking place. When this happened, of course, lineage conflict split the clan.

In Kwangtung, on the other hand, clan wars were openly backed and organized by clan leaders because this was one important way for them to increase their own power and the clan's control over ritual land. The ritual land in turn provided a means of payment for the struggle. Ultimately, the values that were invoked and the rewards that were promised strengthened clan solidarity and the hold of the wealthier sublineages.

By the nineteenth century, clan warfare was endemic in Kwangtung.

Parts of the province were in a state of "chronic anarchy," characterized by embattled villages, high walls, mud embankments, arms warehouses, semiprofessional fighters. Around Whampoa, for example, two clans feuded almost continuously during 1835 and 1836, writing out vengeful scrolls with their own blood, defacing each other's graves, and employing the same "bands of devoted men" or "forfeits" described in the eighteenth century. Most of these wars began as struggles over water rights or land. The clans preferred to fight rather than turn to the magistrate's court, where they would be subjected to extortion and the vagaries of Chinese justice. For each belligerent was fairly certain what his clan's military losses would be in advance. It was a calculated risk. Unfortunately, the area of violence tended to spread. Mercenaries were hired, or clans extended their network of alliances by calling on other, unrelated lineages of the same surname. Even the militia offered means of extension. "Lineage members, for the purpose of common defense, banded together forming a *pao-chia* organization which raised local militia and posted sentries. All these matters were dealt with by the ancestral hall, which thus necessarily became a military headquarters and assembly point for the militia." For clan and *t'uan-lien* were mutually intermingled in Kwangtung during the 1840's and '50's. The militia of a uniclan village was nothing more nor less than a clan organization. Its leaders were clan leaders. The wounded or dead were rewarded with the clan's ritual land, and above all, honored by inclusion in the clan's ancestral hall.

The word for ancestral hall in that part of China is *tz'u-t'ang*. Because of the stress on geomancy, propitious sites were very desirable and therefore hard to acquire. Only wealthy lineages could afford the land for such a shrine. The *tz'u*, therefore, was intimately related to the process of lineage segmentation and clan formation. Since ancestral tablets were removed from the domestic shrine once they were four generations away from the descendant who maintained them, "no segment higher than an extended family could find a focus in them." However, they could be replaced by another sort of tablet which was placed, not in the household shrine, but in the special ancestral hall, the *tz'u-t'ang*. This, in turn, could lead to a more expanded kind of social grouping: intermediate lineage segments, one step above the regular extended family. Then as the lineage formed around a *tz'u-t'ang*, and incorporated other intermediate segments, more economic resources were commanded, and a clan would emerge, growing geometrically. Thus, in a rural district with only one or two surnames, there might be one *tsu* containing over one thousand people with twenty or more *tz'u-t'ang*, and one main clan shrine called the *ta-tsung-tz'u*.

However, the clan shrines, like the clan fields, both unified and divided the lineage. For while the rich families built their temples and maintained extended families, the poor lineages, without ritual foci, remained divided and alone. In short, the shrine unified the expanding, aggressive lineage, and separated it from the less powerful households.

Since the tablets hung in the *tz'u-t'ang* had none of the immanent sanctity of the actual ancestral tablets in the domestic shrine, they represented ascribed social values, not personal religiosity. These tablets actually conferred genuine social status on those enshrined there, and on their descendants who came to pay ritual respect. No wonder, then, that inclusion in such an ancestral hall was so powerful an incentive to members of the local militia. In fact, some of the best descriptions of militia activities in the Kuang-chou gazetteers are to be found, not in the biographies (*lieh-chuan*), but in the sections on shrines. Official sanction for such militia was even sought in the guise of laudatory tablets for the shrines. While the *t'uan-lien* may have attracted and abetted rebellious and heterodox forces of disorder, the basic values they invoked were conservative, familistic, and orthodox.

But what of lineage involvement in the gentry-inspired militia leagues that transcended village and clan? Even there lineage may have been just as important. Of the twenty-five leaders of the *Tung-p'ing kung-she*, 60 percent shared surnames. This does not necessarily prove kinship. But the high correlation, as well as the obvious relationship of the Hsieh and the Wang kin, who share generational names, suggest that the militia federations may have been successful in Kwangtung precisely because they were conglomerates of preexisting clan "banners." Could particular militia organizations even have existed in an early form as multiclan alliances? Perhaps. But the really large federations of *t'uan-lien*, such as the *Sheng-p'ing she-hsüeh*, transcended clan alignments. The gentry allied series of vertical lineage groups. Therefore, all of the potentially horizontal ties between the gentry and tenants of one clan and those of another were suddenly linked or strengthened. A peasant from one village discovered that he shared economic or social interests with a poor peasant from another town. Without the militia movement, the mutual hostility of the nucleated countryside, which favored the leaders' control of a clan, would have prevented this realization.

Inevitably, this horizontal mobility pulled the two axes of the class-clan equilibrium against each other with an increased force. As long as the external enemy, the British, threatened Kuang-chou, lineage ties held. When the menace was apparently disposed of after 1849, class began to override clan. For the militia movement had also strengthened the gentry's control within each lineage segment. Ritual leadership among clansmen was not necessarily in the hands of local notables. A clan elder might be a relatively powerless creature, chosen for genealogical seniority and approved because he could not use his powerful position for selfish ends. But because of the militia, it became necessary to elect politically acceptable gentry who then assumed leadership of the ancestral halls and "public offices." The disruption of the balance of control between the district magistrate and local notables eventually affected the clan. As the economic, political, and military roles allocated to the gentry increased, the functions of the clan-village multiplied. Sublineage leaders were drawn into compact political and ritual organizations: "public offices" (*kung-so* or *kung-she*), or "local schools" (*she-hsüeh*). This process, which began in the mid-nineteenth century, was to culminate in almost a total congruence of ritual and political power in the twentieth century. By 1930, "in the present system of rural self-government (in Kwangtung), the chiefs of sub-districts, and the chiefs of villages, as well as their subordinates, are for the most part recommended by the authorities of powerful clans."

All of these changes disturbed the social balance maintained by the clan. By 1845, society began to polarize into wealthy and poor. Class interests were no longer "softened" by the lineage. These interests, though always present in Chinese society, emerged nakedly and boldly from the militia movement. They did not create the movement. Historians like Seiji Imabori have theorized that the gentry's militia were designed to keep the hostile tenantry in economic subjection. Hence, the gentry militia of the Taiping period have been neatly defined as a "counter-revolutionary" force that suppressed the rebellious peasants. On the contrary, the militia originally unified landlord and peasant. Xenophobia and the clan held rural Kuang-chou together during the serious economic crises partially engendered by the Opium War. But the forces described above eventually polarized society, and then the militia changed their function. Instead of being devices of mass defense and popular consensus, they became organs of social control, putting enormous power in the hands of the wealthier notables. As this process went on, the peasantry became disaffected. Greater and greater numbers began to join secret societies that transcended the clan.

This phenomenon was not peculiar to China. The same sort of polarization occurred in certain areas of southern Europe, notably in Sicily.

The coming of the modern economy (whether or not it is combined with foreign conquest) may, and indeed probably will, disrupt the social balance of the kinship society, by turning some kins into "rich" families and others into "poor," or by disrupting the kin itself. The traditional system of blood-vengeance outlawry may—and indeed probably will—"get out of hand" and produce a multiplicity of unusually murderous feuds and embittered outlaws, into which an element of class struggle begins to enter.

As with the Mafia, so with the Triads.

THE SECRET SOCIETIES OF SOUTH CHINA

> The sage Confucius handed down to us the ink and brush. For
> three successive years I have sat for examinations; some day
> Heaven will smile on me, and the names of the Sons of Hung
> shall appear on the list of successful candidates.—Triad initiation
> ceremony

Students of the plot theory of history are prone to attribute enormous
influence to secret societies. The thought of conspiracy is reassuring:
man, after all, is a creature of free will, not a tool of circumstances or a
product of social forces. Impersonal history is thus conveniently anthro-
pomorphized. Besides, secrecy as such holds its own fascinations: esoteric
passwords, hooded figures in the night, subtle handshakes of recognition,
a pervasive world brotherhood reaching into high places. It is tempting to
believe that history pivoted on the machinations of the eighteenth century's Illuminati, Italy's Carbonari, or the Third Republic's Freemasons.

Westerners in the nineteenth century succumbed to the same sort of
romantic notions about Chinese secret societies. After all, they were even
more shrouded in mystery than their European counterparts; and there
was no denying the fact that they were ubiquitous. Kwangtung, in particular, seemed filled with "Triads," a rubric that covered three similar but
separate societies: the *T'ien-ti-hui* (Heaven and Earth Society), which
was most prevalent in Fukien; the *San-tien-hui* (Triple Dot Society); and
the *San-ho-hui* (Triple Unity Society), which flourished in Kwangtung
but was also found in Kwangsi, Fukien, Kiangsi, and Hunan. Time and
time again, isolated revolts pulled aside the veils of secrecy to give the
Europeans a tantalizing glimpse into this fascinating underworld. Early
in the nineteenth century, a Fukienese named Ch'en Li-nan had terrorized
Tung-kuan with his chapter of the Heaven and Earth Society. Nan-hai
and Hsiang-shan counties were often disturbed by local branches of the
San-ho-hui, whose members were known familiarly as "brains" (*nao*),
"old concubines" (*fang-chang*), "willow branches" (*liu-chih*), or "iron
sticks" (*t'ieh-pan*). By 1838, even the Triple Dot Society had begun to
recruit members openly in the delta area.

Nomenclature hardly mattered. Regardless of chapter or branch, each
society behaved in about the same way as far as the southern Chinese
themselves were concerned. To the Cantonese the groups were collec-
tively known as the societies of the "vast gate" (*Hung-men*), for these
were individual, autocephalous bands, without central control, acting
under different names at different times. This diffusion was at once the
order's weakness and its strength. Because there was no ultimate headquarters, the societies found it difficult to sustain a large uprising for
long. Over the years, the history of the Triads was a tale of futile,

scattered rebellions, without any semblance of union or coherence. On the other hand, the cellular nature of the organisms made it almost impossible to break up the societies, unless one could wipe out all of the "dangerous classes" that joined the chapters in every market town of southeast China.

The one thing that each society shared with the other was a common initiation rite and history, which was usually transmitted orally. For obvious reasons, there were differing versions of the Triads' origins, but most agreed on certain crucial details. During the initiation, the Grand Master told the neophytes how, in 1674, the monks of the Shao-lin temple in Fukien, all adepts in the martial arts, answered the K'ang-hsi Emperor's call for volunteers to help him drive off the Eleuths of Galdan. Thanks to divine help, the barbarians were defeated, and the Emperor rewarded the Abbot with a special seal. Sixty years later, the villainous prefect of Foochow coveted the precious seal still held by the nearby monastery. First, he managed to convince the Yung-cheng Emperor that the monks of the Shao-lin temple were planning a rebellion. Then, helped by a treacherous monk named A-ch'ieh, he fired the temple and killed all but five monks, who escaped with the seal to another temple high in the mountains of the province. There they discovered a porcelain censer floating on a stream and bearing the slogan, *Fan-ch'ing fu-ming* (Oppose the Ch'ing dynasty and restore the Ming dynasty). Out of the censer shot a red light, which revealed a magic sword. After these discoveries, the five monks were suddenly and mysteriously joined by five new men, the "Tiger Generals," and—some versions insist—the fourteen-year-old grand-son of the last Ming emperor. All pledged a blood oath and raised the righteous banner of revolt. In their first encounter with the Manchus, however, they were defeated and routed. The brotherhood, hunted like dogs, split into five Grand Lodges, which spread across South and Central China, swearing to carry on the struggle against the nefarious Ch'ing.

This legendary potpourri had little to do with the societies' real history. There was a Shao-lin temple, famous as the home of Chinese boxing; but it existed in Honan in the T'ang period. There were tales of thirteen warrior-monks helping an emperor; but the ruler was T'ang T'ai-tsung, the enemy Wang Shih-ch'ung, and the time the seventh century. There was a revolt in 1674; but the leader was Chu I-kuei, a Ming loyalist en-sconced on Formosa. Still, some historical associations do emerge from the ritual myths. It seems clear that the Triads originated on Formosa, since the first verifiable historical reference associates them with Lin Shuang-wen's rebellion on that island in 1786. From there they moved to Fukien on the mainland, where the apocryphal temple was supposed to have existed. After the White Lotus revolts at the end of the eighteenth century, they spread throughout South China, periodically roiling the surface of society along with some of the other sects descended from the

Buddhist societies of Yuan times: Green Lotus (*Ch'ing-lien*), Inactivity (*Wu-wei*), Eight Diagrams (*Pa-kua*). After 1800, every minor rebellion usually incited some Triad activity—always in the name of restoring the Ming: the *Pa-kua* revolt of 1813, Chu Mao-li in 1814, Chao Fu-ts'ai's *Yao* rebellion in 1832, and so on.

The legendary accounts say nothing of this later history. Yet, in a way, the closely guarded ritual is much more revealing than a bald historical description of the Triads' activities. Its secrecy contrasted sharply with the openness of village life in China. Like the walled yamen, or the Forbidden City, the secret society surrounded itself with a complex of awe-inspiring ritual forms. Within the rural confines of that agrarian empire, the Triads existed as a kind of counter-state, a political organism *within* society. More than that, the secret societies represented an artificial but complete social subsystem. To join the brotherhood was to be reborn, to enter a new set of eternal relationships. Social distinctions would be abolished. A great unity would emerge.

"We revere the heavenly doctrine of being united in one, and therefore desire to overthrow the Ch'ing and restore the Ming so that the will of Heaven and that of Earth shall be once more united. . . . Tonight we pledge ourselves before Heaven that the brethren in the whole universe shall be as if from one womb, as if begotten by one father, as if nourished by one mother, and as if they were of one stock and origin." These were ties that nothing could sunder, once the oaths had been sworn, each man's blood drunk, and the special signs of identification learned. "As thus I strike off the head of this white cock, so may my head be struck off if I, like A-ch'ieh, prove to be a traitor." This was genuine blood brotherhood, an artificial sib functionally analogous to the family.

The ideal Chinese social unit was the extended family. Usually, only the stem family proved financially feasible. Extra sons had to create their own conjugal units or become one of the loose, floating population known as "dangerous classes" in Confucian social commentary. This inner proletariat automatically helped turn any minor social or economic crisis into a disaster. But so impregnated were they with the ideals of familism that the very organizations of revolt sedulously copied kinship and guaranteed these artificial ties with elaborate rites of passage. The candidates were always cleansed, then dressed in white clothes to symbolize the purity of the new man—white, also, to symbolize the pure Ming against the forces of darkness. For the rebirth was total. The neophyte washed off the dirt of the old order to enter a new age. "Wash the filth of Ch'ing from off your faces with the water of the three rivers, that your true countenances may appear, and your mouths be closed. Divest yourselves of the clothing of Ch'ing, an emblem of servitude, and in place thereof, don the raiment of Ming." This was restorationism: not revolutionary, but revolutionist. After all, not only did the Triads wish to restore the Ming;

they also derived their charismatic legitimacy from the K'ang-hsi Emperor's seal. Their rebellions were always justified specifically because local officials had let their avarice override Confucian duty, and generally because the dynasty had violated the legitimate order represented by a monarchical paradigm, the Ming. In fact, the only element in their ideology that distinguished the secret societies from sanctioned Confucian protest was their anti-Manchuism; and even that was traditional. Ethnocentrism had been an ingredient in secret-society ideology since the days of the Southern Sung, when the regime insisted on the right of native Chinese to rule over foreign barbarians. Whether Juchen, Kitai, Mongol, or Manchu, the barbarians became a target for the hatred of the "purer" Chinese. This was particularly true for Kwangtung. Who could forget the eleven-month siege of Canton in 1650, when the Tartar troops finally battered down the walls with cannon and killed over one hundred thousand people in a brutal bloodbath of revenge and fury? These popular memories did not die early. In fact, anti-Manchu revolutionaries like Sun Yat-sen felt that hatred of the Ch'ing formed the essence of the Triads' ideology.

By the era of K'ang-hsi, the Ch'ing dynasty had already consolidated itself, and the loyal remnants of the Ming were either dead or exhausted. The two or three remaining elders realized that their great forces had vanished and that there was nothing to return to, and so—wishing to keep nationalism (*min-tsu chu-i*) as their root and source—they passed it on to later generations. Thus, "Oppose the Ch'ing and restore the Ming" became their testament, leading to the organization of societies, so that later rebels could find future help awaiting them.

Nevertheless, it is hard to believe that this ethnocentrism represented some form of "protonationalism." Even overseas, the secret societies were formed into rival speech groups, which split the Chinese communities vertically and hindered the development of nationalism. Their useless retention of the Ming ritual long after the Manchus were overthrown proved that ethnocentrism and restorationism served other purposes.

First, the dispossessed could find pride and self-esteem in their own racial purity. Second, restorationism corresponded to a "rational perpetuative nativism" which looked back to the good old days when officials were just, food was in plenty, and society was not out of kilter. Third, the Manchus diverted social anger from the native upper classes. Fourth, during periods of actual rebellion, restorationism permitted the Triad leaders to pretend to more than banditry—it gave them a sense of political significance. For there were really three levels of "rebellion" in South China: banditry, outlawry, and actual revolt.

The bandits (*tao*) were *ad hoc* rural gangs which gathered in small bands to rob at random. Membership fluctuated. A peasant might join for one raid and abstain from the next. Only occasionally were larger confederations formed for temporary plundering. Seldom was secret-society membership claimed, as there was a clear distinction between mere robbers (*t'u-fei*) and dangerously rebellious societies (*hui-fei*). If there was any ideological consensus at all, it was the notion that these forces were limiting social oppression.

The outlaws (*tsei*) were permanent brotherhoods living outside the villages in mountainous or wooded areas. There was little cooperation with the peasantry. In fact, villages often had to pay protection fees to keep the *tsei* away from their walls. The outlaws, in turn, lived in a state of permanent social insurrection, levying tolls, kidnapping travelers, collecting harvest taxes, and sometimes even attacking small administrative centers. Many of the outlaw bands of Kwangtung emerged from the irregular militia of the Opium War. One contemporary Chinese scholar wrote: "If righteous braves assemble, then they feed themselves from the rations of the militia. If they dissolve, they form secret societies, to lurk in the mountains and valleys, waiting to rob and plunder. The homes of the gentry are thus harmed. . . . The high officials have nourished a cancer." Like the Mafia of Sicily, Chinese outlaws relied on secret-society ties to hold them together through good and bad times. Unlike the Mafia, their leaders were not rural landowners. Only in the districts around Ch'ao-chou, where the local notables were seldom officials, or else headed warring clans, did secret societies boast prestigious or wealthy heads. In the richer and more settled Kuang-chou delta area, peasants opposed the *tsei* whenever possible.

Finally, there were the secret societies in rebellion. When local economic conditions grew intolerable, increasingly larger numbers of normally peaceful peasants found themselves forced to steal for a living, and the line between *tao* and *tsei* was erased. Ineffable rumors hinted that the dynasty had run its term. A single outlaw band, acting in the name of the Ming, would unite multiple gangs of bandits and begin to recruit openly among the sedentary peasants. Government and justice had failed: the "Way of the Gods" was about to emerge. Political change, not gang enrichment, became the expressed goal.

This political strain distinguishes Chinese secret societies from the Christian sects of medieval Europe. There the Church was universal. The sects, aiming at direct personal fellowship, renounced universalism and physically or spiritually fled from the City of Man. They were not an alternative. They were an escape or a rejection. The secret societies, on the other hand, did not renounce a universal world-view, or compatibility with the greater society in which they existed. True, in the long history of China there have been "pure" sects whose adherents represented an ideological or social fringe: the vegetarians of the T'ang period, or the tantric followers of certain twelfth century White Lotus (*Pai-lien*) sects. But usually, no matter how bizarre the origins of a cult, its pretensions quickly became temporal and political. Chang Ling, leader of the *Wu-tou-mi-tao* (The Way of the Five Pecks of Rice) sects in the late second century A.D., may simply have created a faith-healing offshoot of Taoism. But his son, Chang Heng, quickly used the cult to carve out a satrapy for himself in Szechuan. Even the most potentially revolutionary of Chinese secret societies, the antitax (*k'ang-liang*) movements of the Southern Sung, did not engage in utopianism. While the charitable Franciscans and communal Beguines had morally revolted against the very institution of property, the Chinese brotherhoods simply sought its redistribution.

This distinction between utopian escape and perennial political engagement explains the continuing involvement of Chinese secret societies in dynastic change, as well as their perpetual inability to provide any alternative to the Confucian system. In that sense, Chinese social thought —whether part of the "Great" or "Little" tradition—was holistic. European Christianity, on the other hand, was only apparently integral, actually embodying two great currents of social thought. The first was conservative and best symbolized by Thomism, which used *lex naturae* and Aristotelian forms to explain the social system existing outside the City of God. The second was radical, characterized by chiliasm, "generous love," and a bent toward primitive communism. Rome tolerated this second, anti-institutional set of doctrines by creating the monastic orders. But the history of the Catholic Church from the ninth century to the sixteenth century can easily be viewed as a continuing failure to "enclose," disarm, or destroy the potentially revolutionary beliefs of the sects and heresies: Albigensian, Franciscan, or Taborite. The Church's ultimate defeat occurred with the Reformation. Both sects and secession were "pure" protests against the institutional and hierarchical nature of the temporal papacy, with its emphasis on order, law, and restraint. The history of the sects themselves was not a series of alternatives offered to that hierarchy, challenging the Church as a particular manifestation of accepted values and beliefs. Rather, the sects represented a series of alienations. The beliefs that inspired them were nurtured by emotions that the Church could never hope to meet, because of the fundamentals of the Thomistic social doctrine which lacked the necessary degree of "magic" to allow for shared belief.

Not so with traditional Chinese thought. The marvelous syncretism of Han Confucianism, with its "five agents," its cosmic trinity, its charismatic emperor-priest, its theory of omens, allowed it to absorb many potentially antinomian and rebellious strains of thought. Thanks also to Mencius' espousal of the right to revolt and the later Kung-yang thinkers' mystic *chün-tzu* (sage), there were enough safety valves to contain everything but new and powerful doctrines imported from outside the civilization. The really revolutionary element in the history of the secret societies and sects of China was the introduction of millennial Maitreyan Buddhism.

In times of famine or distress, the Buddhist theory of the three Kalpas brought hope and solace to the demoralized. Since the transition from one cycle to the next was supposed to be heralded by calamities, the doctrine corresponded perfectly to the real historical cycles of irrigation breakdown or invasion. The self-righteous were promised deliverance, and their tormentors, extermination. Spiritual power, in short, would triumph over temporal authority. However, the Confucian political system was so arranged that no one doctrine could claim a monopoly of that spiritual power. Once a new emperor donned the dragon robes of state, he was endowed with magical control over the cosmos until fresh calamities should arise. Thus, this Buddhist belief in the intervention of Spirit in history ultimately allowed a ruler oriented to Confucianism to stabilize chaos. The world had not ended. The discontented, the alienated, the rebellious, were pulled back into the ever-renewing, never-ending whorls of Confucian history. Even Buddhism only predicted the Ultimate Void, Kunyata: not a solution to the world, but an issue from it. Amitabha's Buddhist Paradise was never secularized. History remained process, and never became progress. In this context that was the most fundamental difference between Western and Chinese thought. When the Seventh Seal was opened, the secular world would vanish. But rationally with Vico and Condorcet, mystically with Joachim of Floris or Boehm, Paradise was secularized: Swedenborg's heaven emerged as a Big Rock Candy Mountain. This promise of rewards in this world was to prove the most explosive social force of the nineteenth century. Saint-Simon, Fourier, and Marx linked history as progress with the industrial revolution, and modern socialism was born. In China, this kind of historical view was not introduced until Hung Hsiu-ch'üan founded the *T'ai-p'ing* Heavenly Kingdom. Only after that could K'ang Yu-wei change the "Great Unity" (*Ta-t'ung*) of Kung-yang Confucianism from Arcady to Utopia, from the halcyon past to the glowing future. By then, however, China wanted a Western, not a native, paradise. Marxism-Leninism emerged, and Confucianism gave its last gasp.

13

The Rise of Land Tax and the Fall of Dynasties in Chinese History

WANG YÜ-CH'ÜAN

ISTORIANS have not failed to note the importance of the exorbitant rate of land tax at the end of the Ming dynasty of 1368–1643. For more than fifty years before the fall of the dynasty, the agricultural economy of China was being bled to exhaustion by special land taxes levied on the peasantry and known by such names as "Liaotung supply," "expedition supply" and "training supply," which were supposed to finance and provision the armies fighting against the Manchus in South Manchuria. Excessive taxation and corruption in the levying of the taxes provoked in the end peasant risings all over China. It was the leader of a rebel peasant army who actually took Peking and caused the suicide of the last Ming emperor; only then, taking advantage of the collapse of the central government, did the Manchus convert their attacks into a permanent conquest.

Knowing that their main problem was the desperate condition of the peasantry, the new Manchu rulers undertook at once to allot land to peasant-owners and to diminish the rate of land tax, and the success of their efforts makes the first period of Manchu rule notable for the restoration of social stability. The most important measure was the "permanent settlement" decree of 1713, under the emperor K'ang Hsi, giving the assurance that for the future there would be no variation in the rate of either land tax or poll tax. Later in the history of the Manchu dynasty these two taxes were consolidated as one, ominously known as "one single whip."

Good intentions cannot however deflect the course of social history. The Manchus had imposed themselves as a privileged class at the apex of a society which, in spite of the temporary lightening of abuses, remained exactly what it had been under the Ming dynasty. No imperial decrees could eliminate the forms of exploitation inherent within the

Wang Yü-ch'üan, "The Rise of Land Tax and the Fall of Dynasties in Chinese History," *Pacific Affairs* (June 1936), pp. 201–20. Reprinted by permission. Footnotes omitted.

system. The Manchus, whose own privileges were rooted in the system (or had been grafted on to it), became corrupted by the same decay which had rotted the Ming dynasty. When they fell it was because they had allowed and participated in a predatory exploitation of the basic agricultural economy of China which made easier the collapse of their empire in peasant revolts when they became subject to the pressure of the West—itself a totally new force in Chinese history and armed with powers deadly to the old Chinese society.

The record of the Manchu dynasty, beginning with the redistribution of land and the lightening of taxes and ending with the degeneration of the ruling class, the swollen accumulation of estates in the hands of private, privileged, tax-evading landholders, extortionate taxation of the poor peasantry, and helplessness in the face of foreign invasion, is an epitome of Chinese economic and social history. It cannot be understood except by stating the mechanism and principles of the abuse of power in the exploitation of the Chinese agricultural system. The process of corruption may be described briefly as one in which the central government was robbed of real wealth and power, which were transferred to the very individuals who, as members of the ruling class, controlled the government. They could not possibly be restrained because, while responsible as officials and as a class for protecting the interests of the nation, they were as private individuals the sole beneficiaries of corruption. While some of them, as officials, understood what was wrong, the most that they could accomplish as a class was to try to protect both the government interest and their class interest by trying to make up for the taxes which they themselves evaded by increased taxation of the poor and unprivileged classes. Naturally, as the history of the times was also written by the privileged classes, the methods of abuse were never coldly expounded as an organized system. Nevertheless, from the records of memorials to the throne concerning separate and widely scattered cases of abuse, it is possible to discern what the system was, and to document it from official sources.

When the Manchus entered China, the first necessity was to bring under unified control the provinces which had broken apart through the collapse of the Ming central government. The Bannermen, who provided the Manchu military power, naturally constituted a first charge on the revenue. The Manchu nobility and high officials were not only a charge on the government, but at the same time for all practical purposes were the government. In proportion as they succeeded in diverting the rewards of power to their personal uses, they weakened the government, but this did not make them cease to be the government, and the investment and managing of their private fortunes soon united their interests with those of the Chinese officials who entered the government service.

The basic source of wealth being the exploitation of the land, the interest of the government was to obtain the greatest possible volume of land tax; but since the interest of the landlords was to extract rent and to evade taxation on their own lands, the volume of land tax revenue could only be kept up by an increased rate of levy on the decreasing acreage of land held by peasants. This in itself forced many peasants to part with their land and become tenants, thus increasing the burden on the remainder, with the result that the process of combined state decay and local corruption gathered momentum at an increasing rate.

By the middle of the nineteenth century these processes had gone so far that they made all the easier the defeat of China in the Opium War of 1840–42. Huge expenditures were necessary, but the only reward for the peasants was an increase in the demand for land tax, and for China the humiliating Treaty of Nanking, which destroyed national independence and legalized the importation of opium, again increasing the burden of the people. The process of collapse was thus moved forward a stage, and in 1851 there began in the south, in Kuangsi, the T'aip'ing Rebellion, followed a year or two later in the north by the rebellion of the Nien Min, in Shantung, together with a Moslem rebellion in Yünnan in the southwest.

Then came the British and French occupation of Peking in 1860, when vast amounts of money had to be raised to meet war expenses and an indemnity of 18 million taels. In 1862 the Moslem rebellion spread to the northwestern provinces, with the result that more than half of China was beyond the control of the central government. The people in the regions of revolt were relieved of government taxation, but the burdens of those within the restricted taxable regions that remained became by so much the more crushing. By this time, also, wealth began to be drained from the agricultural interior to finance the building of steamships in the south and textile factories in Shanghai and Nanking, to be followed later by expenditures on railways, a telegraph system, and other new enterprises. The annual revenue had increased to over 60 millions—20 millions more than it had been under the reign of Tao Kuang, from 1821 to 1850—but there was still an annual deficit of more than 10 millions.

In the next reign, from 1875 to 1908, China was defeated in 1883–1885 by France in Annam; in 1894–95 came the Sino-Japanese war, and in 1900 the allied Foreign Powers took Peking and demanded an indemnity of 400 million taels. The financial resources of the Manchu dynasty were wrecked. In spite of every effort, and the assessment of new kinds of levies, there was still a great deficit. Foreign loans were negotiated, from Britain and Germany and from Russia and France, a financial expedient unknown in previous Chinese history, and plainly designed to saddle foreign control on the nation.

Yet the Manchu ruling class continued to indulge themselves insanely. The Empress Dowager built a summer palace with funds that had been raised to create a navy, with the result that in the war with Japan the navy was hopelessly weak. Outside of the capital, from provincial governor to district magistrate the officials and scholar-gentry scrambled for money and position. The customs tariff imposed on China by the foreign powers was limited to a conventional five per cent; the salt gabelle, under a monopoly system, could not be rationally reorganized in a short time. The land tax was the sole major source of revenue. Between 1851 and 1861, therefore, the collection of surcharges on the land tax began. At the beginning of the reign of T'ung Chih (1862–74) another surcharge was assessed; and further and more cruel surcharges were demanded in the reigns of Kuang Hsü (1875–1908) and Hsuan T'ung (1909–10). Moreover, in the later years of the reign of Kuang Hsü, the central government allowed provincial governors to collect land taxes and surcharges at their own discretion, with the result that the rate of increase in the collection of the land tax began to accelerate rapidly.

The yearly land tax of Ssuch'uan province had been 669,131 taels at the beginning of the Manchu period. To this was added a "minting fee" of 110,000 taels, to cover the commutation from grain-tax to silver. In 1854 the rate of this surcharge was raised to tael per tael of the basic tax. In 1862 another surcharge of 100 per cent was assessed, so that the total land tax became three times what it had been before. In 1901 a new surcharge of a million a year was added, so that the total annual levy came to more than 3,500,000 taels, or five times the original. In Kiangsi, the surcharges were comparably heavy. Though a reduction of more than 10 millions was made in 1865, when this province was affected by the T'aip'ing Rebellion, there was still a surcharge of more than 660,000 taels on the *ting-yin* or poll tax. On the *ts'ao-liang* (also called *ta'ao-mi*) or grain tribute, which in practice was always commuted to silver, there was a surcharge of more than 460,000 taels. The total of surcharges in 1873 was no less than 1,400,000 taels, exclusive of the basic tax.

Surcharges were collected under various names, of which some came into use as early as the reign of Tao Kuang (1821–1850), such as *chung-p'ing*, "weighted measure" or "extra weight"; *hsien-yü*, "extra margin"; *ch'ou-pu*, "provisional margin"; and *tsa-fei*, "miscellaneous charges." As the names indicate, the nominal purpose of these charges was to ensure that a full complement of grain was delivered at the ultimate collecting center, loss or shrinkage in transit and all incidental expenses being charged not to the government but to the original taxpayer, who was thus made responsible not only for the tax but for the expense of collecting and remitting it. Costs of this kind, being variable, could easily be manipulated to the advantage of the tax collector. From the reign of Tung Chih (1862–1874) such exactions became more and more intolerable.

The increase in the land tax noted for the provinces of Ssuch'uan and Kiangsi may be taken as a rough but fair indication of what went on all over China. The most significant information now available relates largely to illegal overcollections and similar abuses and is therefore of a kind that cannot be reduced to consistent statistics covering the whole country or even a whole province; but this does not impair its importance in indicating that there was an exceedingly great difference between the tax as finally delivered to the central government and the amounts actually gouged out of the peasants. The official figures of 48 million taels for the yearly land tax collected in the reigns of Kuang Hsü and Hsüan T'ung (1875–1908 and 1909–1910) at the close of the Manchu dynasty, which represent a nominal increase of 18 million taels a year over the earlier Manchu period, can positively be stated to be far below the sums actually collected from taxpayers. The rich margin between the land tax nominally listed and that extorted in practice was exploited not only by tax collectors and officials, but by all who invested in land and evaded their taxes by passing them on to the peasantry. The real land tax cannot be statistically presented, because the methods used made for concealment of the real figures; but its relative importance can be gauged, and the mechanisms by which the margin of profit was exploited can to a great extent be described.

At the present day, under the Nanking government, the taxes due from landlords are collected directly from the peasants. That an equivalent system was in use under the Manchu dynasty may be inferred from a decree of 1846, in which it is stated that "the rich gentry are called Ta Hu (great families) and the common people are called Hsiao Hu (small families). The shortage [in tax payments] of the Ta Hu is always compensated for by surcharges on the Hsiao Hu." No documents have yet come to light showing the burden of land tax paid by the peasantry in statistical proportion to the evasion of tax by landlords, but there can be no doubt that a vicious process of this kind was at work, which was cumulative in its effects. The possibility of tax evasion made for a more and more disproportionate concentration of land in the possession of landlords (including rich merchants and officials who were absentee landlords), thus increasing the power of those whose political influence in local administration was already great enough to enable them to evade taxation. The more powerful they became, the less they paid, and the less they paid, the more insistent became the pressure on the decreasing number of small peasant proprietors.

It is clear therefore that the abuse of the agrarian system was a vital part of the methods of exploitation used by the privileged classes. The decay of the real political and military power of the Manchu dynasty in the nineteenth century produced a general slackness in administration. Governors of provinces could do as they pleased, and even local magistrates could disregard an imperial decree. This condition was confirmed, instead of being remedied, by the ruling already mentioned, which transferred the responsibility for collection and supervision of the land tax from the central government to the provinces. It was a part of the traditional system, as taken over by the Manchus, that both civil and military officers were underpaid. As a supplement to the small salaries which they drew from the central treasury, they were allowed to grant themselves, out of the local land tax, a form of payment which was known as *yang lien*. This, in theory, covered their living expenses, and divided the cost of administration into salaries, paid by the central government, and living expenses, contributed by the district which benefited by the administration, at the same time cutting down the expense of remittances to and from the central treasury. In practice, this right of local levy made it possible to demand, from the payers of land tax, additional assessments which nominally were government surcharges but actually were a direct private tribute to the officials.

Thus Hu Lin-yi, then governor of Hupei province, attacked the corrupt practices prevalent in 1857, stating that:

> In the transport of grain tribute to Peking, the *pang-fei* [additional tax to cover cost of transport] has now been cancelled; but the Provincial Grain Intendant demands his *ts'ao-kuei* [grain fee, grain perquisite]; the Grain Commissioner [equal in rank to a viceroy, and charged with the transport and disposal of tribute grain from the eight provinces adjacent to the Yangtze, to be shipped to Peking by the Grand Canal] demands it; even the Deputy Prefects and Magistrates—all demand it. The office of the Prefect demands a lodging fee; the office of the Provincial Treasurer demands a lodging fee; the petty officers of the Grain Commissioner—they all demand it.

From this it can be seen how the demands of the higher officials prepared the way for petty but even more cruel exactions by *ya-i* or yamen runners and other underlings. The higher officials even stooped to profit by these malpractices, which gave them the opportunity to accept bribes for "correcting" abuses on which they themselves grew rich. When the date for the collection of land tax had been proclaimed, the petty officials and their hangers-on went to each village, forced their way into the cottages of the peasants, and compelled them to make immediate payment of the tax. If there was any delay, the peasants would be lashed till the blood spurted, unless they paid, as a bribe, what was known as *pao-erh-ch'ien* or "pocket money," in earnest of full payment later. Payments of this kind might have to be made more than once, and might even, in the end, amount to more than the total tax due, but as they were not discounted against the tax, the full amount remained still to be paid. A memorial of 1885, condemning this custom, describes the land tax collectors as "living on the blood they suck from the peasants."

Peasants who had enough grain to pay their tribute promptly, brought it to the yamen, the whole family of each peasant attending, including the women. They had to appear actually before the due date, so that there should be no delay on the day of payment. If it rained while they were waiting, they had to protect their rice as best they could, for fear that the dampness would make it change color. Even if the collectors received it on time, various demands for "wastage charge," "light weight charge," "cargo-charge," "transport charge" and so forth might still have to be met, so that it was regarded as not abnormal for a peasant to pay his tax at the rate of 250 per cent of the assessed amount. When the collectors measured the grain, they usually managed to get a considerable surplus (later to be deducted privately for their own benefit), by "trampling the measure," to pack it tight, and by heaping a cone on the top of it so that, in the biblical phrase, it should be "pressed down and running over." When this had been done, even the spare grain which the peasant had brought with him to meet the surcharge was likely not to be enough. If the grain was measured with a discount of 30 per cent (a frequent practice), the shortage would be all the greater. Disputes between taxpayers and tax collectors were therefore common, which gave the collectors a further opportunity to extort hush-money, on the ground that the peasant had refused to pay. Hu Lin-yi, in the memorial already quoted, declared that the peasant paid, in surcharge, as much as three times the principal tribute.

Feng Kuei-fen, a statesman of the nineteenth century who proposed many reforms in the collection of the land tax, not only suggested that the rate of taxation be diminished, but urged that it be distributed more equitably as between peasants and landlords:

> In the past, when the collection of land tax began, the local officials used to send several strong men to guard the official grain measure. Now, however, they openly declare a discount of 30 per cent [in measuring the grain]; and on top of this another 20 per cent is demanded. Besides heaping up the surface of the measure, trampling it down, and "seizing the pig," they demand food-money and a transport fee, a tax-roll fee, a fee for stamping the seal, a fee for sifting rice, a granary door fee, and a granary fee, amounting in all to two *tou* [20 per cent on the *shih*, the unit of measurement]. The taxpayer has to pay more than 2.5 *shih* for each *shih*.

The grimly apt expression "seizing the pig," refers to the "squealing" of the peasant when seized by the tax collectors to force him to pay up. The landlords, however, belonged not with the pigs but with the butchers. The advantage of their position enabled them to refuse to pay all the extortionate surcharges, and even the principal land tax. Another device of the collectors was to advance, on behalf of a peasant, the amount which he would have to pay on the date of collection, taking as security the official "summons to pay," which was the evidence of legal assessment. When, however, the peasant appeared to pay this tax, he would find that he could not recover his official summons; and the collectors, taking advantage of this, would then demand an extra surplus. A memorial of 1844 declares that "there are often taxpayers who ought to pay one *sheng* or one *tou,* who cannot settle their tribute with several *shih*"; and as one *shih* contains 10 *tou,* and one *tou* 10 *sheng,* it is evident that extortions could amount to more than 10 times the assessed tribute.

In addition to exactions of this kind there was the heavy charge on exchange between copper and silver, and also on the commutation of grain tax into money. Owing to the indemnities paid to foreign invaders, the importation of foreign manufactures, and especially the sale of opium by the British, the silver of China began to leave the country after 1840, with the result that its price in China rose. In the reign of Hsien Feng (1851–1861) the shortage of money in circulation became even more acute, as the result of heavy military expenditures and the cost of foreign indemnities. To meet the need for money in circulation, three new denominations of "big money" were coined, with the nominal values of 10, 50 and 100 pierced copper cash. This was followed by the issuing of "iron big money" and "lead money." All of these coins depreciated rapidly in value, while the price of silver continued to rise and that of grain to fall. A *shih* of rice, measuring approximately 16 gallons, which had formerly sold for three taels or Chinese ounces of silver, declined to the value of 1.50 taels, as attested by Tseng Kuo-fan, one of the most important viceroys of the time:

In the past, the tax on one *mu* of land (about a sixth of an acre) could be settled by selling three *tou* of rice (three tenths of a *shih*), and there was still something to spare; now the sale of six *tou* is not enough to pay the same tax. The government receives the same amount of tax as before, but the peasant's burden is practically doubled.

Another official illustrated the same situation in different terms:

Since the reign of Tao Kuang (1821–1850) opium has been imported by foreign merchants, who carry silver away from China with them, so that the price of silver has risen very high. Formerly an ounce of silver was worth 1,500 pierced copper cash; suddenly the rate rose to 2,000 cash, then to 2,200, and now the people have to pay 2,500 cash to settle each tael of the land tax, whether principal or surcharge. Their payments are more than twice what they were before.

Tseng Kuo-fan, as one of the highest of the officials concerned in putting down the T'aip'ing Rebellion, was fully aware of the increased hardships of the peasants and the danger which they threatened to the state, on which he commented as follows:

Since the rise in the price of silver, the people have suffered more bitterly in paying their land tax, while the demands of the tax collectors have become increasingly urgent and brutal. They often arrest a rich member of a clan, to press him to pay for a poor member, or arrest members of the family of a poor man, and even put his neighbors into prison. Therefore the people have become full of hatred; they rise and rebel.

As if the increase in the tax through deflation was not enough, the insatiable tax collectors also took advantage of the rising price of silver to manipulate the rate of exchange between silver and copper. The rate of exchange tended to rise in any given region, as already noted; but there was also a wide variation as between regions. A decree of 1828 states that:

The land tax of Shantung province during the reign of Chia Ch'ing (1796–1820) was collected at the rate of from 3,100 to 3,200 cash per tael. Now, in many places, the rate has been raised to 4,000 cash, which compared with the market rate means a doubling of the surcharge . . . The commutation rate increases from day to day. In Ninghai [district] it is 4,000 cash per tael, in Chuch'eng [district], 4,260.

The arbitrary raising of the commutation rate continued into the reign of Kuang Hsü (1875–1908). In a decree of this reign it is stated that:

The price of silver is now about 1,100 cash per tael, but the local governors still fix the commutation rate at from 2,800 to 4,000 cash, with the result that the exchange surcharge amounts to more than twice the original tax.

The conditions referred to in these decrees and memorials differed from place to place, but they reveal a general similarity which makes it possible to understand the system of exploitation as a whole; and it need only be added that there was a further margin of profit in the manipulation of exchange by merchants, to take advantage of the demand for ready cash at the harvest season and when the land tax was collected.

The prevalence of corrupt practices made it possible for all kinds of subsidiary extortion to flourish, providing for the livelihood of parasites who lived on the official parasites. Among these were the *tiao sheng* and *lieh chien,* "corrupt graduates" and "depraved scholars." They were members of the scholar-gentry who had passed the first degree of the civil service examinations (*sheng yüan*) or had been enrolled as students of the imperial academy (*chien sheng:* a status that could be obtained by purchase) but had not been appointed to official positions. Their social rank as members of the bureaucratic class enabled them to thrust themselves between officials and people and live on lawsuits and black-mail. If the local magistrates and even governors did not give them a share of the perquisites of tax collection, they would accuse them of extorting illegal surcharges and ruin their careers—this being possible because, in a thoroughly bureaucratic system, an official is assumed to be honest so long as complaints are not heard, real honesty being less important than peace and quiet.

Before the date of tax collection, therefore, it was common for local magistrates to feast all the "unemployed scholars" of their districts and fix with them their share of *ts'ao kuei* or "tribute perquisites." With the assent of the unemployed members of the bureaucratic class, the bureaucrats in official positions could then proceed openly to abuse their power. The "corrupt graduates" and "depraved scholars," if not satis-fied, used other devices. They could take advantage of the discrepancy between "great families" and "small families," or important people and common people, to gather a number of poor peasant families together and represent them as being one solid clan, owning a large estate and therefore to be taxed only with caution. Poor peasants could by this device escape from paying some of the many surcharges, while the unemployed scholars collected part of the difference between the light tax on important people and the heavy tax on common peasants. The fees demanded by scholars who organized this kind of tax evasion were known as *sung mi* or "lawsuit rice." In Hupei province, scholars of this kind were called "locusts" by the peasants, and the "lawsuit rice" was known as the "locusts' fee." A governor of Kiangsu province, in a petition demanding the rooting out of this kind of practice, asserted that:

There are many who have no land at all who pay a land tax of several hundred *shih,* and many others who do not produce a hundredth or a thou-sandth of a *shih* of rice who receive "tribute perquisites" of from several tens to several hundreds of taels . . . There are as many as three or four hundred *sheng* and *chien* [unemployed scholars of this class] in a single district.

Tax evasion, when organized in this manner, was easily converted first into a system of private taxation and then into a system that was not alternative to the official tax, but additional to it.

The examples that have been given are enough to show that toward the end of the Manchu dynasty the total of taxation centering around the land tax had swollen to the almost incredible proportion of 20 to 30 times the "permanent and unalterable" tax determined at the beginning of the dynasty, and the conditions which had attended the fall of the Ming dynasty had been reproduced in full. The "sifting fee" ran to as much as three times the basic land tax; the "pocket money," for allowing the payment of tax to be deferred, to as much as 10 times; the arbitrary commutation rate doubled the basic tax, and the rise in the price of silver doubled it again. If the "lodging fees" demanded by the collectors as they made their rounds through the countryside be added, together with the "locusts' fees," the basic tax was multiplied about 30 times. No statistical statement of a twenty-fold increase is, however, adequate. What is really significant is that by the end of the dynasty the original strong centralized power of the Manchus had broken down into a system of arbitrary and suicidal exploitation by the whole of the ruling class, for the individual and competitive benefit of the separate members of the class.

While, however, the life of the peasants had become desperate, it is clear from the decrees, memorials and other documents, including the memoirs of contemporary statesmen, that the landlords had not been similarly affected. Most modern research has been directed toward discovering discrepancies in the land tax under the later Manchu dynasty as between provinces, but not toward distinguishing the discrepancies in rate of taxation as between landlords and tenants and peasants. There is, however, no lack of this very significant evidence. As far back as the reign of Chia Ch'ing (1796–1820) the evasion of land tax by landlords had become serious. A decree of 1815 declares that "the bad gentry and great families refuse to pay land tax, and the collectors do not even dare come into their villages to demand it." By the end of this reign the annual shortage in collection of land tax already amounted to 19 million taels. In 1846 the admonition to the tax-evading landlord-gentry was repeated, but again without result. In the reign of Hsien Feng (1851–1861) tax evasion had become even more serious, and Feng Kuei-fen wrote that "there are many of the gentry in every district, owning large and extensive amounts of land, who do not know what it is to pay land tax." In the reign of T'ung Chih (1862–1874) there was no sign of improvement, and in 1873 Liu Lu-chüeh wrote to Tso Tsung-t'ang, then governor of Hupei province, who had taken an important part in the suppression of the T'aip'ing Rebellion and was later to be still more prominent in the suppression of the Moslem Rebellion in Kansu and Chinese Turkistan, proposing a remeasurement of land. "If not," he said, "there will still be land tax without land, and land without land tax."

By 1846 the pressure on the peasants had already become so severe that, in the words of an imperial decree, "they murmured like boiling water and rose against the government." Among statesmen of the first rank, such as Li Hung-chang, Tso Tsung-t'ang and Tseng Kuo Fan, there was not one who did not urge radical reforms to cope with the situation. From orders issued by Hu Lin-yi, then governor of Hupei province, an idea of the methods used by large landholders in evading taxation may be gathered. In the first place, when a landlord bought additional land, instead of entering his name at the registration office of the local magistracy, he could give a false name to the subordinate in charge of tax-rolls, who was at the same time an underling in the tax collection service, and lived in the village. The land might thus remain for generations in the name of the seller instead of the new owner; the landlord bought the land, but did not incur the obligation to pay land tax.

If, again, an important man owned land in an irrigated district, he could arrange through subordinate officials who were under his influence to have his land registered in an adjoining unirrigated district, where it would be assessed at a lower rate. Similarly, if he lived in one district and bought land in another, he could have it registered in the district in which he lived, if the tax rates there were lower. Big families could, moreover, appear under several names on the tax-rolls, thus avoiding the obligation for corvée on public works, which was demanded of large families according to the number of men of working age. Finally, when a rich man advanced money as a loan and took land as security, the land tax continued to be collected from the borrower, not the lender, even when the mortgage had been foreclosed. Still another means of evasion was direct bribery of local officials, as illustrated by the following statement of Feng Kuei-fen:

> Local magistrates habitually take advantage of stating civil affairs in ambiguous terms. They hate, especially, to make the land tax clear. The most evident evil result of this is the evasion of tax and acquisition of land by unscrupulous people and strong and oppressive families, who bribe the petty officials.

The effectiveness of the influence of unimportant local officials, when bribed, as indicated in this passage, is at the same time an indication of the extent to which the authority of the central government had declined.

The ease of evasion, for those in a suitable social position, was increased by the lack of accurate tax-rolls and uniform standards of measurement. Land-measures varied not only from province to province but from district to district, and even from one piece of land to another, fertile land being subject to a smaller measure (so as to produce a higher tax) than poor land. This device could, however, easily be inverted by those who had suitable influence, in order to classify rich land, if it belonged to a rich man, as poor land. In the same way, when the tax-rolls were admittedly incomplete and inaccurate, an influential man could easily keep his name off them, and large tracts of land, belonging naturally to those who could best afford to pay the taxes, thus escaped taxation altogether. In the transfer of land by purchase there arose a form of abuse whose effects might persist for generations. If a poor man were hard enough pressed for ready cash, he could be forced to sell his land without transferring the obligation to pay taxes on it, himself retaining the liability for future taxes. It was from this kind of transaction that there arose the phenomenon of "land tax without land and land without land tax." The legal discrimination between the ownership of land and the liability to pay taxes on it could be endlessly manipulated in favor of those who had power, influence and capital.

With the decline of central power in the later years of the dynasty, the district magistrate tended to become inferior, in real power, to the important landowners of the district which he nominally administered. He did not dare to challenge a landlord who was an important official, or the son or grandson of a man who had held high rank, and still had important connections in the official world. Landlords of this class not only saved money by tax evasion, but acquired fresh land and mortgages, by advancing money for the payment of land tax to poor peasants. It was because of the abuses arising from lack of accurate land surveys and tax-rolls that Feng Kuei-fen so strongly urged the necessity of remeasuring the land; and it was for the same reason that any reform of the kind was persistently opposed by the "great families" which held the real power in every district. Their influence was great enough to force Li Hung-chang himself to order the abandonment of the attempt; beginning his career as the strongest supporter of the central government against the landlords, he ended, under the pressure of agrarian rebellion, as a supporter of the propertied classes against the peasants.

While the majority of landlords did not succeed in escaping the land tax altogether, they were able as a class to pay at a very much lower rate than the unprivileged peasantry. Thus Li Hung-chang admitted that:

In Soochow and Sungchiang [in the rich, irrigated Shanghai region], corruption is worse than in other provinces, and among the greatest injustices is the classification of "great families" and "small families" . . . The rate of the land tax is assessed according to the social rank of the payer—the noble and the commoner, the strong and the weak. The gentry settle their tax for one *shih* only, while the common people pay three or four *shih* for one *shih* of assessed tax. The same hundred *mu* of land will yield not a single cash of tax, or be assessed at several thousand cash [according to ownership]. In general, the surtaxes on the Hsiao Hu go to make up the shortage of tax collected from the Ta Hu.

Tso Tsung-t'ang and other great statesmen bore witness to the same state of affairs, and the evidence is clear that the great landowners were not, in proportion to the land they held, an important source of revenue to the state.

The powerful families had an advantage not only in the computation of the land tax itself, but in arranging the rate at which the grain levy was commuted to a money tax. "The richer the family," according to Li Hung-chang, "and the more it ought to pay, the lower its rate of commutation." Poor peasants paid as much as four taels in settlement of one *shih* of grain tribute, while the gentry paid only two taels. The maximum injustice was in the case of land tax payers who owned no land at all, as commented on as early as 1820, and again later:

In Kiangsu there are poor people who do not own a single strip of land, and yet pay a land tax of from several taels to several tens of taels a year; while many who have only a few *mu* of land pay enough land tax for several tens of *mu*.

As a result of all these converging pressures, there took place the "flight of the Hsiao Hu to the Ta Hu," of which Li Hung-chang wrote that "the number of the 'great families' is increasing daily, and that of the 'small families' is rapidly diminishing." Faced with starvation, the poor peasants had only one direction of retreat: they had to come under the "protection" of their oppressors the landlords, as landless laborers with no social position and no economic safeguard of any kind. Beyond this there was only revolt; and revolt came, in due course.

Because the increase of the local power of landlords and district officials and the decay of the power of the central government were overlapping and interacting processes, the effects of the collapse of the internal economic structure and the pressure of foreign nations on the Manchu government accentuated each other. In proportion as the peasants lost their economic independence and it became more impossible to extract wealth from them, the pressure of the effort to squeeze the last few coppers from them became more cruel. A large part of the land tax collected nominally for the upkeep of the civil administration and for the privy purse of the imperial household was diverted to the payment of indemnities to the foreigners hanging on the flanks of China. The Manchu rulers became process-servers and executioners for the Western powers engaged in nineteenth-century imperialist expansion.

The peasants got no benefit whatever out of the taxes wrung from them. By the end of the century landlords, merchants and usurers were drawing profits from moneylending as well as from rents, and often they were officials as well, or at least related to the swarm of officials who held tight the net of exploitation drawn 'round the peasant. The cultivation of land had become subject to a predatory system. The peasant who escaped the surcharges on the Hsiao Hu, the small, unimportant, uninfluential families, could not hope also to escape all the demands of the Ta Hu or landlord families, and the private taxation system of the "unemployed scholars" who lived on "lawsuit rice"; nor could the landless peasant escape both the penalties for delay in payment of his land tax and the demands of the merchants for a high profit and of the usurers for a high rate of interest. Increased payments to meet the extravagant needs of the imperial household and the foreign indemnities were not enough; still further payments were exacted from those least able to defend themselves, in order to make up for the taxes which the rich and powerful were able to evade.

The officials, the gentry and the merchants who invested their profits in the purchase of land took advantage of the weakness of the harassed peasantry to acquire larger and larger estates. The poor peasant, forced to mortgage his land at a high rate of interest, lost it eventually by foreclosure, but without being relieved of the obligation to pay land tax. The landlords leased their additional lands to the former owners, at rentals which took 60 and 70 per cent of the crop. The great private landholders grew fat as the government grew lean; but the richer they got, the less they were able to defend themselves against either internal rebellion or foreign aggression. The methods of exploitation which nourished their private wealth made agrarian revolt inevitable; and when it began, the government was unable to defend the ruling class which had robbed it of power.

The peasants' desperate condition was well known to officials, as witness a memorial of the end of the reign of Tao Kuang (1821–1850):

Peasant families have long had no surplus of food. Even in a year of abundance they have to eat the chaff of the wheat. This evil is the result of surtax collections. . . . If they abandon the land handed down by their fathers, they have no better way of making a living; if they keep it, the whole product yielded is not enough to pay the land tax.

Nor, on account of the heavy land tax, was anyone willing to cultivate, as a small peasant proprietor, land that had thus been abandoned. When Teng Chia-hsi, the grandson of a former viceroy of Kuangtung and Kuangsi, asked Shen Pao-cheng, then the viceroy, to receive his lands as public property because he was unable to pay the land tax, Shen was moved to say, in a memorial to the throne:

Even a family of noble rank is unable to pay the land tax and abandons its land as lost. How can we bear to imagine the condition of the poor peasants, who suffer very much from the extortion of tax collectors?

The question, however, was not only one of the illegal extortions of tax collectors, but of the legal distinction between ownership of land and liability to pay the land tax, the innumerable surtaxes, exorbitant rents, the high rates of profit demanded by merchants and usurers (which increased with growing economic instability) and the loss of the economic independence of the peasants, all of which combined to wreck both the agricultural system and the structure of the state, of which it was the foundation. Tseng Kuo-fan, in a memorial in the reign of T'ung Chih (1862–1874), after describing the cruel methods of the tax collectors, went on to state the causes of rebellion as follows:

Therefore the people, growing full of hatred, rise and rebel. The four cases in various provinces [listed in the memorial], were the result of the double increase in the price of silver, surtax collections by the local officials, and cruel punishment of the peasants by yamen underlings. It is difficult for the people to live under such conditions.

Shen Pao-cheng, in 1877, admitted similarly that a riot of the previous year "was really due to the fact that they hoped to diminish the grain tribute"; and an imperial decree of 1799, long before the agrarian situation had become acute, also admitted that the system of administration was partly at fault:

Living for centuries under the mercy and beneficence of the Dynasty and in a state of peace, none of the people would abandon their families and turn to insurrection if they could help it; revolts are due solely to the insatiable avarice of the local officials, who suck the peasants dry.

These explanations are, however, inadequate. There can be no doubt that it was not the delinquencies of tax officials alone, nor foreign aggression alone, nor any other single abuse or calamity, but the structure and method of operation of the ruling class as a whole, from emperor down to landlord and yamen runner, that exhausted the peasantry on which it lived and drove it to revolt.

Sporadic insurrections began in the reign of Tao Kuang (1821–1850), the most serious of them being in Hunan, in 1844, and at the same time there were scattered risings in Chekiang, where the slogan of the peasants was refusal to pay the land tax, as it had been at the end of the Ming dynasty two centuries before. The great T'aip'ing Rebellion began in 1851, in Kuangsi, and before its defeat in 1865 had occupied two thirds of the country. In 1853 began the rebellion of the Nien Min, starting in Shantung and spreading widely through the north, where it dragged on for years; and in 1871 there was another general rising in Shantung against the collection of the land tax. The Boxer Rising of 1900 stemmed, therefore, from what was by then an established tradition of peasant revolts, and there is no doubt that the Boxers were recruited largely from poor peasants who had rebelled, originally, against payment of the land tax.

The Manchu dynasty fell chiefly not because of foreign invasion but because its ruling class had wrecked the peasant-agrarian foundation on which the state was built. Its end was not wholly like that of the Ming, because no one power among the foreign nations pressing inward on China was strong enough both to take and defend the whole of the rich booty that lay waiting. Instead of conquering and occupying, they exploited at long range. There is no doubt that by their intervention at the time of the T'aip'ing Rebellion they actually propped up the Manchu throne when otherwise it would have fallen. Their policy was to uphold the Manchu emperor with one hand, and with the other to relieve him of part of his profits as the apex of the ruling class. Even when the dynasty did at last fall, the influence of the foreign powers brought in a patched-up republic which maintained practically unchanged the system of the ruling class, and the super-tribute paid out by the ruling class on foreign loans, armaments and so forth. The result has been that the agrarian crisis of the end of Manchu rule, relieved but not remedied by the Republican Revolution of 1911, and deferred but not eliminated by the Nationalist Revolution of 1927, has reappeared in a new climax. The old factors are all there; the hopeless peasantry, the foreign pressure, and the all-devouring ruling class, which ramifies through the civil and military services, the old and new banks, the old and new merchant enterprises, the factories, and finally the landlords, who are closest to the peasant and most active in repressing him, and from whose families come the military officers, government officials, factory owners and bankers.

14   *When sentiment for social revolution spread in the 1920's (and when the national revolutionaries, the Kuomintang, tried to keep the lid on society), the Communist Party galvanized the sentiment. It did so by claiming the mantle of "the Chinese people"—against the "Chinese bourgeoisie" and against imperialist foreign peoples. For there was certainly a foreign side to the war against exploitation. The West was charged with conniving at a continued domestic repression, in the interests of foreign profits. The Chinese exploiters (so went the charge) were humbled by the West, then sustained against "the people" so as to spike its revolutionary potential, in either the social or the national cause. When China was opened by the West, a bridge was thrown across from the West to the Chinese elite, but the bridge went down between that elite and "the people."*

The Opening of China

FREDERIC WAKEMAN, JR.

WHEN I first began thinking about this paper, I was tempted to indulge myself in hyperbole by calling it "The Tyranny of Historical Metaphor." The metaphor in mind was the Sino-centric world order, ideally regulated by imperial virtue and power. Its tyranny was double-edged. In its time it determined the conduct of Chinese diplomatists to the point of national disservice. And, long after its destruction in the nineteenth century by European imperialism, it maintained its hold over historical imagination. Western historians, perhaps in quiet reaction to Marxist theses of economic imperialism, have even singled out the tributary system as a major (if not *the* major) cause of the Opium War (1839–1842), believing that the kowtow may have suited earlier Asian monarchies, dominated by Sinic culture, but that it had become dangerously anachronistic by the Palmerstonian era. This is not an outmoded thesis by any means, but both of the assumptions behind it have been questioned closely during the half-century since Henri Cordier and H. B. Morse wrote their diplomatic histories of China. In

Frederic Wakeman, Jr., "The Opening of China," paper delivered at the December 30, 1968, meeting of the American Historical Association. Printed by permission of the author. Footnotes omitted.

fact, it was Morse's young friend, John Fairbank, who first pointed out over thirty years ago that the opening of China was less of a rupture with the tributary mode than had been thought. Most recently he has written that the temper of that era "was actually more traditional than modern. . . . The Western powers, coming from outside the tradition, intent on their own aims, did not realize how closely the treaty system was built within the framework of Chinese tradition." Other historians have shown that even before the age of the European nation-state, tributary theory had to accommodate itself to international reality. Granted, there were a few powerful reigns in China's long history which had inspired or realized the system, but usually there was a continuing tension between "psychological myth and reality." While this did force pragmatic adjustments onto the system, making tributary diplomacy a much more subtle instrument than it first appeared, it also created contradictions between "theory and fact" which have led some historians to wonder how much an ideologically rigid theory of international relations could have been credibly retained by the Chinese.

This puzzlement would not persist if the traditional Chinese notion of a centrally dominated world order were taken to be a genuine metaphor, dictionary-defined as "the figure of speech in which a descriptive term is transferred to some object to which it is not properly applicable." In other words, it was precisely the fictional element which made tributary theory such a compelling vision to the Chinese. This is not to say that it was merely an instance of what Mannheim called the "cant mentality," which reacts to social or political denial by insisting all the more strongly on its own cherished verities. Rather, tribute theory was a symbolic "template" used to order events and forces essentially disturbing to Confucian world views. In confident times it supported the expansionism of Chinese rulers; in darker days it eased the doubts of those committed to an ordered world of Confucian cultural supremacy. We can speculate, of course, as to tributary ideology's precise position within that imaginal sphere. Should it be seen as a projection of the internal order onto an external and possibly hostile world? Or would it be more realistic to think of the imperial-bureaucratic system as partly dependent upon tributary relationships for symbolic corroboration? Inner-outer or outer-inner? The two are so closely intertwined that distinctions may be tautological, for in either case Confucian ideology was unashamedly universalistic. We should not conclude from this, however, that its spokesmen always felt obliged to deny inconsistencies. A willful belief in the *probability* of world order could carry assurance in itself to reduce the impact of disturbing events.

The greatest shock to this Chinese cultural self-confidence before modern times was Mongol rule. Yet instead of being abandoned, tribute theory received its final formulation in the succeeding Ming dynasty, which was at the same time possibly the most culturally paranoid of any of the major ruling houses of Chinese history. Over its period of rule, and continuing on into the early Ch'ing, these anxieties over imperial weakness before outer enemies were historified into familiar (and therefore comforting) frames of reference. The dilemmas of the Southern Sung court, the Mongol problem during Ying-tsung's reign in the fifteenth century, or the sixteenth-century debates concerning Anda: these historic confrontations with barbarians were woven by historians into acceptably repetitive patterns on a traditional warp.

For this reason it is very difficult for modern historians to determine whether or not Chinese officials sensed any difference when they encountered a new form of barbarism in the eighteenth and early nineteenth centuries. Partly because of the development of a ritualized vocabulary, partly because of crudely conceptualized theories of barbarian behavior, Ch'ing bureaucratese hardly seems to distinguish at all between English and Oyirads. Yet there were certainly at least three categories of foreigners in eighteenth-century visualization: East and Southeast Asian monarchies, nomadic Asians from the North and West, and an outer zone of maritime barbarians from the "western seas." In officials' minds the last of these were most divorced from the Chinese world order. They were also the least comprehensible, the most "foreign," as evidenced by the quasi-hysterical repetition of *i-ch'ing p'uo-ts'e* (which should really be translated as "*these* barbarians' natures are unfathomable"). What they could fathom, though, was in some ways more disturbing than the traditional threat of tribal invasion from the North.

During the general nativist reaction which set in after the relative cosmopolitanism of the early years of K'ang-hsi's reign (1662–1722), Christianity became regarded as a foreign ideological contaminator. After about 1717, when the religion was explicitly linked with European traders at Canton, this fear was extended into a general revulsion against the commercialization of South China that accompanied the overwhelming increase in trade over the century. At first the object of attack was the exchange of valuable silver sycee for foreign clocks and mirrors, "worthless objects," in the eyes of Chi-ch'ing, Governor-General of the Liang-kuang in 1799, who feared that "there is no way to prevent a slight weakening of our economic constitution." Actually, of course, the sycee was being bought with Mexican silver dollars—less fine than ingots but so much in demand by the internal Chinese money market that they sold at a profit of 22 per cent. By the early eighteen-hundreds the nature of this exchange had been recognized by the Chinese for what it was, and foreign coins were singled out as concrete symbols of both barbarian contamination and the seduction of the Chinese peasant into unhealthy, non-agrarian ways. It was maintained that the "morality of the Cantonese is rather low . . . because foreign money is used for business and is circulated throughout the province. . . . Bad habits such as disseminating opium in the interior, building gambling houses to seduce good people, and propagating the heresy of western religion which can allure the hearts and minds of the people, are perhaps the results, all due to the fact that foreign money corrupts the people of Kwangtung."

But even these alarming developments could be rendered more familiar through historical analogies. The anti-Christian memorialists might cite Han Yü's attack on Buddhism in the T'ang period, while tirades against worthless luxuries recalled physiocratic arguments of Sung Kao-tsung's reign. I might add that this did more than reassure the Chinese. The memorialists' *déjà vu* sensations disposed them to react quickly to familiar-seeming problems. The only trouble was that they were too often content to employ equally familiar solutions. Within a limited recognition range, Ch'ing foreign policy was therefore extremely responsive—but frequently bewildered once it had exhausted routine alternatives.

I do not wish to imply here, though, that mid-Ch'ing bureaucrats buried their economic problems under classical allusions. On the contrary, I would contend that they did indeed sense, however dimly and murkily, that they were faced with a dangerous threat to their hegemony. The threat was identified at first as being *internal*, though it only became prominent because of its identification with the Europeans. An account of the maritime districts of Kwangtung written about 1600 reads:

All sorts of barbarians frequently come among these districts. They are intent upon trade, not piracy, but they hire traitors who pursue the ways of profit of the barbarian ships and do not devote themselves to a basic occupation. Some thereafter go on to plunder and rob.

What is being described here are the symptoms of a fundamental social change that accompanied the partial commercialization of the southeastern littoral in the period from 1500 to 1850. No historian has yet been able to quantify this social change; but some, like Fu I-ling, have assembled hundreds of Ming and Ch'ing impressionistic references to the rise of a class of native merchants engaged in the junk trade with Annam, Japan, Indonesia and Malaysia.

There seem to have been two basic types of mercantile groups, with less exchange of personnel between them than one might expect. The first, centered originally at Amoy, Foochow and Ningpo, was composed either of rural landowners who formed combines to diversify their in-vestments by outfitting trading vessels, or else of petty *k'o-shang* (traveling merchants) who had managed to amass enough capital to settle into trading organizations like the famous Fu-ch'ao junk guild of Canton. The second sort was far less respectable. The inhabitants of entire villages dotting the southeastern shoreline or sprinkled on small offshore islands became professional seafarers. For them the line between piracy and trade was indistinct, particularly when all forms of maritime commerce outside of certain kinds of genuine tribute trade were declared illegal in the 1590's and again after the 1640's. Like the prohibition of opium, this drove even the wealthiest of guildsmen into collusion with corsairs. And that cooperation in turn confirmed scholar-official impressions that overseas commerce, piracy and smuggling were not only mutually synonymous, but also somehow involved with foreign interests. As far as the state was concerned, the first discernible connection was with the Japanese, thanks to the illegal navies of merchant-smugglers like Cheng Chih-lung or Li Tan who operated out of Hirado, Formosa, Tongking and Macao. This was a *mestizo* world of Sino-Japanese, Achinese, Fukienese, even Portuguese—who all stood equally condemned as either foreigners or barbarized Chinese "traitors" conducting the busy traffic in drugs, textiles, raw silk, condiments, porcelain and metals between the entrepôts of Asia. And over the years this exchange stretched not only across Asia but around the world, as Atlantic seafarers met Pacific brethren in competition and collaboration to create a truly new maritime civilization. In the broadest sense, this new "fringe" civilization meant the end of the great ecumenes of Europe and Asia, for it was a deviation from the continental heartland on both sides of the world. In the West it accompanied the rise of the modern nation-state, redefining the medieval concept of community. In the East, however, it was momentarily denied, both by Tokugawa Japan and by Ch'ing China.

For the Ch'ing, the denial occurred twice. The first time was the most dramatic because it involved sealing off the coast and removing its population at various times between 1661 and 1683. There were tactical reasons for this, since the Manchus were then at war with Cheng Chih-lung's descendants, who maintained themselves by coastal raiding and a monopoly trading system. But by 1683 the last Ming loyalists were long dead, surrendered or resigned, and the K'ang-hsi emperor decided to permit legal trading once more. His immediate justification was that local officials along the coast were actually using the prohibition to extort fees from an illegal trade which they secretly allowed to continue. Why, the emperor asked, has the central government not recognized this sector in order to tax it? State revenue would thereby increase without burdening the peasantry. Though its justifications were physiocratic, this was still an eminently practical decision which came to apparent terms with the reality of maritime commerce. However, this pragmatic policy ended with that particular reign, and a second denial of the coastal fringe culminated in the restriction of European trade to the single port of Canton in 1759–1760. There were two reasons for this: a more orthodox application of tribute theory by both the Yung-cheng and Ch'ien-lung emperors; and, secondly, higher and more complex forms of collusion between Chinese merchant groups and Western traders. In my view, of course, the reasons are inter-related simply because the greater the threat, the more necessary the insistence on Confucian order.

The heightened collaboration between native and foreign mercantile interests was a direct result of a fundamental transformation in Sino-Western trade relations during the eighteenth century. Since Roman times China's major exports had always been luxury goods. But during the seventeen-hundreds, the inhabitants of England suddenly became tea drinkers. By 1785 the average London laborer was spending 5 per cent of his income on that beverage, and during the following decade, the E.I.C. sold over seventeen million pounds' weight of leaves. The Honourable Company had finally found a mass staple like tobacco which could be marketed against almost elastic demand. The extent of the trade, however, demanded a huge and constant supply of tea year in and year out, and the E.I.C. was therefore forced to ensure delivery of the following season's ladings by apportioning future shares of the trade to individual guild merchants who were advanced 50 per cent of the price of the leaves in goods and silver. This drew the hongists and factors into a tightly knit Anglo-Chinese monopoly, mutually allied against the Hoppo, the Imperial Superintendent of Trade at Canton. Since 1736 the Hoppo had used the security merchant system to hold the hongists as fiscal hostages for the port's trade. Crimes committed by the crewmen of vessels guaranteed by a given hongist gave the Hoppo a pretext for extorting tens of thousands of taels from that single individual. Junior merchants thus found themselves perpetually skirting bankruptcy; and the East India Company factors—who were obsessed with the fear of seeing the joint Cohong replaced by a single Chinese merchant powerful enough to set his own prices—began to advance more and more capital to keep weaker hongists afloat. The Hoppo in turn no longer found it necessary to increase his direct exactions upon the foreigners, because all that he had to do for his "squeeze" was threaten one of the merchants with disgrace and imprisonment. Since the English had already advanced, or loaned, a considerable amount of money to that particular individual, they could not afford to sacrifice him. His life, his existence as a merchant, was their collateral; and even more funds were handed over by the E.I.C. to the hongist to satisfy the Superintendent. Monopolists of both cultures saw common ground in sheer self-defense against Chinese official interference.

But at least this form of collusion was committed to maintaining regular trade under state license, and it was therefore unlikely to challenge government controls. The second group of collaborators, though, were relative newcomers and restive. On the foreign side stood entirely modern economic interest groups, the country firms and free traders whose ready capital supplanted monopoly advances in 1813, and whose parliamentary lobbyists went on to destroy the E.I.C.'s China trade after 1833. Their presence in Canton announced a second great revolution in Sino-foreign economic relations. First with Indian cotton, then with opium, the country firms transformed China from mere supplier into a consumer's market. True, the aim for many years was just to sell enough to buy more tea; but then a strategic alliance was effected between Scotch brokers in Asia and Manchester manufacturers in England. The Midlands' mills might never really add that mythical extra inch to every Chinaman's shirt-tail, but it was believed they could. This dream alone was enough to change the thrust of discontent. No longer was it a question of getting produce out through the narrow but reliable funnel of Canton. Rather it was felt the time had come to tear down all the barriers so carefully erected behind the tribute system, and let manufactured goods pour in.

Unlike earlier mercantilists, though, Manchester liberals found no counterparts within China. But they did become closely involved with the meaner commercial elements of the water world. Listen to Mao Hsiang-lin, a Shanghai scholar of the mid-nineteenth century, describe his city just after it became a treaty port.

Many of the inhabitants are transients, gradually setting a new style of life . . . [and making] the people think of nothing but profit and trade, material wants and licentious adornment. . . . As foreign merchants thrive more and more, the Concession grows larger, and the workmen they hire—mainly drifters from Fukien and Kwangtung—rely upon their protection to behave outrageously. The local authorities dare not detain them.

Indeed the eighteen-hundreds saw an acceleration of what we have glimpsed earlier in the seventeenth century. Along the coast, the fringe, there burgeoned ever more petty merchants, seamen, smugglers, longshoremen and transport clerks who moved restlessly from entrepôt to entrepôt. In Fukien they found a secret organization which perfectly suited their need for self-protection or concealment, and by 1802 had introduced the brotherhood of the Triads to Kwangtung. Violently anti-Manchu on the one hand, and intimately connected with the opium traffic on the other, Triad cells helped confirm the dynasty's anti-commercial prejudices. Whether collaborating with Gutzlaff at Ningpo in 1842, or seizing Amoy and Shanghai in 1853, this *lumpenproletariat* was no friend of the state. But then, once China had been opened to the treaty system, neither was it a friend of the newly self-confident Western commercial establishment. During those years of European ambivalence towards Chinese rebels, some Western merchants did supply insurgents with arms, and foreign soldiers of fortune occasionally joined their ranks; but formal offers of alliance from the Triads and Taiping were rejected. In fact, by 1860 the Western powers were quite prepared to cooperate with the Ch'ing in restoring order within the country to make the treaty ports safe for established trade.

But what of the Chinese world order in this startling new alignment of apparently traditional and modern interests? In his classic study of trade and diplomacy on the China coast, John Fairbank suggested that:

Further analysis of the Western century in China should make it plain that the treaty system gradually became a basic component of the power structure of the Chinese state. The Westerner in this period was a partner in a Sino-Western rule over China, which by degrees came to supplant the Manchu-Chinese synarchy of the Ch'ing period.

That was written twenty-five years ago. Since then Professor Fairbank has added another element to his analysis. Employing a heuristic distinction between power structure and culture, he shows again how Sino-foreign domination was established, but stresses the fact that Europeans did not participate in the traditional culture. "Thus," he concludes, " 'Western conquest' proved abortive. Instead of being taken over by the new invaders, the Chinese world order finally disintegrated."

Of the last phrase there is no doubt, though the disintegration took time. That ruling metaphor was kept artificially alive long after its fatal seizure, because the Ch'ing could not face its demise without a substitute. And of substitutes there were none; for tribute symbolism was too much a part of a traditional order in which bureaucrats, not consuls, called the tune. Thus when it did die in the 1890's, it died abruptly, finally leaving room for politically autonomous ideologies. But this cultural vision did not perish because the West lacked appreciation. It disintegrated precisely because the West *did* form part of that power structure, even determining it. Fairbank himself has shown with great skill just how the forces of order—an alliance of compradores, English bankers, treaty-port consuls and high officials like I-liang eager to tap new sources of income—all combined against the rabble of both cultures. This was a social alliance versus disruption, directed against some of the very groups the West had used before when it once was forced to look for more clandestine allies. Now they would retain their gains, as segments of the traditional Chinese elite began to see that self-perpetuation demanded they finally come to some terms with that maritime fringe, that new, *literally* bourgeois order. If I may end by suggesting a different metaphor, let it be that Western imperialism forced nineteenth-century Chinese power holders to choose between the heartland and the periphery. The decision was never easy, as the desperate and momentary return of the dynasty to Boxer nativism shows; but elites eventually shifted and compromises were made. The irony of it all, the historical poetic if there need be one, is that traditional China never combatted that urban, cosmopolitan, coastal world as desperately as revolutionary China does now.

15

". . . that new, literally bourgeois order. . . ." Where was the novelty? And what was broken down, and only indifferently reassembled, with admixtures, so that nineteenth-century economic growth was not growth to maturity, but to ineffectuality? The past's arrangements were all but dissolved. But the present, as of 1911–1914, the inception of the Chinese Republic, offered no place to stand. Only the future, the subject of passionate visions, would seem to promise resolution.

Economic Change in Early Modern China: An Analytic Framework

JOHN K. FAIRBANK, ALEXANDER ECKSTEIN, and L. S. YANG

I. THE CHINESE ECONOMY IN THE PERSPECTIVE OF WORLDWIDE ECONOMIC DEVELOPMENT

THIS paper tries to characterize broadly the process of economic change in China during the century of disturbance which ended with the collapse of the Ch'ing dynasty in 1911. In approaching this task we focus particularly upon the factors that retarded growth. In order to gain perspective upon this century of economic transformation in China and place it in the context of world economic development, we first outline briefly and schematically several paths which industrialization has followed since 1750 in different parts of the world.

A. Phases of the Industrialization Process. Although the process of industrialization has characteristically moved through certain definite phases, both the number and the sequence of these phases have varied in different countries. At the risk of oversimplification we may distinguish two basic models, with the early starters, and particularly England, falling into one pattern and many of the underdeveloped countries of today fitting into the other.

The industrialization process among these latecomers may be divided

John K. Fairbank, Alexander Eckstein, and L. S. Yang, "Economic Change in Early Modern China: An Analytic Framework," *Economic Development and Cultural Change*, IX, No. 1 (October 1960), pp. 1–26. Reprinted by permission of the University of Chicago Press. Footnotes omitted.

into five phases characterized by (1) traditional equilibrium, (2) the rise of disequilibrating forces, (3) gestation, (4) breakthrough or as some prefer to call it, take-off, and (5) self-sustaining growth. Typical features of these periods may be generalized as follows:

In phase one, minor growth, innovation and technological change may occur but they are not sufficient to break the rigid and inhibiting bonds of the traditional framework of social and economic institutions.

In phase two, disequilibrating forces which arise are typically exogenous, originating outside the society and subjecting it to the shocks of war, invasion, colonial rule or the like.

In phase three, these shocks weaken the traditional forms of political, legal, social and economic organization, while new institutions and modes of production are introduced and clash with the old. Disruption is mingled with construction to produce increasing tension between the technically possible and the institutionally feasible. Gestation is evidenced in the creation of certain external economies (e.g., transport, modern commercial or banking facilities), certain industrial nuclei and technically skilled labor, all prerequisite for a breakthrough.

Phase four sees a rapid spurt in the rate of industrial production based in turn on increased rates of investment. Typically industrial growth tends to be most rapid during the breakthrough or take-off, since it is at this stage that the shifts in the production functions are most marked; for many of these are based on once-for-all economies exemplified by shifts from handicraft to machine methods of production. Usually the active leadership in this process is in one or two sectors—textiles, mining, or foreign trade. Industrial growth is accompanied by continuing changes in agriculture.

In phase five, the new industrial economy eventually enters a stage of self-generating growth which continues at a higher rate than under the old order, although less rapidly than during the period of breakthrough. As the growth of established industries slows down, new industries arise to take the lead in the process, indicating that the economic institutions of the society have now become truly industrial—that is, such factors of production as labor and capital have acquired a high degree of mobility and the institutional obstacles to change have been minimized. Economic change and growth, in short, have become institutionalized.

This model fits the experience of India, China, and most other Far Eastern areas (with the exception of Japan) better than it does the experience of the West European countries. For them, the British model is much more applicable. Professor Rostow's three-stage model outlined in his most stimulating article on "The Take-off into Self-Sustained Growth" applies mainly to this British experience.

The distinguishing feature of the British model is that the traditional preindustrial order itself provided a framework for gestation. The commercial revolution of the mercantile period and the agricultural revolution following it were the necessary precursors of the industrial revolution in England. Endogenous, i.e., internally generated, forces played a dominant role in the rise of disequilibrating forces in the form of new inventions, advances in technology and innovations. Precisely because the disequilibrating forces in the English case arose as the culmination of a long process of preparation, they led directly to a breakthrough, rather than to a prolonged pre-industrial period of tension and gestation as in the Far Eastern case.

In between these two patterns or models are a number of intermediate cases in which intricate interplays of exogenous and endogenous factors produced the disequilibrating forces. For instance, in Japan gestation (in the form of growing commercialization during the late Tokugawa era) evolved endogenously as in Britain; but at the same time, unlike the British case, disequilibrating forces arose exogenously in the shock of foreign contact after Perry "opened" Japan. However, with the period of previous preparation, the Western impact on Japan—unlike that on China —led directly to a breakthrough during the Meiji era.

B. *Phases of Industrialization in China.* The above scheme can be applied to China by assuming that the Chinese economy of the early nineteenth century was in the first phase, that of traditional equilibrium. The old order had already begun to be disturbed by the population growth of the eighteenth century (the process of domestic decline, which became manifest in rebellion, awaits further appraisal). Meanwhile, the best known agent of change in the nineteenth century was exogenous— the growth of Western trade at Canton, which drew China into the network of expanding world trade. The disequilibrating force of the Opium War of 1840 and the Western political and commercial impact thus coincided with the growth of domestic problems of population pressure and administrative decay typical of a period of dynastic decline. These changes began a century-long process of disintegration, transformation and slow gestation within the traditional Chinese order. During this long period, as we shall see, new institutions grew up side by side with traditional ones, a modern economy was built up on the periphery of the old economy, and there was sporadic and scattered growth in some areas (export trade and railroad-building), paralleled by decline or collapse in other sectors (rural handicrafts, particularly cotton spinning). These developments in the latter part of the nineteenth century began to generate an acute degree of tension, in the minds of proud conservatives and later in the minds of modern patriotic Chinese—a tension between the vision of changes which seemed technologically possible for the growth of national strength and the betterment of Chinese life, and the frustrating realities that prevented national self-realization and industrialization within the institutional structure of the old Chinese society. This tension gradually built up to explosive proportions, until the shackles of the old order were violently broken and the Chinese economy erupted at long last into an industrial take-off under totalitarian control which we are witnessing today.

The vigor and violence of the present breakthrough under Communist auspices seems to have been exacerbated by the unusually prolonged period of gestation. China's remarkable early slowness in responding to the Western economic impact may lie behind her present rapidity of change. The fact that the rise of disequilibrating forces and the period of gestation, according to our model, together occupied at least a century suggests a major problem in the study of Chinese economic history—namely, the institutional stability of the old order, which remained remarkably inert long after the traditional equilibrium had been disturbed.

Two concepts may be suggested to account for China's tardiness of response. One is the view that the traditional Chinese order, within the limitations of its inherited technology and value system, had become over the centuries a strongly integrated society with institutions which, developed over long periods, had attained a high degree of sophistication. The old China was thus a firmly-knit and thoroughly tested society with a culture of great vitality. It was also enormous in size, as well as far removed from the aggressive Atlantic society at the other end of the Eurasian land mass. It could not easily adopt Western ways without a fundamental remaking of the entire social order.

The second concept explains China's slow response in terms of political institutions: it suggests that China's political tradition inhibited the growth of a nation state. The Middle Kingdom had remained a universal empire in Eastern Asia, subject to the periodic control of non-Chinese dynasties whose alien rule at Peking frustrated the growth of modern nationalism. Hence China lacked both the public sentiment and the political leadership necessary for a Japanese type of rapid Westernization.

However China's slowness may be explained, the modern century of her economic history presents us with a record of retarded development. While this cannot be called a period of "stagnation" in the literal sense of "standing still," it was at least one of far-reaching social and economic disorganization, which may even have resulted in an actual decline of per capita product. Should further research support this hypothesis, such a decline could be viewed as a concomitant of this period of disturbance, representing the price China had to pay for future growth. Perhaps the disturbance and decline constituted social and economic costs the country had to bear in order to create the preconditions for subsequent economic growth.

II. THE OLD ORDER

Before we proceed with an analysis of the Chinese economy of a century ago, certain generalizations are necessary. First, while the old order in China exhibited many characteristics typical of a pre-industrial economy, there were some notable differences between the pre-industrial economies of Europe and China. The Chinese economy existed in an institutional and cultural framework distinctly different from that of Western societies. For example, the single fact of a rice economy based on widespread use of water had far-reaching implications affecting the relationship between land and labor, the density of population, and the forms of village, family and kinship organization. These cultural and institutional differences affected the capacity of the economy to adapt itself to change, to grow and to industrialize.

A second general point is that the economy of early nineteenth-century China approximated rather closely Malthus's and Ricardo's model of a "stationary state," with a population pressing against resources close to the margin of subsistence. The prevailing level of technology remaining more or less static, both the Malthusian population checks and the law of diminishing returns were operative. In sum, the China of the early nineteenth century had a circular-flow economy in which production was absorbed in consumption, with very little if any net saving, so that the economy merely reproduced itself without advancing.

Finally, one basic general factor in China's economic destiny was the rapid population growth in the eighteenth century which led to a doubling, or more, in the mere number of the Chinese people, without much immediate change in the character of their economy, culture and institutions. This demographic growth had been made possible by agricultural expansion in the early Ch'ing period of the seventeenth and early eighteenth centuries, which was facilitated both by the peace and order established under the strong Manchu dynasty after 1644 and its comparatively efficient administration, and by the earlier introduction of new crops like maize, sweet potatoes and peanuts in the period after 1500. The new crops greatly widened the food base by making previously marginal soils productive. By the early nineteenth century, however, the margin or reservoir obtained through the introduction of new crops and varieties was probably exhausted, so that population was pushing against the limit of available resources at the prevailing level of technology. While living standards may have risen in the eighteenth century (on this we lack data), it seems probable that they were forced down in the early nineteenth century. The population expansion had not been accompanied by an agricultural revolution comparable to that of eighteenth-century England, while the growth of foreign trade and a money economy during the late Ming and early Ch'ing periods (manifest, for example, in the "single-whip" tax reform) had been contained within the traditional social order.

In effect, the period of the late Ming and early Ch'ing can be characterized as one of extensive, rather than intensive, growth based on expansion of cultivated land area and population. The new crops were not in the category of major technological innovations likely to affect the basic modes of production in either agriculture or processing. While there was some commercialization of the economy, it was not a major or disequilibrating change.

Thus we begin with the general assumption that the Chinese peasantry, through their adaptation to environment, had attained an optimum efficiency in resource use and allocation at a more or less stationary level of technology.

We divide the old Chinese economy of the period 1800–1850 into three levels: (1) the agrarian (rural) level, (2) the commercial level, which is superimposed on the agrarian, and (3) the governmental level which is superimposed on both the agrarian and the commercial.

A. The Agrarian Level. The agrarian level was that of the village where seventy to eighty per cent of the Chinese people lived.

The capital equipment of the economy at this level included a large accumulation of man-made installations which had been inherited over the centuries—for example, paddy fields with their embankments, dikes and sluiceways, as well as terraced fields for dry farming, irrigation canals of all sorts together with the wooden contrivances for lifting water, wells, the usual village and farmstead buildings together with groves of mulberry trees, tea bushes, and other resources for handicraft production. Accumulating over many generations, these installations represented an extensive and long-continued investment of labor and in turn made possible a more efficient application of manpower to the soil. It was noteworthy that among these items of capital equipment such as wooden plows and stone grain-grinding rollers there was a minimum of metal equipment and machinery. Irrigation water might be lifted, for example, by a rather simple foot treadle, or, alternatively, by a mere bucket with ropes held by two persons. Technical devices commonly in use were geared to the ready availability of cheap manpowers.

The natural resources available to the agrarian economy, combined with the capital installations mentioned above, set the character of economic activity. After the eighteenth-century extension of cultivation, the additional resources of water and soil available for an increase of cultivation were not great. Similarly, by that time the destruction of forest cover had proceeded very far while the degree of reforestation was insignificant. Coal deposits, although abundant in the northwest and other areas, were not developed and coal was used only on a small scale for local industries.

Among the extractive industries, fisheries were rather well developed, both inland and on the coast. Copper, tin and lead were mined in the southwest but had perhaps reached diminishing returns. Iron mining was comparatively undeveloped. In short, the Chinese peasants' use of natural resources was pretty much at the bamboo and wattle level.

Labor in the village was comparatively plentiful per unit of cultivated area. The population increase, under way since the eighteenth century, had left a high proportion of the people in the younger age brackets. Rich culture in South and Central China and the comparable garden-farming methods of North China created a high seasonal demand for hands, and a corresponding need for handicraft production to absorb farm labor power in the off seasons. Cropping systems, ranging from the double-cropping of rice in the far south to the winter wheat of North China, made use of this farm labor power, but its year-round employment was made possible only by the subsidiary handicraft industries—especially cotton, silk, and tea production. These industries in South China, together with the longer growing season, provided the basis for somewhat higher consumption standards than in North China, where seasonal unemployment and chronic underemployment were more prevalent. The abundance and cheapness of labor fostered and perpetuated the labor-intensive methods of farm production—for example, those used in the tea, silk and cotton industries, in hand or manpower irrigation, in transplanting and harvesting of rice and other crops; and also in the use of manpower for transportation by pole, barrow, chair, or the rowing, sculling or tracking of vessels. In other words, not only agriculture but also transport was labor-intensive.

Farm technology, through an age-long and continuous process of adaptation between land and labor, had come to be based on highly intensive land use with comparatively high yields per unit of land but a low yield per unit of labor. The stability of this technology was posited on the whole economic and institutional structure. The relative abundance of labor tended to minimize the inducement to innovate, while the scarcity of capital impeded the capacity to do so. At the same time, the traditional assumptions of the peasantry and the landlord-gentry militated against rapid technical change.

Land tenure, based on a general freedom to buy and sell land, cannot be called "feudal" in the Western European sense, and there were few legal shackles on the peasantry (such as serfdom or villainage). Yet the hard facts of the population-resource balance, aggravated by the prevailing systems of agricultural taxation, credit and marketing, kept the peasant near the margin of subsistence. As the nineteenth century wore on, owner operators were in increasing danger of having to sell their land to make ends meet in a bad year. Tenants were in similar danger of getting so heavily into debt that absconding into pauperism or banditry was their only way out. The system of land tenure lent itself to an increasing concentration of land holding, tenancy and absentee landlordism in modern times.

The social structure and customs, although they provided a stable matrix for the various factors of farm production, included certain institutions which particularly inhibited an increase in the efficiency of production. For example, the lack of primogeniture and the customary fragmentation of land holdings among all the sons, and the comparatively enormous expenditures expected for marriage and funeral ceremonies, all served to inhibit saving. Above all, the distinction between the literate upper classes of landlords, merchants, officials and city-dwellers on the one hand, and the great mass of the illiterate peasantry on the other hand, set a limit to the latter's capacity for innovation. The difficulties of the ideographic script kept the Chinese peasant at the coolie level, able to use his manpower with certain time-tried techniques and devices, but unable to rise easily into the upper strata of society. Conversely, men of trained intelligence with leisure to innovate would not often be found in the fields or workshops. The Chinese class structure, reinforced by Confucian ideology, made a sharper division between hand-worker and brain-worker than in Western Europe. Thus the philosopher Chu Hsi might make his famous observation that the stones on a mountain-top had once been in the sea, but he was in no position to become a Francis Bacon. None of China's great painters, though *ipso facto* scholars, could become a Leonardo.

Entrepreneurship had little opportunity to develop at this rural level. The manufacture of consumer goods like cloth shoes, cotton textiles for clothing, silk and tea were naturally subordinate to agriculture and were generally geared to supplying a strictly local market by using limited capital resources, except as we shall note below. Extractive industries like mining, fishing and lumbering, while somewhat more specialized for the market, shared the same difficulties of being fragmented, labor-intensive and capital-poor, with little chance for expansion of production or of marketing.

B. *The Commercial Level.* This level of economic life served as a sort of highway or bridge linking the agrarian with the governmental level. It performed the distributive and exchange functions which met the closely related needs of inter-regional trade and rural-urban interchange.

The market structure of old China was extremely complex. The agrarian level of economic life was of course self-sufficient only in a relative sense: the share of the agricultural product entering trade channels was rather small, while the dependence of the rural sector upon non-farm purchases was also only of marginal importance. Broadly speaking, rural self-sufficiency was broken in two ways: (1) through unrequited shipments of tax grain and (2) through an exchange of a variety of special products for salt and similar necessities, the few important staples that had to be purchased, and for a few luxury products. On the other hand, trade in the traditional economy can be considered as the supply system for the Chinese upper classes—that combination of large land-owners, scholar literati, officials and merchants who constituted the mobile top strata over the inert peasant mass. These people provided the chief market for luxury products, just as they were also the population groups not directly engaged in the process of agricultural production.

Trading activity took place within a quite complex, inefficient and highly fragmented market organization characterized by a marked pro-liferation of middlemen. The market structure was inevitably peppered with strong monopolistic and monopsonistic tendencies. Trade in staple commodities, the demand for which was quite inelastic, was mostly subject to government monopoly. However, the system of official regula-tion and licensing frequently broke down in practice, as illustrated by the operation of the salt monopoly, where as much as half the salt might be distributed through illegal smuggling channels which were not secret so much as connived at by the lower officialdom. Of course, breaches of this type in the power of monopoly, far from leading to invigorated competition, merely involved a change from an official to an extra-legal system of licensing. Within this framework, commodity flows ran through an interlocking maze of local, regional, and to some extent even inter-national markets.

Local trade, to begin with, was part and parcel of rural life, centered on the local market towns with their fairs and periodic (typically, tenth-day) village markets to which merchants regularly brought their wares. This local trading activity had a regularity and rhythm comparable to the other cycles of rural activity which carried the villagers through their daily routines, through the seasons of the year, and through the span of human life in an established context of goals, expectations and tech-niques. Local trade distributed necessary consumer goods like salt, metal ware and paper to the peasant households, together with items considered to be luxuries, like porcelain, tea or silk. This distribution was effected with an extensive use of barter and personal credit arrangements. In ex-change for goods brought in through local trade, the farm surpluses, if any (pigs, fruit, etc.), and special local products like wood oil or opium, were shipped out. Our typical picture of local trade is that it radiated out from the market town or fair about the distance that goods could be transported in one day on a round trip by carrying a pole or sampan. This created a cellular pattern of local economy in which a region could survive indefinitely when nature was favorable and similarly might be devastated by natural calamity.

Interregional trade was superimposed on this cellular and interwoven pattern of local trade. Interregional trade was in part merely one aspect of the general urban-rural interchange, i.e., the aforementioned bridge between the agrarian and official levels. However, over and above this, it was a reflection of a certain amount of regional specialization. Among such regionally traded commodities were salt, which was made by a variety of means in some eleven officially established production areas and distributed thence by licensed merchants; tea and silk, which in much of South and Central China were local products of low grade but became goods for regional trade when produced in their highest quality (for example, the teas of Northern Fukien and Kiangs; and the silk of the Huchow region inland from Shanghai); porcelain, which was specially produced under imperial auspices at Ching-te-chen in Kiangsi; copper, tin and lead which came particularly from Yunnan; or heavy timber such as was brought down the Yangtze.

International trade, against this background, may be viewed as merely a special, and from the point of view of the Chinese economy a rather unimportant, form of interregional trade. Chinese commodities which had gone abroad from ancient times had included the silks which crossed the ancient Central Asian route to Rome; Sung porcelain and copper coins, which went by sea throughout the Indian Ocean region; and brick tea, which was taken from the Wuhan region up the Han River route toward Mongolia and Russia. Over the centuries the balance of trade had generally favored China, where the wide range of latitude from the tropics to Manchuria made for an essentially self-sufficient economy. There had been a general flow of gold and silver bullion from Japan, and especially from Mexico by way of the Philippines, with some later increments from Europe and India directly. The early Portuguese had facilitated the exchange of Chinese silk for Japanese silver through Macao. Meanwhile the major commercial development of pre-industrial China was carried on over the junk routes. The fleets of Ningpo exchanged a wide range of produce with the Korean peninsula and southern Manchuria. The main southern route centered on Amoy and went around the Southeast Asian coast to the straits of Malacca. Over this route came a variety of woods, spices and edibles, including sugar. However, none of these forms of international trade had dealt in staple consumer goods until the late eighteenth century, when raw cotton began to be imported from India.

The transport network which made possible this regional exchange within China as well as abroad was well developed within the limits of prevailing technology. The paths suitable for carrying-poles or barrows between villages were supplemented in Central and South China by waterways. Where the North China coolie might compete with donkeys and on the northern border with camels, the chief carrier in the Yangtze basin and southward was the sampan powered by human muscle. Large gangs of transport coolies were available for the portages on the water routes—for example, the tea coolies who after 1850 carried shipments from Northern Fukien into the water network of Kiangsi. The water transportation of South and Central China by river, lake and canal served the great bulk of the Chinese population. The accumulated public works of centuries had produced a nexus of canal and sampan routes, fed by the broad continental system of rivers and lakes which were in turn nourished by the heavy precipitation over the hills and mountains of South China. As a result it was possible to move persons and goods by water routes that were continuous or almost continuous from Canton to Peking and from the southeast coast to the borders of Tibet.

The efficiency of Chinese inland water transport was remarked upon by the early Western embassies to China in the late eighteenth century. Both the British Macartney embassy of 1793 and the Amherst embassy of 1816 on their return from Peking used the canal barge route all the way to Canton except for the brief portage of twenty-four miles or so over the Meiling Pass north of Canton. The Dutch embassy of 1794–95 used this route in both directions. These European observers estimated that Chinese rafts could carry twenty tons on one foot of water.

Meanwhile, coastal transports by the seagoing junk fleets, which totaled on the order of 10,000 vessels, also provided a channel of domestic transportation all the way from Hainan Island to Manchuria. Sea transport of the grain supply for Peking by junk fleets around the Shantung promontory provided an alternative to the Grand Canal even before the decline of the latter after 1852. While not capable of the speed of clipper ships, Chinese junks with their lateen sails were remarkably efficient carriers, especially when using steady seasonal winds on established coastal routes.

All in all, we may regard the complex and pervasive network of Chinese water transport as comparable to the traditional farm economy—that is, highly developed within its technological limitations.

The supply of capital for the operation of this economy was comparatively limited. Savings might be accumulated by the enlarged family in the form of real estate, particularly land, but such savings were not liquid and were seldom available as a basis for credit creation except as security against loans. Rural moneylenders secured high rates of interest but did not become institutionalized as bankers or even as professional moneylenders. The most common kind of rural credit was that granted by landlords to tenants against the security of future crops. Towns and cities naturally had more institutions for capital accumulation. For example, the pawnshops did a lucrative business and were extensively invested in by wealthy officials. Typically, this was a nonproductive type of investment. The hoarded capital of merchant guilds and licensed merchant-guild members (like the large salt merchant families or the family firms in the Canton Cohong) was sometimes used to finance commercial operations. One of the most rewarding forms of investment was to purchase a licensed position in one of the many monopolies sanctioned by the government—for instance, in the salt gabelle. In other words, money was to be made less by producing goods than by transferring or handling goods or funds, including taxes and fees.

Typical of this situation was the fact that the famous Shansi remittance banks, which were simple partnerships with branches elsewhere in China operating on capital funds on the order of 100,000 or 200,000 taels, were engaged not in deposit banking or lending of funds for productive enterprise but rather in the simple remitting of funds from place to place, mainly for the official class. These banks were developed in the late eighteenth and early nineteenth centuries to replace the more primitive escort agencies (*piao-chü*) which had been established to escort and protect the movements of bullion funds from place to place. However, in the course of performing this transfer function in its more sophisticated form—through drafts—they did not become agencies for the creation of credit in the fashion of modern banks. With credit formation thus handicapped, the commercial economy was all the more dependent on the supply of currency, in the form of copper cash or silver bullion. The fluctuations in the rate of exchange between these two media greatly complicated the difficulties of trade in nineteenth-century China, as we shall note below.

The currency and exchange system, like the system of weights and measures generally, was remarkably complex because the major unit of account, the tael (*liang* or ounce) was not uniform but carried from place to place and trade to trade. The classical description of this situation is that of Dr. H. B. Morse, for the city of Chungking:

Here the standard weight of the tael for silver transactions is 555.6 grains, and this is the standard for all transactions in which the scale is not specified. Frequently, however, a modification of the scale is provided for, depending in some cases upon the place from which the merchant comes or with which he trades, and in others upon the goods in which he deals. A merchant coming from Kweichow, or trading with that place, will probably, but not certainly, use a scale on which the tael weighs 548.9 grains; a merchant from Kweifu, a town on the Yangtze a hundred miles below Chungking, will buy and sell with a tael of 562.7 grains; and between these two extremes are at least ten topical weights of tael, all "current" at Chungking. In addition to these twelve topical "currencies," there are others connected with commodities. One of the most important products of Szechwan is salt, and dealings in this are settled by a tael of 556.4 grains, unless it is salt from the Tzeliu well, in which case the standard is 557.7. A transaction in cotton cloth is settled with a tael of 555.0 grains, but for cotton yarn the tael is 556.0 grains and for raw cotton the tael is 547.7 grains.

This seems confusion, but we are not yet at the end. Up to this point we have dealt only with the weight on the scale, but now comes in the question of the fineness of the silver with which the payment is made. At Chungking three qualities of silver are in common use—"fine silver" 1,000 fine current throughout the empire, "old silver" about 995 fine, and "trade silver" between 960 and 970 fine; and payment may be stipulated in any one of these three qualities. Taking the score of current tael-weights in combination with the three grades of silver, we have at least sixty currencies possible in this one town.

It seems evident that the tael system's complexity suited the interests of exchangers of currency rather than the interests of sellers or buyers of goods; at any rate it favored all of these persons rather than the producer or the ultimate consumer. We must understand it as an institution tied in with the vested interests of the middleman-merchant class and its patrons the official class, rather than with the interests of entrepreneurs seeking to produce goods or to develop new products and markets. Every time goods or funds passed through the commercial network, a percentage was levied for the costs of exchange operations. Half a dozen such levies and operations would not be unusual in an ordinary transaction between one province and another. Furthermore, the complexity of the tael system was so great as to make exchange an esoteric subject, monopolized by specialists and insiders with a knowledge of the system. This facilitated an inefficient proliferation of services, in which the distributive process involved more layers and more manpower than was really necessary. This inevitably must have impeded commodity flows, causing numerous delays, wastage and spoilage. Moreover, the distributive margin between buying and selling prices was thus increased because of the excessive number of persons who derived support from it.

Management and entrepreneurship at this level of the economy were generally inhibited by the subordination of merchants to officialdom. The patronage of the upper stratum of landlords, literati and officials was essential to commercial operations. In theory, the state was expected not only to preempt certain monopolies like salt and iron, but also to regulate commercial and industrial activities by licensing and other means, and in general limit capital accumulation and expenditure by individuals. The merchant had no legal safeguards to protect his property against exactions from the governmental level, since the officials represented the law. Thus while bureaucratic patronage and protection were essential to commercial operations of all sorts, the official class retained the spirit of tax-gatherers rather than of risk-taking entrepreneurs. Their gentry-landlord background and the scholarly disesteem for the merchant class from ancient times, all imposed strict limits to merchant initiative and innovation. Economic enterprise was carried on within a framework in which the power of officialdom was the final recourse, rather than a system of impersonal law which the merchant might invoke to protect himself. By using official patronage and power, a merchant capitalist could secure certain lucrative opportunities represented by licenses or monopolies, the right to distribute salt, contracts for the transport of grain, or sales orders for the imperial household or official establishments. The merchants' aim was to seek comparatively safe forms of profit-making and therefore to secure an opportunity for levying fees and charges, both official and unofficial, upon one of the great staples of commerce. In each case this opportunity had to be secured on a personal basis and preserved with the support of official power. Thus the whole prevailing structure of incentives was such as to encourage and perpetuate established forms and norms of commerce while at the same time discouraging risk-taking, the seeking out of new markets, or innovation.

C. *The Governmental Level.* By this we mean the economic activities organized, superintended, or indirectly controlled by the official class on behalf of the imperial government at the capital and in the provinces.

The role of government in the economy was posited on the fact that the official class retained the ultimate power in Chinese society. The government in one sense was rather active in the country's economic life, but in another sense its role was limited and passive. On the one hand, the dead weight of official and quasi-official forms of taxation bore heavily upon the country's economy, as did also the various forms of state monopoly, licensing and the like. All of these, in effect, entailed a negative type of interference. On the other hand, the services performed for the economy by the Chinese state were minimal—largly confined to the maintenance of the waterworks and the stocking of granaries as a safeguard against famine. The active promotion of mercantile activity, the concept of the development of the economy as a whole—i.e., an implicit or explicit concept of economic growth—or the idea of building up the country's economic power as a prerequisite for augmenting state power, all seem to have been minimal in the Chinese tradition. This accords with the fact that the whole notion of international competition and thus of economic nationalism, even in its mercantilist sense, was absent. This can be illustrated by the fact that there was no idea of a protective tariff, and that similar tariff rates were applied to exports and imports. This general attitude was also clearly reflected in fiscal practice.

The Ch'ing fiscal system was very pervasive, but highly inefficient. It operated within an imposing façade of regulations including quotas for revenue collections by regions, fixed charges on these collections and allocations of payments, both to the capital and to other provinces by transfer directly. Collections were partly in kind but major revenue collections were in money terms. According to the imperial bookkeeping in the statutes, surplus-revenue provinces regularly paid sums to revenue-deficit provinces and all sums entered were allocated to specific purposes. In actual fact, however, it is plain that much larger sums were handled within each province, if only to maintain the bureaucracy and its activities, without being accounted for to the capital. When under pressure for funds, the officials commonly collected contributions, or in other words, made levies upon merchants or indeed upon anyone known to have money. Since such persons usually had secured their funds in part through official patronage, this system of contributions was perhaps not inequitable. Literary degrees and official titles and, in extreme cases, even official positions were conferred upon the contributors. The sums so levied sometimes reached millions of taels from major monopolists in the salt trade or the foreign trade at Canton. But this form of quasi-taxation was certainly not a type of levy to encourage capital formation.

Land tax and labor service formed the backbone of the fiscal system and were aimed at garnering for the government the surpluses of agricultural products and rural manpower which formed the chief economic resources of traditional China. These taxes had a long and necessarily complex history coming down through more than two millennia. In general, by the nineteenth century they had been combined into a complex system of payments in money terms. Expected receipts were listed as quotas, both for provincial and for local areas at different levels. Statutorily, the local quotas were intended to maintain the official post stations, local public works and the bureaucracy, at the discretion of the local officialdom. Provincial quotas were also set for amounts to be made available to the Board of Revenue at Peking. The actual collection of local taxes, as noted above, was several times the statutory amount of the various quotas listed at Peking. The estimation of the amount of taxation actually levied is one of the more important problems awaiting study by economic historians. In general, officialdom was put somewhat in the position of tax farmers, required to report a minimum to their superiors and expected to collect enough in addition to maintain themselves and their activities.

The efficiency of tax collection depended upon the degree of dynastic vigor at the time. During periods of dynastic strength, official corruption tended to stay within bounds and thus fiscal efficiency could be maintained. This frequently meant a lighter tax burden, more equitably distributed, with a larger proportion of receipts finding their way to Peking and with a better performance of public services. However, in the course of dynastic decline, official corruption tended to be reinforced by the growth of local vested interests, by a decline of morale, and by an increased need for official funds. In such circumstances the efficiency of collection would decline, many large households and favored families would get themselves off the tax registers, and in the end a higher tax total would be collected if possible from a dwindling and impoverished segment of the rural population. The classic result would be rebellion followed by a new dynasty and a beginning of the dynastic cycle.

The grain tribute collected in kind in the Yangtze provinces was a special form of tax to provide the stipendiary food supply of the imperial capital. There was a widespread and intricate administrative network for the transport of this tribute grain to Peking. The grain transport administration had to cope with the problem of maintaining the Grand Canal and the lower reaches of the Yellow River dike system so that grain shipments from the Yangtze delta could traverse the regions normally flooded by the Yellow River system—a major engineering problem as well as an administrative one. The alternative to the Grand Canal was the system of sea transport by junk fleets from the Shanghai area around the Shantung promontory, on a route probably as much subject to shipwreck as the canal route was subject to pilfering or banditry. The grain tribute performed several economic functions: it fed the swollen bureaucracy surrounding the imperial court and the Manchu military garrisons in the north and provided supplies for the maintenance of emergency stocks. At the same time, it played an important role in internal trade and in limiting the self-sufficiency of the rural sector.

The military establishment, with its large stipends to maintain garrisons of Manchu and other bannermen and their families, was one of the great vested interests and administrative problems. The local territorial troops, or constabulary, the so-called Army of the Green Standard, were maintained from local land-tax sources. By the nineteenth century, both the garrisons of bannermen and the constabulary had proved ineffective to quell local rebellion. The eighteenth-century expeditions on China's borders and into neighboring regions like Tibet, Annam or Central Asia had drained funds from the government with questionable economic return. In the ten great campaigns under the Ch'ien-lung Emperor we can see at work the ever-present urge to contain the barbarians, combined with a vested military interest on the part of Manchu commanders who led large forces in border operations and requisitioned even larger sums to support them. It is a question whether the financial profit to be derived from these expeditions was not an important incentive for them. After the White Lotus Rebellion at the turn of the century, however, the traditional military forces had lost their capacity and morale and represented a net drain upon the state economy.

III. PRE-INDUSTRIAL CHINA AND PRE-INDUSTRIAL EUROPE

A comparison of the pre-industrial economies of Europe and China may help us to identify the factors and processes that facilitated growth in the former and retarded it in the latter. Such a comparison yields a number of striking similarities and also some major differences:

A. *Similarities.* In both societies a primarily agrarian economy supported a small superstructure. It was based on a "natural economy" of local barter with a low degree of commercialization and minimal use of money. Money served more as a standard and store of value than as a medium of exchange and payment. The monetary system was inefficient. The low degree of commercialization was also indicated by the extensive barriers to trade in the form of tolls, dues and taxes on the movement of goods; the poor development of roads and communications except for water transport; and the general scarcity of capital as measured by high and usurious rates of interest. As a result, these were essentially what Heckscher has called "storage economies," in which consumption largely depended upon accumulated stocks. Such inventories of grain and other foodstuffs were needed not only to meet inter-harvest requirements, but also to serve as a protection against natural and man-made disasters. Thus a considerable proportion of China's current resources were tied up in an unproductive form of investment. Other similarities to the pre-industrial European scene included the low status of the merchant and money-lender, and the extensive use of guild organization to protect and also control merchant activities.

B. *Dissimilarities: Foreign Trade and City Growth*. The dissimilarities between China and pre-industrial Europe are perhaps even more notable: for example, in pre-industrial Europe possibly the two most important factors contributing to the process of economic change were the growth of foreign trade and the growth of autonomous cities. Europe's development and expansion overseas after 1492 were marked by a widening in the extent of the market and the commercialization of the economy to-gether with extensive capital accumulation, all facilitated through foreign trade. These developments also depended upon the growth of urban centers, with their legal status as chartered cities or city states and the special privileges extended to the burghers. The growth of the bourgeoisie symbolized the rise of modern Europe.

Neither of these elements had a counterpart in China. Foreign trade in proportion to the total economy, even during the Sung period, never reached the degree of importance which it had in Europe. The reasons for this smaller role of foreign trade in the case of China are many and varied. First, the geographical configuration of the Chinese setting put its centers of ancient population on the broad irrigated plains of the Wei and Yellow Rivers. Only later did dense populations accumulate in delta regions like those of Canton and Shanghai, after China's social institu-tions had been well established. When seaports eventually developed, their growth was handicapped by China's comparative isolation from other major states. Korea remained an appendage, accessible by land as well as sea. Japan and Annam were comparatively small and peripheral. Chinese expansion was chiefly absorbed in the subcontinent of the modern Chinese area—for example, into the Southwest or into Central Asia. With half a dozen domestic provinces, each bigger than any accessi-ble foreign state, China's trade remained oriented toward the domestic market and not based upon seafaring. Arab traders from Southeast Asia had taken the lead in developing commericial sea contact with Chinese ports. Only afterward, in the Sung and Yuan periods, had Chinese merchants become principal participants in maritime trade. From the Ming period, the cultural and social institutions of China became still more firmly ethnocentric in character, with little emphasis upon voyaging abroad (as in the European crusades to the Holy Land or later to Asia on the track of Marco Polo).

Against this background, the deliberate government policy of regulating and restricting foreign trade in the Ming and Ch'ing periods is quite understandable. The big Ming expeditions into the Indian Ocean were governmental experiments and were discontinued after the middle of the fifteenth century. The Manchu dynasty came down from the north and controlled South China last. Not until the end of the seventeenth century did it resume the Ming system of tributary trade. Even then it was always ready to sacrifice maritime commerce in the interest of maintaining local order and preventing the influx of subversive foreign influences. China remained largely self-sufficient within her own borders between the tropics and Siberia.

At the same time, the Chinese city was under the domination of officials rather than of merchants. The major urban centers were administrative rather than commercial. The tradition of government monopoly or regulation of all forms of large-scale association and economic activity kept commerical growth subordinate to the political, administrative and military interests of the noncommercial ruling strata.

Lying behind the contrast between China and Western Europe are the differing institutional frameworks and cultural values within which their economies developed. The West, except in Egypt, had little counterpart to the irrigated rice economy which had such far-reaching influence on Chinese life. The Mediterranean Basin facilitated the growth of city-states and sea trade, and Western European geography with its radiating peninsulas later fostered the development of nation-states and overseas explorations. These same factors promoted the introduction and diffusion of new technologies and new ideas. In contrast, the Chinese empire from the beginning was turned in upon itself by the Central Asian land mass and the expanse of the Pacific Ocean. It early developed a bureaucratic empire in which the legal system remained a tool of the official class. Feudalism in China was wiped out at the time of the Ch'in unification. From the Han period on, the bureaucratic network and the ideal of imperial unity militated against the rise of detached and particularistic political-economic areas. In spite of the barbarian inroads after the Han dynasties, the geographical environment and cultural and institutional inheritance of the Chinese people were so strong as to lead to a revival of unified empire. This meant that the pluralistic and multifocal institutional structure of Western Europe, with its struggles and rivalries among the crown, the nobles, the lesser gentry, the cities and burghers, between church and state and between nation and nation within Christendom, had no counterpart in Chinese experience. Where European development out of the chaos of feudalism stimulated dynamic and individualistic innovation and adventure, the Chinese empire remained a bureaucratic colossus bestriding all social life. This was reflected in the legal system which did not protect the individual within the family nor the individual property holder nor, least of all, the merchant; and also in the Confucian ethic, which did not give the individual the same incentive as the Protestant ethic.

It would be a mistake, on the other hand, to regard Chinese society, with its dominant bureaucratic overlay, as the equivalent of a modern centralized state. On the contrary, the old China inculcated the particularism of family-centered kinship relations and village or market-town-centered economic relations. At both of these levels personal relationships remained more important than the universalistic and rational criteria which have developed, rather recently, in modern European society. In short, the different economic growth of Europe and China is symptomatic of the total cultural difference between them.

IV. CHINA'S ECONOMIC DEVELOPMENT, CA. 1760–1914

In essence, the disequilibrating forces and the pattern of disturbance in China were similar to those in most underdeveloped areas. Yet in China economic change followed a different path conditioned by extraterritoriality and the rise of the treaty ports. They served as a means for transplanting not only of Western capital and entrepreneurs, but of Western legal institutions and commercial practices as well. This was possible because the treaty ports were protected from the arbitrary exactions of officialdom and the other impediments to economic activity referred to above. These conditions encouraged the accumulation of capital in the ports, both by Western and by Chinese enterprise.

Therefore, in effect, the prime agents of economic change in nineteenth-century China are comparable to those seen earlier in Europe—foreign trade which provided the impetus, and special city status formalized through extraterritoriality which provided the opportunity. However, unlike Europe, China's new economic growth did not radiate out into, and become diffused throughout, the traditional economy. The institutional barriers in the traditional sector of the economy, and the failure of the government's efforts to achieve an industrial breakthrough under official auspices, seriously impeded factor mobility between the hinterland and the treaty ports; growth did not take root outside the ports, but remained bottled up in them. One part of the economy remained based on the traditional order while another grew up in the coastal and riverine cities. Thus industry was concentrated in the treaty ports in order to secure the institutional advantages of greater legal protection of property and investment. The metropolis of Shanghai and its dominant position in Chinese manufacturing at the end of the treaty century are outstanding examples of this phenomenon, as are also Tientsin and Canton.

In analyzing the pattern of economic change during this century of disturbance, it is useful to distinguish several sub-periods.

A. *The Drawing of China into the World Economy, 1760–1842.* The domestic economic developments of this period have been little studied but presumably centered about the phenomenal population increase. Under the stimulus of factors operating in the early eighteenth century which need not detain us here, the population more or less doubled in this period. Present estimates give an order of magnitude somewhere around 230 million for 1760 and 430 million for 1842. The economic implications of such growth can be imagined but have not been extensively traced in the record.

Foreign trade in this period centered at Canton as the sole port. It was based on a barter of Chinese tea and silk for Western silver and Indian produce, carried on mainly by the licensed guild known as the Cohong and the British East India Company within a framework of bilateral monopoly. At the Chinese end this trade was conducted on a bargaining basis with a price solution that was necessarily indeterminate. The triangular Chinese-British-Indian trade, balanced by the so-called Country Trade from India, has been studied to some degree. China engaged in a passive trade, in which the foreigner took the initiative by coming to Canton. After arrival, the East India Company vessels had to dispose of their cargoes of British woolens and other products. Very generally, the Hong merchants could take these goods at a loss and consequently had to raise their tea and silk prices to cover this loss. There was an increasing tendency for the Hong merchants to borrow capital from the East India Company. Hong debts and Hong bankruptcies consequently plagued the British company operations. The increasing tea and silk exports which grew in response to the European demand were made possible only by the imports of raw cotton and opium from India. After about 1819 opium eclipsed cotton as the chief means of "laying down funds" in Canton for the continually growing export trade. But while exports passed outward through the established channels of the Hong merchants and the East India Company, the opium import trade was illegal and centered elsewhere, in the hands of the opium merchants both foreign and Chinese. Thus the Canton system with its British East India Company and Cohong monopolists ceased to be the channel for the major import, and was left standing, so to speak, on one leg only. When the tea exports rose to twenty million pounds a year and above, the result was that opium smuggling, administrative collapse, disorder and friction grew proportionately. All of this culminated in the Opium War and the unequal treaties, which led to the abolition of the Canton monopoly and permitted trade expansion.

The repercussions of the opium dispute of the late 1830's on the domestic economy have not been fully analyzed. The growth of the Shansi banks in the early nineteenth century and the simultaneous accumulations of capital by Cantonese Hong merchants and by salt monopolists in the lower Yangtze and other self-producing regions would suggest that there was a general growth of money economy within China during this period. Another indication is in the increased valuation of silver in terms of copper cash—a complex subject of the Opium War period. Chinese officials ascribed the increased cost of silver to its outflow in exchange for opium, overlooking its attendant inflow to pay for tea and silk. Debasement of the copper coinage, the increased demand for silver as the chief medium of exchange in an expanding money economy, hoarding in a period of disorder, to say nothing of population increase, are other factors lying behind this phenomenon.

B. *Economic Disorganization and Decline, 1842–1864.* The treaty system established a new institutional framework for foreign trade. In the treaty ports the lead was taken by commission or agency houses, like Jardine, Matheson and Co., Dent and Co., or Russell and Co., which developed services for trade expansion through chartering ships, insuring cargo, and buying and selling on a commission basis for Western merchants at a distance. On the Chinese side, these Western treaty port firms used Chinese compradores, who had formerly been merely buyers of supplies, but who now undertook both to collect export cargoes and to distribute import goods on a commission basis. With the assistance of Cantonese compradores inherited from the earlier period, new trade outlets and trade routes were rapidly developed. They centered particularly on Shanghai, which was closer than Canton to the major centers of tea and silk production. While exports continued to grow, the trade remained handicapped by the small Chinese demand for Western textiles and other manufactured imports. The result was a steady increase of illegal but well organized opium imports.

The impact of this treaty-port trade after 1842 upon the Chinese economy as a whole is still obscure. The domestic living standard recorded in literary references seems to have been characterized by a Confucian austerity and frugality among the ruling strata in the seventeenth century, followed by a more lavish display and consumption of goods in the prosperous eighteenth century. Similar literary references suggest an increasing economic stringency and imperial parsimony in the early nineteenth century. Under the impact of population increase, the decline of the dynasty's administrative competence seems to have been evidenced by an increased incidence of natural calamities, the declining efficiency of the Grand Canal transport route, and the growth of piracy and opium smuggling on the coast. At any rate, the impact of the early foreign trade must be fitted into this larger domestic context more persuasively than has yet been done. The Marxist-Leninist contention that foreign imports depressed native living standards by wiping out rural handicraft production cannot be substantiated for the period before the 1860's. On the contrary, it may be argued that with the phenomenal increase of tea and silk exports, per capita product may have risen in some areas. In any case, such estimates must vary according to the regions considered—the lower Yangtze tea and silk areas may have prospered while the hinterland of Canton in Kwangsi may have suffered from the new treaty system.

The Taiping Rebellion of 1851–1864, on balance, must be regarded as a product of domestic causes, with foreign factors playing a minor role. Its impact upon the economy was devastating, though this is another subject that has not been sufficiently explored. The great rebellion and the smaller disorders which accompanied and followed it curbed population growth, and perhaps resulted in an actual decline of population. Key areas of the countryside were ravaged and the channels of trade were disrupted. All of this was made worse by the deterioration of the water control system and consequent flooding of the Yellow River, which changed its course from south to north of the Shantung peninsula after 1852. Thus rice supplies for the capital had to be transported by sea instead of the Grand Canal.

One of the most significant effects of the rebellion was the cutting off of the land tax of South and Central China. In response, the imperial government had recourse to expedients like the issue of paper currency and casting of large copper or iron cash. Its chief recourse, however, was to institute taxes on trade, among which the new Maritime Customs at the treaty ports were most important. Unofficially, new taxes were also levied on opium imports. Most important of all was the new provincial tax on goods in transit, i.e., *likin,* which got started in 1853.

The general result of the rebellion was thus a restructuring of the fiscal system with a shift from direct to indirect forms of taxation. This meant a greater dependence of the imperial government upon foreign trade revenues, at a time when the enforced treaty revisions of 1858 and 1860 made it dependent also on political cooperation with the foreign powers.

C. *The Abortive Breakthrough, 1864–1895.* This was a crucial period during which Japan succeeded in breaking out of the vicious circle of economic backwardness, while similar attempts to bring about a state-led industrial revolution failed in China, for reasons which we shall try briefly to indicate.

The decade of the active restoration of Confucian government, after the suppression of rebellions, was attended by the use of foreign arms and the setting up of arsenals at Shanghai and Foochow to make guns and gunboats. At the same time, the revised treaties opened the Yangtze River and North China treaty ports to foreign trade, foreign steamships developed these new routes, and China now lay open to complete foreign access by water, along the coast and in the interior. The power of the foreign trade impact was signalized by the growth of such port cities as Shanghai, Tientsin, and Hankow, and the rise of foreign banks, like the Hongkong and Shanghai Banking Corporation formed in 1864.

Foreign trade in this period increased steadily, and the treaty port cities began their economic domination of the commercial hinterland, into which their goods were flowing. The decline in staple exports led to a diversification of trade as reflected in the export of a variety of new products—tung oil, dried eggs, bristles, and similar products of the agrarian economy. At the same time, kerosene and tobacco began to develop their mass markets, symbolized later by the wide distribution networks of the Asiatic Petroleum Company and the British-American Tobacco Co.

Technology and training in industry were given some stimulus from translation programs and from the dispatch of students abroad. Yet here again the traditional social structure and cultural values kept the trained men of superior intelligence from pursuing mechanical or even mercantile aims.

Under the impact of all of these developments combined, domestic handicraft production now began to be subjected to the competition of Western textile imports, while at the same time the transplanting of tea plants to India led to serious competition with Chinese tea exports, and the opening of Japan to foreign trade stimulated Japanese competition in silk exports. China suffered in this competition because the standardization of product and organization of marketing and finance were more advanced in India and Japan. It is extremely difficult, however, to get a balanced estimate of the trends of Chinese farm economy and subsidiary handicraft industries of this period. For example, one imponderable factor was the degree of destruction inherited from the period of rebellion. Government efforts to replant mulberry trees for silk production and to revive agriculture generally, and the evidence of widespread destruction in the countryside of the lower Yangtze provinces indicate the magnitude of this factor. In these decades Indian opium imports began to be displaced by steadily rising domestic opium production, so that in the 1880's these imports actually declined.

This is the period which also signalizes the early efforts at industrialization under official sponsorship. Many industries were begun. The China Merchants' Steam Navigation Company under government auspices and compradore management began to compete with foreign shipping after 1872. The Kaiping Mines were developed north of Tientsin from the late seventies to provide coal for the steamship lines and for Shanghai.

Eventually China's first railroad line was built to service these coal exports under central government auspices. The institutional mechanism for these developments in general was that of "official supervision and merchant operation" (*kuan-tu shang-pan*). This in effect was an attempt to make an industrial breakthrough while leaving the institutional framework essentially untouched. The reasons for the failure of this attempt have now been assessed by Dr. Albert Feuerwerker's volume on *China's Early Industrialization*. They will also be clearly illustrated in a forthcoming study by Dr. Kwang-Ching Liu which analyzes the failure of one of the leading enterprises under this system, the China Merchants' Steam Navigation Company. The precursor of this system of "official supervision and merchant operation" had been the traditional Chinese salt administration, a government salt monopoly which was essentially a fiscal institution. The attitudes and practices characteristic of such an institution consequently affected the management of all the enterprises set up under this system. They were viewed by the officials as a source of "squeeze" and personal income; this attitude was typical of all the levels of officialdom, all the way up to the imperial court. At the same time, enterprises operating under this system were used as instruments for broadening the regional power of the different cliques which vied for primacy within the nineteenth-century Chinese state. This attitude then spread to the managers of these enterprises, who viewed them basically as objects of despoliation. Thus both the sponsors and the operators of these would-be-modern enterprises were motivated by a tax-farming rather than an entrepreneurial spirit.

If we look more closely at the function and the role of official sponsorship under the *kuan-tu shang-pan* system, we see that it first of all provided encouragement and sanction for the founding and initial promotion of the enterprise. This encouragement might take several concrete forms: the granting of certain monopoly rights by the state or its organs to the new company (e.g., shipment of tribute rice); government loans or other types of grants of government capital to the enterprise; and protection of the enterprise by its official sponsors against exactions by other officials. In return the official sponsors would appoint the managers of the enterprise, thereby assuring effective supervision. This inevitably affected the character of management. Managers usually held official rank, and at the same time represented the shareholders. They therefore faced two ways, toward their official sponsors and toward the shareholders. In this situation management tended to be particularistic.

Similarly the investment and financial policies of the company were likely to be characterized by short-term borrowing at high rates of interest, by guaranteed dividend payments, and by inadequate allowances for depreciation. These attitudes and practices were not confined to the late nineteenth century alone, but were widespread in Chinese business and government up to the very advent of the Chinese Communist regime.

Thus the system of "official supervision and merchant operation" was self-defeating. To overcome the dead weight of stagnation in nineteenth-century China a massive effort was required, involving large outlays on capital-intensive projects with low prospective rates of return; by raising the marginal productivity of capital such projects could then create a more favorable economic milieu for the growth of private business enterprise. However, an effort of such magnitude could only be mounted by the State and in reality the enterprises fostered by Chinese officials at the time in shipping, mining, communications, etc. were precisely of this type. But because of the very nature of the state and its officialdom, they were doomed to fail.

D. *Economic Imperialism and the Beginnings of Industrialization, 1895–1914.* The economic repercussions of China's defeat by Japan in 1895 were immediately apparent in the large foreign loans which China had to contract in order to pay the war indemnity. Japan used these funds to develop heavy industry and to build up her monetary reserves prior to a shift to the gold standard, thus forging further ahead of China. The foreign loans were secured on the Maritime Customs revenue and, from this time onward, ate into that reliable and increasing source of central government income. Japan's victory also touched off the scramble for concessions, which were extorted mainly in economic terms. The spheres of interest secured over various regions of China by the imperialist powers included ninety-nine year leases of major ports like Dairen, granted to Russia, or port sites like Tsingtao, granted to Germany. Running inland from these ports were railroads financed by, mortgaged to, and run by, the foreign powers. The Chinese Eastern Railway cutting across Manchuria to Vladivostok, as arranged in 1896, was now joined to the South Manchurian Railway running to Dairen under Russian control. The Germans developed a railroad in Shantung on similar lines. In both cases, mining rights along the railroad right of way were also granted the foreign power. In effect, these concessions permitted the imperialist power to invest in China's industrialization, mainly in the form of transportation and extractive industry. In retrospect it may possibly appear to future students that the imperialist powers on balance invested more than they profited from these arrangements—at least this may be true of Germany in Shantung.

The Japanese treaty had also permitted foreign industrial establishments to be set up in the treaty ports on Chinese soil. Thus the last bar to direct foreign leadership in China's industrialization was removed, but it was a leadership which also meant control over large sectors of the economy. In these same years under government auspices leading officials began official enterprises—for example, the textile mill at Shanghai under Sheng Hsuan-huai or the coal and iron complex at Han-yeh-p'ing in the Wuhan area under Chang Chih-tung.

The Boxer Rebellion of 1900 was another disaster which diverted still more of China's revenues to pay debts to foreigners under the Boxer indemnity. In the decade which followed, the central government reform program created new administrative and economic institutions, such as government banks and a central ministry of commerce and communications. A new army was built up with native and foreign equipment, the provision of which constituted a new industry. Railroad building had its first major decade of accomplishment under Sino-foreign auspices, and there was a considerable degree of economic growth, the extent of which has not yet been estimated. This process involved the rise of new industries and economic institutions and the decline of old ones. For example, the century-old Shansi banks began their final decline, being unsuited to modern banking needs. The new and enterprising merchants of Japan and Germany pushed their distribution networks among the Chinese mercantile communities of the interior and developed their markets with less dependence on Chinese compradores. Groups of provincial gentry, merchants and officials initiated railroad projects in competition with those of the central government, although they usually failed to secure adequate finance and management. A few individual entrepreneurs emerged from the Chinese upper strata, like the top scholar Chang Chien, who developed his own cotton mill and other enterprises in his native place of Nantung, Kiangsu. Remittances from overseas Chinese communities began to flow back to China, playing an increasingly important role in the country's balance of payments. Capital accumulated by overseas Chinese from the Canton and Fukien areas was also flowing back into such investments as department stores in the treaty ports. Naturally there was great regional differentiation in this scattered and sporadic economic growth. It centered undoubtedly in the Canton and Shanghai areas. But there was also, for example, a forward movement under official leadership on the Inner Mongolian frontier, where Chinese agricultural expansion was facilitated by the completion in 1910 of the railroad from Peking through Kalgan to Suiyuan.

Evidences of the continued growth of foreign influence over, if not actual domination of, the Chinese economy can also be seen in the first decade of the twentieth century. Financial development agencies like the Peking Syndicate or the British and Chinese Corporation were formed with funds invested by the Hongkong and Shanghai Banking Corporation and the British firm of Jardine, Matheson and Company. British interests secured control of the Kaiping Mines. British funds were used to build the Shanghai-Nanking railroad and other lines in the lower Yangtze as a British sphere. Negotiations for American financing of Manchurian railroads were prosecuted (to little avail) by Willard Straight and others, and for the Hankow-Canton railroad by an international consortium of bankers. This era of "dollar diplomacy" and projected financial developments under foreign control in various parts of China was climaxed by the collapse of the dynasty in 1911. The foreign bond holders were immediately reassured when the inspector general of Chinese Maritime Customs, Sir Francis Aglen, for the first time took actual receipt of Chinese customs revenues and deposited them for safekeeping in the foreign banks in the treaty ports. This was followed by the Reorganization Loan of 1913 to the new ruler, Yuan Shih-k'ai, from which the United States abstained. The era of financial imperialism was cut short only by the outbreak of the First World War.

As evaluated half a century later, financial imperialism may have seemed more threatening to Chinese patriots in the early twentieth century than it might actually have become in the unfolding of its own operations. Possibly the bark of imperialism was worse than its bite. The fact remains, nonetheless, that from 1896 until the Second World War China's payments abroad on loans and indemnities constituted a sizable and constant financial drain which inevitably impaired her capacity for domestic capital formation, both governmental and private.

E. *The Example of Railroads.* The various factors facilitating and impeding economic growth may be seen in the history of railroads. In most countries railroads served to widen the extent of the market, stimulate the rapid commercialization of agriculture, the growth of cities and of a money economy, while at the same time the railroad itself provided a market for the iron, steel and engineering industries. But in the crowded countryside of China proper the coming of the iron horse was in no way comparable to its role in the opening, for example, of the American West.

Among many obvious reasons for this, the following may be suggested: First of all, the abundance of water communications in South and Central China, which reached to the capital, serviced by abundant manpower, maintained a severe competition for any railroad enterprise. In the densely populated countryside, land values for a right of way were costly and public opinion on geomantic grounds was superstitiously opposed to railroads. Another factor was the lack of sufficient capital and credit in a society where capital could not easily be mobilized by bond issues or other measures of credit creation. Moreover, the railroad, coming as the tool of the foreigner, met a rising patriotic opposition which was explicitly stated by leading officials: unless and until the Chinese government could build its own railroads and control them, it was preferable to have none. From the beginning it was realized that railroads under foreign control provided strategic means of military as well as economic ingress and invasion.

The railroad pattern which actually emerged was in part a product of the strategy of commercial exploitation through imperialist spheres of influence. Railroads were built under foreign domination from treaty ports inland through the peninsula of southern Manchuria and the peninsula of Shantung, as well as from Shanghai over the Yangtze delta. The Chinese Eastern Railway in the north, for Russia, and the Hanoi-Yunnan Railroad in the south, for France, served as the most obvious strategic spearheads. A similar plan was evident in the Peking-Suiyuan line, the first one to be built by China, which facilitated the "secondary imperialism" of China's expansion into Inner Mongolia.

Geography constituted an added barrier to railroad development—first, in the form of mountains which, for example, kept the railroad effectively out of Szechwan until recently. Meanwhile the Yangtze itself is so preeminent a highway that, as the geographer George Cressey has noted, the railway lines tend to be at right angles rather than parallel to the river. It is no accident that the Chinese railroad network has been built more extensively in North than in South China. We suggest, in short, that the retardation of railroad development was due to the interplay of a variety of factors, a study of which may serve to demonstrate in microcosm the impediments to China's industrialization.

In sharp contrast, we see an entirely different course of development in Manchuria. In that region the railways assumed the role of "leading sector." They turned out to be highly profitable, almost from the very beginning of their operation. At the same time, unlike the situation in China proper, these profits were largely plowed back into investment, not only in the railroads themselves but in other enterprises as well. Consequently railroad earnings constituted one of the important sources for financing the development of other social overhead facilities and also contributed to the founding of other industries. This railroad development greatly stimulated the commercialization of Manchurian agriculture, drawing it into the world trading network. At the same time the railroads themselves provided an important market for engineering, repair, and machine-building services. Railroad development thus became the center of a broadening pattern of economic growth, which spilled over into agriculture, industry, and trade. Moreover, and again unlike the situation in China proper, this growth did not remain confined to the coastal strip of Manchuria. The example of railroad development illustrates the difference in the course of Manchurian, as opposed to Chinese, economic development in general. This difference may be viewed as the result of three categories of factors: (a) the much more favorable population-resource balance in Manchuria; (b) the comparative absence of institutional barriers to modernization such as prevailed in China proper; and (c) the injection of Japanese control and entrepreneurship coupled with large-scale capital imports into Manchuria.

V. CONCLUSION: PATTERNS OF RETARDATION

The preceding survey has touched upon two central questions: (1) what were the active agents of economic change in nineteenth-century China? and (2) what were the chief factors that retarded economic growth? By way of conclusion, let us summarize briefly the roles played by the treaty ports, as principal centers of change, and by certain Chinese institutions as factors of retardation.

The Western impact transmitted through the ports was a multiple challenge, military, political, economic, social, ideological and cultural. The new influences were inevitably subversive of the old order. Thus the Chinese leaders were plunged into a dilemma. They felt the necessity to meet the challenge, but were unable or unwilling to understand that this could not be done without a radical remaking of practices and institutions, even ideas, in every sphere. This was, of course, one of the great differences between nineteenth-century China and Japan.

The transformation of Chinese life was accompanied by an erosion of the traditional economic order which was evidenced, for example, in the decline of handicrafts and later in the displacement of native banks. This decline of the old was paralleled by the creation of a new order in the treaty ports and in Manchuria. The result was a century of growth and decline occurring side by side.

The data now available do not permit the drawing up of a net balance sheet. We cannot measure the rate of growth in the expanding sectors and the rates of decline in the contracting sectors. In our present state of knowledge, we cannot determine whether the Chinese economy as a whole was expanding or contracting during this period. Foreign trade appears to have been the most important disequilibrating force in the economic realm. It performed the role of a "leading sector," generating an almost classic text-book-type process of cumulative economic growth which, however, remained confined to the treaty port segment of the Chinese economy.

The growth process here was interacting and cumulative. The gradual rise of foreign trade in the early nineteenth century stimulated a demand for the development of financial facilities. Up to the middle of the century, foreign trade had to be financed by the trading firms themselves. This necessarily limited the scope of the trade and the number of firms that could enter it. However, the rise of modern banking and insurance companies, particularly between 1858 and 1864, facilitated the entry of smaller merchants into foreign trade. We see here a sequence—the growth of foreign trade giving rise to a demand for banking facilities, which in turn facilitated the further expansion and widening of foreign trade which led to the processing of export products, such as tea and silk, in the treaty ports, and also to the processing of certain import products which were consumed in the treaty ports. The latter involved the growth of such food-processing industries as flour-milling, sugar-refining, and brewing. In turn, the development of the treaty ports, with a growth of foreign trade and of allied industries, necessarily led to population growth in the ports. This stimulated the demand for public utilities such as water, gas, electricity, and local transport. The development of public utilities and of shipping both stimulated the demand for coal. At the same time, there was a need for engineering shops and small works to service all of these enterprises. The expanding population in the treaty ports naturally demanded housing services. This stimulated housing construction, which gave rise to a growing demand for cement and other building materials. Meanwhile as the market for imported textile manufactures widened, it became increasingly profitable for foreign firms to build and operate textile mills in the treaty ports. A similar development occurred with respect to cigarettes and tobacco, canned goods and certain other consumer products.

However, the question still remains as to why this self-generating process of economic growth remained largely bottled up in the treaty port segment of the economy and why the multiplier effect of investment was thus largely confined to that segment. The precise reasons, the factors and variables, that may account for this require further exploration. On the basis of presently available evidence we surmise that there were three types of factors that hindered the spread of economic stimuli from the treaty ports to the Chinese hinterland: (1) institutional as well as physical (transport) barriers to the movement of goods and, even more important, to the movement of factors of production; (2) leakages from the treaty ports to foreign countries through the medium of profit remittances, so that some of the multiplier effects of investment upon income and employment were felt in the home countries of the foreign firms rather than in China itself; (3) the development of public utilities, banking facilities and other "external economies," which raised the marginal productivity of investment and thus reinforced the economic advantages already enjoyed by the treaty ports as compared with the economy of the Chinese hinterland.

On balance, the treaty port performed certain very important historic functions in China's long-run development. First of all, it created the aforementioned "external economies." It built up the modern commercial network, not only external but internal. It fostered the development of railroads and provided a framework within which modern factory production could be initiated, with primary emphasis upon light consumer-goods industries.

Secondly, as a result of this factory and business development, the treaty ports provided a training ground for Chinese technical and managerial personnel and for Chinese entrepreneurship. It is important to bear in mind that the Chinese compradore and his successor, the Chinese merchant and entrepreneur, built up the Chinese portion of the modern economy under the wing of the foreigner's privileges. In fact the treaty ports became jointly administered centers of joint economic growth, from which the Chinese entrepreneurial class were by no means excluded. On the contrary, the ports attracted Chinese talent and capital. Even socially the bifurcation between natives and foreigners became less distinct than in colonial countries.

Through the Chinese merchant and official classes, the ports also served as a means for mobilizing Chinese savings and channeling them either into the modern banking system or into direct investment in treaty port enterprises. To the extent that these enterprises did not remit profits abroad or invest some of their earnings in enterprises abroad, they too created pre-conditions for a later take-off into industrialization.

Thus a more meaningful view of the significance of the treaty ports might see them as the spearheads of a modern Sino-foreign economy, which was encroaching upon the traditional scene. In a physical sense the treaty ports served as entrance points into the traditional network of Chinese water-borne communications. The aim of the foreign merchant from the beginning was to get his goods flowing into this already well-developed distribution system. Western steamers on the Yangtze plying all the way to Szechwan, symbolized this process. It is significant that the British in the late nineteenth century were carrying three-fifths of China's steamer cargo.

This process was similar to that by which the foreigner joined with the Manchu-Chinese official class in such administrative institutions as the Imperial Maritime Customs Service or the Salt Revenue Administration and Post Office. In a comparable fashion the foreign merchant teamed up with his Chinese compradore and the growing Chinese merchant and banker class to dominate the modern sector of the economy, and spread its influence over the hinterland.

To say all this does not resolve that underlying question: Were the treaty ports in the long view a help or a hindrance to China's economic growth? Many considerations must be brought to bear on this thorny question. It involves among other things that difficult task, to prove a might-have-been—that China could have broken out of her traditional order and achieved a modern industrial growth in the absence of a Western impact such as was actually delivered through the treaty ports. We suspect that when another generation has finally gleaned and winnowed all the evidence it will be found that the influence of the treaty ports on Chinese economic life varied markedly over time: that they were a stimulus in the nineteenth century, becoming by degrees more of a hindrance in the twentieth.

Capital accumulation in the age of imperialist domination centered increasingly in the treaty ports for reasons mentioned above. On balance it seems plain that after 1895 a considerable proportion of the capital surplus in the Chinese economy was siphoned off to meet indemnity and loan payments abroad. Such payments must be taken as net withdrawals from China's economic resources, in other words, a tax on the economy. The effect was probably to handicap economic growth.

Yet, without minimizing the evils of imperialism, it would be short-sighted to place the center of China's economic development *outside* of Chinese society. Its retardation, like the long slow process of dynastic collapse, was in large measure a function of the interplay of domestic institutions and conditions. It is these that must be studied to gain further insight into China's economic growth.

If we define "institutions" in the broad sense as long-established patterns of social conduct, we may see their inhibiting influence primarily under the subheads of state activity and the administrative practices of the official class. First of all, the Chinese state failed to provide certain of the minimum pre-conditions essential to economic growth outside the treaty ports. For example, the Chinese authorities singularly failed in the maintenance of peace and order during the whole modern century. They were also unable to create a uniform currency and unified monetary standards. There was no uniform system of weights and measures. There was no stable administrative framework within which an effective market organization could develop. Transport and communications remained poor. Education, health and welfare measures were minimal. The inability of Chinese leaders to create the minimal pre-conditions for economic development was most clearly evidenced in the *kuan-tu shang-pan* system for "official supervision and merchant operation."

PART FOUR
The Sense of the Future

16

The last century of Chinese history, with its attrition of Confucian thought and society, saw a heightening sense of the future. Confucianism was oriented toward the past. Communism, devoted no less than Confucianism to history as the field for its world view, is oriented toward the future. Confucian views were continually challenged, or eccentrically developed, in earlier Chinese history, but the old versions of utopian thought show us futurism as archaism.

FROM

Egalitarian and Utopian Traditions in the East

JEAN CHESNEAUX

SOCIALISM was born in the West in the 19th century, be it the Utopian visions of Saint-Simon, Owen or Fourier, or the system, at once theoretical and militant, founded by Marx and Engels. It was the heir not only of the philosophers and economists of the modern age, Diderot, Hegel and Ricardo, but also of a more ancient egalitarian and Utopian tradition, which constitutes its "prehistory" and its "proto-history": social movements such as the Bohemian Taborites, the Münster anabaptists or the English diggers; and similarly the Utopian outlooks like those of Thomas More or Campanella or, still more ancient, Plato himself.

During the 19th century socialism spread from the West into the East; timidly at first, as an echo of the activity of the second International; and far more vigorously in the frame of the Komintern from 1918–1920 onwards. By "into the East" one means, for example, the "major East-west project" of UNESCO. That is to say that it spread into a series of societies which includes the Far East with its Confucian tradition, the Buddhist countries of South-East Asia, India, the Islam countries. These societies differ widely from one another in their history, religion, political

Jean Chesneaux, "Egalitarian and Utopian Traditions in the East," *Diogenes*, No. 62 (1968), pp. 76–89, translated by Simon Pleasance. Reprinted by permission. Footnotes omitted.

system, but they have in common the fact that they had not evolved in the modern age towards an industrial society, that they had not followed the same route of historical development as the Christian West in the Middle Ages (which until the 16th century was just one among many of the great pre-industrial civilizations of the Old World). Distinguished from the West in this way, this "East" does not become confused with the "Third World"; it is hallmarked by written cultures, by complex politico-religious systems which are deep-rooted in an explicit history, by a higher technological and economical level, and by vast state constructions.

Judging from the manner in which socialism implants itself in this "East" in the 20th century, is it no more than a graft, a purely exogenous development? This characteristic of exteriority and novation is certainly fundamental. But one cannot shrug off the fact that socialism has also had an effect on a whole series of egalitarian and Utopian traditions that belong to the East, particularly to China and the Islam countries.

Contrary to what took place in the West, these muddled traditions of justice and equality are certainly not connected with modern socialism by a continuous series of historical intermediaries. But for the first socialists of these countries they made precedents and "national legitimizations" which they felt to be all the more vital because they were living in an East dominated by the West, an East impatient to free itself. And so in Tokyo in about 1905 the first groups of Chinese students favorably inclined to socialism discussed its possible Confucian "ancestors": Mencius, the minister of the Sung Wang An-shih, the collective granaries of the Tai-ping. The first Arab socialists devotedly compiled the *hadith* (words attributed to Mahomet) which could be interpreted in the sense of social justice. The socialising reform plan of the Siamese minister Pridi in 1932 was put under the patronage of the Messiah *Maitreya*, whose coming, in Buddhistic tradition, should promote a just and happy society.

Even if implanted in the East by an external process, socialism has shown itself capable of carrying out and realising the confused dreams that had been entertained by men for generations. In this sense it is not as "foreign" to the East as one might sometimes think. Sun Yat-sen, for example, has several times spoken of the continuity that links modern socialism to Taoism and Confucianism: "When the people has communalized everything that concerns the State, we shall have really realised the objective of the 'well-being of the people' (which is the third principle of Sun Yat-sen); we shall have realised this *ta-t'ung* world of great harmony wished for by Confucius," he says in the conclusion of the second lesson on the well-being of the people.

Mao Tse-tung has likewise insisted on several occasions on the idea that the historical mission of Chinese communism was to achieve the old Confucian Utopia: "The power of the State and political parties will disappear quite naturally," he says of the future communist age, "and thus allow mankind to enter the era of *ta-t'ung.*"

In return, particularly as the 20th century advances, these "pre-socialist" Eastern traditions have been used by the political *milieux* in Asia which are hostile to communism; today one talks of "Islamic socialism" in certain traditionalist *milieux* in Algeria, Syria and Egypt; it is upon "Buddhistic socialism" that certain leading *milieux* in Cambodia, Burma or Ceylon want to found an ideology that would be capable of rivalling Marxism. A similar preoccupation was also doubtless present in the mind of Sun Yat-sen when he insisted on the specifically Chinese sources of socialism which he proposed in his *Three Principles of the People.*

These egalitarian and Utopian traditions hold an important place above all in China, in the Buddhist countries of South-East Asia, and in the Moslem countries; they count far less in India and Japan.

In China, the *locus classicus* of social Utopianism is represented by a very ancient text in the Book of Rites (*Li Chi*), chapter vi, article 1, the terms of which were familiar to any literate Chinese in those days as they are to any cultured Chinese today:

When men walked in the path of virtue, the world was a community. Those who were talented were chosen (as leaders). Their voice was sincere and they exercised harmony. Men treated others' parents as their own, and cherished others' children as their own. Old people were given shelter until they died, men in their prime had work, and the young education. Widows, orphans, the childless and the sick were shown tenderness and compassion in the way they were cared for. Every man had his work, every woman her hearth. People hated to see goods wasted, but did not want to procure them for themselves. They liked to work to their full capacity, but without seeking private gain. That is why individual ambitions had no chance to develop. There were no thieves or brigands, and the frontdoors of the houses were always open. It was the period of so-called Great Unity (*ta-t'ung*).

The same ideal of a fraternal society where mutual interest takes the place of private interest can be found in Mencius (6th century before our era), with the idea of the priority of the people over the sovereign, a phrase which is likewise often quoted. Mencius also describes (Book iii, chapter 1) a state of primitive agrarian communism, where the fields are divided into nine parts, the eight lots on the outside going to families, the ninth, in the center, cultivated commonly for the prince. It is the system of the "field in the shape of a well" (the Chinese ideogram that means "well" is drawn with two horizontal and two vertical lines which make nine divisions), that is *ching-t'ien,* "those who cultivate the same *ching,*" says Mencius, "will always be together wherever they go; they will share among themselves the job of defence and keeping watch. In case of illness they will help each other. In this way all the inhabitants will love one another and live intelligently together." This Utopian myth of agrarian communism, the *ching-t'ien*, is extremely vital in China until the 20th century.

Mo Ti, another master of classical Chinese philosophy, based his philosophy on mutual aid and universal love. The ideal Mohist society is based on the principle of similarity; people love what is profitable to all; everyone works and the gain is divided.

But it is the Taoist school (5th-6th centuries before our era) which puts forward the richest traditions of social Utopia and egalitarianism. The Taoists are filled with nostalgia for a Golden Age "based on co-operation, not on acquisition" (Needham). They condemn class distinction and urge mutual aid. They are opposed to State power and private interest.

"In ancient times," says Chuang-tzu, one of the fathers of the Taoist system, "the human condition was identical. Men wove their own clothes and every one cultivated the land to subsist. There was the Virtue of all men living in the same manner (*t'ung-te*). They were united in a single social group, which is what we call freedom given naturally from heaven. In that age of perfect virtue, men lived with the birds and the wild animals and all creation was one family. How could they know the distinction between prince and subject?" (Chuang-tzu, chapter 9).

The Taoist philosopher Yang Chou glorified the physical strength of the labourer and the love he had for his work; for him the principal factor is "everything that renders calm the man of the fields, everything that gives him joy." He is the author of the famous paradox of the benefit which becomes its own opposite, by the intermediary of glory and profit: benefits and above all "distributions" bring "glory." This latter leads to "gain" because of the respect that is earned. Aspiration to gain is accompanied by the violation of the rights of other men, "strife"; "benefit" becomes an evil. . . .

Another classical Taoist, Lieh-tzu, describes, as if in a dream (Book II, chapter 1) a mythical kingdom where "there are no leaders, and everything happens by itself; the people have no desires, everything comes about naturally," a text which Sun Yat-sen considered to be a precursor of modern anarchy. This whole Taoist tradition is impregnated with an Utopian egalitarianism, which J. Needham and E. Balazs have been particularly insistent about. Such ideas as *tai-ping* (great harmony), *p'ing-chün* (equalization), *chün-t'ien* (equal fields) belong to this Taoist fund, from which, as we shall see, peasant revolts and Utopian reformers borrow heavily throughout the history of China. In the words of L. D. Pozdneieva, in ancient China "the religion born from the doctrine of certain ancient Taoists was nothing more than a heresy capable of advancing for the first time the demand for the equality of all men, in the face of god, and consequently the equality of goods, contrary to Confucianism, that religion for the privileged."

Egalitarian movements similarly make the best of the Buddhistic tradition of charity and the condemnation of riches, and most particularly of the myth of the Buddhist Messiah, the *Maitreya* (in Chinese *Mi-lo-fu*) whose coming is supposed to be the beginning of an age of justice, plenty and well-being.

In fact, this brief sketch of the "pre-socialist" elements of the traditional Chinese heritage must make way for another philosophical school of ancient China, that of the agrarians (*Nung-Chia*), which J. Needham connects with the English diggers of the 17th century. The agrarians, who are close to the Taoists, desire a society where everyone works the fields, leader and subject alike. They attacked the views of Confucius on the necessity of having wise men, exempt from manual labour, to direct the State. In the ideal country they describe, the leaders cultivate the land with the simple folk, and prepare their morning and evening meals themselves, and at the same time carry out their official duties. But the classics of the agrarian school are lost, and are only known about through the allusions of other authors, notably Mencius.

This rich egalitarian and Utopian tradition is perpetuated throughout classical Chinese history and right into the 19th century by two quite distinct tendencies, two currents of social protest against the established order: the protest of the literate Utopian reformers and the protest of the egalitarian peasant movements.

In fact, repeatedly throughout Chinese history there have been literate men with Confucian backgrounds and members of the ruling class who have been in conflict with the established order. Some were content to express in words their criticisms and their dreams of a more just society. Others, taking advantage of favorable circumstances, tried to put their social reform projects into practice, to translate Utopia into facts. But both categories borrowed constantly from the traditional heritage, the content of which has just been briefly outlined; they referred to the Golden Age of *Ta-t'ung;* they called for an equal distribution of wealth and land especially; they attacked private interests and profiteers.

In this way a real school of social Taoist-inclined criticism, full of energy, was formed under the dynasty of the later Han (during the first two centuries of our era). Wang Fu (90–165) expresses a nostalgia for a *t'ai-p'ing* era of great harmony, and condemns the concentration of wealth; he prefers the secluded life of the hermit to glory. T'ung Chungch'ang (born in 180) sanctions a return to the state of *t'ai-p'ing* by reintroducing the ancient system of a communal cultivation of fields "in the form of the well" (*ching-t'ien*); the evils of society, in his eyes, stem from the fact that "the fields are distributed without restriction among private people." Pao Ching-yen (3rd century), a disciple of Chuang-tzu, is the "first political anarchist in China, and a bold thinker who goes far beyond the muddled Utopianism of popular Taoism" (Balazs). He levels the Golden Age when "there was neither master nor vassal" against the regime of oppression that reigned in China in his lifetime.

The same dream of the Golden Age is expressed in the famous Utopia of T'ao Yüan-ming (365–427) entitled *The Source of the Peach-Garden*. In this imaginary journey, the author describes a land beyond the world and beyond time, the people of which preserve the primitive customs of ancient China, day-to-day life, work and leisure take place in a communal atmosphere; government, officials, taxation, public forced labour and war do not exist.

But it was not simply a matter of intellectual constructions. From the end of the first Han dynasty, in the first years of our era, the usurper Wang Mang (who reigned from 9 to 23) had attempted a general re-distribution of the land, in line with the *ching-t'ien* system. He added a whole series of antiquating reforms, made legitimate by the ancient Utopian canonical books, particularly the Book of Rites: thus the system of the "six monopolies" (salt, metals, mines etc.) and the "five zones of equalization" (in which State offices fixed the prices, purchased the surplus and resold when prices were rising). His reforms died with him.

Another great reformer, Wang An-shih (1021–1086), appeared under the *Sung* dynasty. He likewise appealed for the communal traditions of very ancient China, in order to impose agrarian measures which would equalise the land-tax in terms of the productivity of the land. Together with Wang Mang he was considered as the father of Chinese socialism by the first socialist intellectuals at the beginning of the 20th century. But Wang An-shih is not an isolated figure. Another thinker of the *Sung* dynasty, Li K'ou, came before him in the path of antiquating Utopian-ism (1009–1059); he had written a book in which he proposed to set up a regime of social harmony (*t'ai-p'ing*) by reintroducing the mythical system of the Chou dynasty and by putting into practice a radical agrarian reform.

The 17th century is similarly a period of profound political crisis in China, both intellectual and social, with the fall of the Ming dynasty and the rise of the Manchus. A thinker such as Huang Tsung-hsi (1601–1695), who took an active part in the resistance against the northern in-vaders, is the author of a famous work "Plan for the Prince" (*Ming-I T'ai fang lü*), proposals for a more propitious age, written in 1662. In it he systematically criticises the function of princes, "the greatest enemy of humanity." He is nostalgic for antiquity when there was less disorder because the laws were less severe. "If there were no governments, every man would live for himself. . . ." He too favors a return to the agrarian system of *ching-t'ien*.

In the 18th century this Utopian tradition is represented by Li Ju-chen

(c. 1763–1830), author of a famous novel of a hundred chapters on which he worked for ten years, the *Ching-hua-yüan* (The Mirror of the Flowers); the novel is set in the 7th century under the T'ang dynasty, and describes the adventures of a hundred talented women in imaginary kingdoms; the description gives rise to an acid criticism of China under the Manchu dynasty. In these kingdoms women have the right to sit for public examinations, they study, they marry freely, they do not have to bind their feet or serve as concubines. This feminist Utopia is still very famous in China.

Hou Wai-lu, the great specialist in ancient Chinese philosophies, has proposed a classification of these intellectual Utopia into two main categories. Those which, in the tradition of the Taoist fathers, describe an ideal imaginary world, the evocation of which presents an opportunity to level accusations at the injustices of real society, but which cannot be put into practice; this is the case of Lieh-tzu, Pao Ching-yen, T'ao Yüan-ming and Li Ju-chen. And those which, by departing from certain archaic texts such as the page by Mencius on *Ching-t'ien,* envisage a restoration of social order by a return to antiquity: this is the case of Wang Mang, Wang An-shih and all their rivals.

Parallel with this long series of intellectual Utopia, Chinese peasant revolts had for centuries also borrowed from the old traditional Utopian and millenary heritage. They referred themselves to Taoist egalitarianism and to Buddhistic Messianism. Their leaders readily proclaimed themselves to be the *Maitreya* incarnate and the old themes of *t'ai-p'ing* (great harmony) and *p'ing-chün* (equalisation) often recur in their vocabulary and slogans.

Thus in the 3rd century of our era the revolt of the Yellow Turbans and that of the sect of the Five Bushels of Rice, which provoked the fall of the later Han dynasty, referred themselves to a Golden Age in which there would not be two different prices in the markets, and there would be no thieves on the highways. They attempted to create "a double communal organisation with a hierarchy based on merit and a will to realise a perfect state." The rebels had to set up in the province of Ssuchuan, which they had held for several years, the system of "equity inns" (*I-she*), where meat and wine were hung at the disposition of the traveller on the condition that he ate only what was strictly necessary. If the traveller contravened this, he was considered a sinner, and had to expiate his sin by working on the roads. In these phalansteries, then, the economic community went cheek by jowl with a severe moral law. The Yellow Turbans referred themselves to an age of prosperity and equality (*t'ai-p'ing*) and proclaimed its imminent advent.

These same themes were taken up by other peasant risings. At the end of the T'ang dynasty, for example, in the 9th century, the chief peasant, Wang Hsien-chih, proclaimed himself as the "great general delivered from

Heaven to re-establish equity." Under the Sung (11th–13th centuries), another peasant, Wang Hsiao-p'o, chief of a jacquerie in Ssuchuan, announced that "he is weary of the inequality that exists between rich and poor; and that he wants to level it out to the benefit of the people." From the outset of the movement, he confiscates all the surplus from the rich and distributes it among the poor; "with us, declares another rebel peasant of the Sung dynasty, Yang K'o-shih, everything we possess in the way of clothes, food, livestock, cloth, grain is not the object of private accumulation, we hand it out fairly to everyone, which is why we represent a true community" (*t'ung-ch'u*).

These egalitarian and millenary aspirations also characterise the "secret societies," groups of religious dissent, social agitation and political opposition, which have been so active throughout Imperial Chinese history (in particular under the Mongol and Manchu dynasties). The society of the White Lotus (*Pai-lien-chiao*), for example, was profoundly marked by the millenary expectation of the Buddhistic Messiah, *Mi-lo-fu*. Groups such as the society of Heaven and Earth (Triad) or the Elders and the Ancients (*Ko-lao-hui*) had an egalitarian organisation (including benefits for women) and their fictitious hierarchy (Great Dragon etc.) was such that it compensated for the inequalities of actual society. The secret societies were furthermore closely connected with peasant egalitarian agitation.

This latter continues with the peasant revolts that provoked the fall of the Mongol dynasty in the 14th century, and the Ming dynasty in the 17th century. This leads directly to the primitive egalitarian communism of the T'ai-p'ing in the 19th century, the great peasant revolt, the very name of which evoked those Taoist traditions that have already been cited. The T'ai-p'ing, who established a dissenting state in central China from 1851 to 1864, the "Celestial Kingdom of Great Harmony" (*T'ai-p'ing T'ien-kuo*), had promulgated an extremely radical agrarian law:

All the land beneath Heaven will be cultivated in common by the people beneath Heaven . . . the land will be cultivated by one and all, rice eaten, clothes worn and money spent. There will no longer be inequalities and no one will go without food or fuel."

In the system of the T'ai-p'ing the harvest had to be stored in communal granaries (celestial granaries) and artisan production was assured by "celestial" battalions of State craftsmen.

This egalitarian character of Chinese peasant movements, an Asiatic version of "When Adam delved and Eve span, who was then the gentleman?", that the English Lollards chanted in the 14th and the peasants of Rhineland in the 15th centuries, has strongly marked the whole of Chinese social history. It is this that explains why every new dynasty, brought into power by the wave of elementary peasant agitation that had overthrown the preceding one, considers itself obliged to realise at least a semblance of agrarian reform. Chinese communism, above all in the thirties, and again round 1955–1960 with the popular communes, develops against this backcloth of peasant egalitarianism.

To what extent have these two currents of egalitarian and Utopian protest, the literate and the peasant, mutually supported and influenced each other? Naturally enough our sources indicate only very exceptional participation by literate men in peasant movements, for example the figure of a certain Li Yen, an educated man who draughted the egalitarian proclamations of the peasants in revolt against the Ming in the middle of the 17th century. But one must bear in mind that Chinese historical documents are all of mandarin origin, and that they were thus quite naturally inclined to hush up any literate opposition to the established order and support of the rebel movements.

These two tendencies, however, represent but a series of isolated episodes and solitary figures. All things considered, the old Chinese regime did not really have to put up with all these protests. But one also wonders to what extent traditional Chinese society, as a whole this time and not as seen through marginal and exceptional cases, is not marked by certain community tendencies which similarly provided favorable ground for the development of modern socialism. This view of an East less marked by individualism than the West has been developed by many sinologists, J. Gernet, L. Vandermeersch, P. Fitzgerald, and especially by J. Needham in a resounding article which tries to show that communist China is nothing more than "the realization of a whole series of community traditions which go back as far as Classical China."

In fact the general climate of classical Chinese society tends far more to integrate the individual in the collective than to oppose him to it, as is the case in the West. The individual is part of his family, his guild, his clan and his village. The word *kung* (collective) opposes what is "private" (*ssu*) in the economic sense of the term. But the word *ssu*— which is a significant fact—has at the same time a pejorative moral connotation: it indicates a "private," that is furtive, appropriation with a view to profit, and more generally all that is secret, dishonest, clandestine, contrary to what is done in a collective and public manner, that is in broad daylight and in the general interest (*kung*).

Classical Chinese society did not offer a favorable ground for private enrichment and lucrative activities. This fact is also clear from hierarchy of social values, in the order of precedence of the "states," such as the political moral of Confucianism defined it: first the literate (*shih*), in possession of knowledge and power, then the peasants (*nung*), their work being the basis of any society, then the craftsmen (*kung*), and right at the bottom of the social scale the "treacherous merchants" (*shang*).

The importance of the traditions of public management of the economy is another aspect of this collective climate of ancient China. This management deals not only with dams and canals, but also with iron and salt, State monopolies since the Han dynasty; in Needham's words it is a "tradition of nationalised production," which one could doubtless link with the "manner of Asiatic production." All the same a strong state hold over the land still exists, and private ownership of land, even if it exists, never has the absolute and unlimited character that Roman law recognizes, the *Freies Eigentum* of the West; F. Schurmann has shown how it is tempered by such customs as the joint rights of the other members of the family, rights of preemption and rights of tenure.

Marxism—a Vietnamese intellectual has remarked—in no way led Confucian intellectuals astray by focussing man's thoughts on political and social problems . . . the Confucian school thought of nothing else. By defining man by the totality of his social relationships, Marxism hardly shocked the literates who considered the supreme aim of man to assume his social obligations correctly. . . . When he moves from traditional to socialist society, the Confucian adopts a new social discipline, but at heart he had never been hostile, like the western bourgeois intellectual, to the principle itself of collective discipline, considering it indispensable to the development of his own personality.

But the objection one can level against all these "transcontinualist" analyses of the historical relation between imperial China and Chinese socialism is that they rest on facts which in reality contribute to a defense of the Chinese *Ancien Régime* and its social inequalities. Such is the sense of the hierarchy that gives political and moral supremacy to the literate over the merchants; the social cohesion implied by the contrast between *kung* and *ssu* helps the established power, and the "natural" authority of the emperor and the body of mandarins who govern in his name (we have already pointed out the basic ambiguity between *kung,* common, and *kung,* prince). It is the same with the tradition of public management of the economy, a tradition which consolidates imperial and mandarin power as well. Classical Confucian society is founded on the opposition of power and the people, on the submission of the one to the other, on the inequalities of fortune and condition that this submission engenders. In this sense it is absolutely opposed to the egalitarian and Utopian traditions that have been analysed above, and it is against this society that the latter have developed. . . .

17 *We conclude with four grand sweeps through the issues of Chinese history over the last century. How did communism, futurism as futurism, come to be the current end of the process? Let us first consider the general record.*

Modern China in Transition, 1900–1950

MARY C. WRIGHT

Most Americans had little occasion to think seriously about China until Communist China began to emerge as a major power. Even those who were especially interested in China seldom gave systematic attention to the current scene. Scholars nearly all studied periods before—usually very long before—1900. Missionaries, government officials, businessmen, and military personnel were absorbed in pressing daily tasks. Most lacked the training, even if they had the time and inclination, to observe perceptively and to gauge accurately the momentous changes occurring around them. A handful of journalists made outstanding efforts to find out what was really happening, to set it in its epochal context, and to report it in readable English. Yet even among these, a working knowledge of the Chinese language and a familiarity with recent Chinese history were rarities. No one doubted that a grasp of the background was essential, but the background grasped was a strange blend of conflicting myths that have remained to block our comprehension of contemporary China.

COLLAPSE OF THE MIDDLE KINGDOM

Everywhere in the world the headlong changes that marked the first half of the twentieth century dwarfed the slower changes of earlier centuries; but nowhere did these changes so stagger the imagination as in China. The longest lived and most populous polity in world history had changed so slowly over millennia that sometimes it seemed not to have changed at all. Certainly there had been nothing remotely comparable

Mary C. Wright, "Modern China in Transition, 1900–1950," *The Annals of the American Academy of Political and Social Science,* Vol. 321 (January 1959), pp. 2–8. Reprinted by permission of the publishers.

to the steady and accelerating transformation of European life beginning in the late Middle Ages. Then suddenly and nearly simultaneously China was struck with equivalents of the Reformation, the French Revolution, and the Russian Revolution. Marx and Darwin were new, but no newer than Aristotle and Rousseau. Young Chinese discovered them all at the same time.

This unprecedented telescoping of history was at first obscured by the continued and obviously vigorous persistence of the many ancient ways that so delighted all visitors. In the midst of a living antiquity unparalleled in the modern world, the signs of the progressive stages of a great revolution were generally discounted. Our experience had not prepared us for a society marked both by strong tradition and by powerful revolutionary drives. The signs of tradition were plain to see and comforting. The signs of revolution could be dismissed as superficial. There were such very wide troughs between the waves that at the time we could not see that there was any cumulative build-up. Today in retrospect, the classic French and Russian sequence is clearly outlined. The Chinese timetable, however, was so different that by the time we began to suspect that we might be seeing the beginning of a great social revolution, the revolution was already far advanced.

The basic thread of Chinese history during the first half of the twentieth century was the search—sometimes ebullient, often heartbroken—for new institutions in every sphere of public and private life, institutions which would connect the pride in a great past to high hopes for a great future. In the tumultuous controversies of fifty years, the Chinese centered their attention on one or another facet of a few great questions: What of the old is worth keeping? Can we keep it and survive in the modern world? What of the new is desirable? Must we take the undesirable too in order to survive? Or can China make a future for herself on lines not yet tried elsewhere? These questions were of mounting urgency, for the Chinese state was prostrate and Chinese life seemed to be disintegrating.

THE FORCE OF NATIONALISM

Because vigorous nationalism provides built-in incentives which a successful government can use to spur and control its people, the growth of nationalism was one of the most significant features of China's recent history. When the twentieth century opened, the power of the Chinese Empire was a very recent and live memory. Hence the shattering series of stunning defeats at the hands of the Western powers and Japan was especially galling. We did not give enough attention to the sharp and swift rise of fighting nationalism. Daily observation of the polite and humorous Chinese, plus a little dabbling in Chinese philosophy, led to the myth that the Chinese were only interested in their own families, that they had no conception of country. Everyone could tell a story to illustrate the point, from the embassy to the kitchen level. Opposite conclusions were drawn from this alleged basic characteristic of twentieth-century China: The Chinese were venal and lacking in decent feeling for the public good, or the Chinese were charming sages happily free of the lusts for power that had wrecked what had been European civilization until 1914. But in either case, the basic analysis was dreadfully faulty.

There was in fact a genuine ground-swell of Chinese nationalism during the first half of the twentieth century, and for its element of xenophobia there were clear historic roots. So much has been written lately of Chinese popular good will toward foreigners until they were brain-washed en masse that at the risk of gross oversimplification, something should also be said of Chinese bitterness and hatred toward Americans and Europeans in recent decades. The crude fear of the white peril that the last imperial dynasty had been able to exploit in the Boxer Rebellion of 1900 had been submerged but not overcome, and the expanding special privileges of foreigners were irritants in increasingly wide spheres of Chinese life. These fears and irritations provided a mass sounding board for what might otherwise have been rather arid denunciations of imperialists. It is well to remember that both Nationalists and Communists have struck this note; that Chiang Kai-shek and Lenin described the tangible effects of imperialism in remarkably similar terms.

THE SEARCH FOR POLITICAL STABILITY

The increasingly patent ineffectiveness of political leadership and institutions was a no less important characteristic of twentieth-century China. This phenomenon was obvious to all, but it was misinterpreted because we did not attach enough importance to the fact that political decline was accompanied by repeated efforts to reconstitute a powerful central government. When government was weakest, the pressures for strong government were greatest, for it was then that both traditional culturalism and modern nationalism were most offended. The various movements and programs that expressed these pressures struck us as rather silly, and the myth grew that Chinese politics was horseplay among warlords with silver bullets. Warlordism was of course a fact, but we were wrong to conclude from this that the Chinese people opposed strong government, or that no central power could be effective throughout so vast and undeveloped a country. The imperial tradition of strong central government never died, and now in retrospect one is struck by how much authority the central government did in fact retain until 1917. Even the "warlord period," 1917–27, was no era of general collapse of centralized authority, for the warlords themselves operated effective political machines over substantial territories. More important, the major contenders for power aimed consistently at the reconstitution of a powerful central state. As external dangers and internal crises mounted, the population of the country did not remain as apathetic and cynical as was thought in Treaty Port circles. On the record of performance it is clear that increasingly wide sectors of the population were prepared to throw their support to whoever gave most promise of effective central government.

The terrible strains of the period notwithstanding, the country remained vigorous, and tremendous new potentials were created in spite of war and inadequate leadership. We were too given to pity for a suffering and downtrodden people, and the pity irked. Widespread suffering there was indeed, but at its lowest point twentieth-century China was no beaten and stagnant country. Rather it offered the world the remarkable spectacle of a people whose ancient institutions had retained great vigor and effectiveness until very recent times; a people with a well-justified pride in the record of a great and prosperous state as well as in their intellectual and artistic heritage; a people who were learning modern skills rapidly and well and yet who with all this promise felt themselves in danger of national extinction because they had found no way to mobilize this latent strength for defense against aggression and foreign special privilege, for raising the standard of living, for a cultural renascence.

AGRARIAN CHINA: PEASANTS AND POLITICS

During the first half of the twentieth century, China remained an overwhelmingly agricultural country. Although the proportionate position of the agrarian sector of the economy declined somewhat, the peasant's produce remained the chief source of revenue and his tax burden increased steadily with the rising cost of more elaborate arms, proliferating government offices, and the service of foreign loans. The terms of rural credit were devastating and tenancy increased, especially in the vicinity of modernized cities. The increased acreage planted in cash crops undermined the traditional self-sufficiency of the village, and cottage industries, once an important source of supplementary income, either disappeared or were bought by merchants. The self-employed artisan all but disappeared, and there was little to mitigate the harsh consequences of the imbalance between the high market value of manufactured goods and the low market value of agricultural products.

No patriotic Chinese could remain insensitive to the plight of the peasant base of society, even if the interest was only theoretical. The programs of the warlords regularly mentioned the need for reforms. The Kuomintang, which came to power in 1927, also had an elaborate rural program; its implementation was unfortunately delayed until threats from the Chinese Communists and from Japan could be removed. Perhaps more important as a symptom of the same kind of guilty uneasiness that drove prerevolutionary Russian intellectuals into populist movements, there was a rash of local experiments in rural reconstruction, sparked mainly by liberals of the minor parties whose programs lay somewhere between the Kuomintang and Communist poles. These efforts were important signs of the times; yet the country was so vast that major accomplishment could not really have been expected without strong government support. They were obliterated in the holocaust of the Japanese invasion.

One barrier to the implementation of the Kuomintang land reform program was the landed wealth of its members. There were exceptions of course, especially among Kuomintang members from the modern business and professional classes. Even among these, however, there was fear that a land reform program, once launched, might gain too much momentum and turn against the Kuomintang. After 1937, with the loss to Japan of the modern cities these men represented, the Kuomintang became increasingly dependent upon the rural economy and thus upon the support of ultraconservative landlords in the hinterland.

Meanwhile, the Chinese Communist Party, founded in 1921, moved rather quickly away from the classic Marxian distrust of the peasantry. The party line shifted tortuously on this as on other points, yet within a few years Mao Tse-tung and others were demonstrating their skill in peasant agitation. Kuomintang realization that peasants when aroused would almost certainly swing to the Communists was a major cause of the breakup of the first Kuomintang-Communist united front and of the Kuomintang's swing to the right after 1927. Driven back into the countryside by the victorious Nationalist armies, the Communists began a long series of land reform experiments, varying according to circumstances from moderate rent reduction to wholesale confiscation. By degrees the Communist party learned how to mobilize peasant support. The Chinese peasant loved his land, but by the third and fourth decades of the twentieth century it could no longer keep him alive without radical changes, and only the Communists offered these.

During the civil war, 1946–49, the Communists succeeded in using land reform as a major political and military weapon. The national government, threatened on all sides, was not prepared to take any very drastic steps. The Chinese-American Joint Committee on Rural Reconstruction struggled manfully to improve agrarian technology in the hope that, with an increased harvest, the peasant's plight could be eased without damage to landlord interests. The conclusion of the outstanding Chinese official chiefly responsible for the effort was that nearly everywhere technological change proved impossible without fundamental institutional change; that indeed without social reform, the peasant could not take advantage of improved methods, and his position often actually deteriorated.

URBAN DEVELOPMENTS

Before 1950, the modern sectors of the Chinese economy lagged so far behind the West, Japan, and even India that one did not usually notice how great the development had been between 1900 and 1950. Beginning in the 1890's, Chinese of a new type, scholar-officials who were also entrepreneurs, began to build substantial modern factories. Mining, railroads, and shipping developed rapidly. The physical plant, the labor force, the managers and technicians required for a modern economy began to appear in increasing numbers. The potential was there for anyone to see, and yet it could not be realized. To the Chinese, this was infuriating. The chief barriers seemed to be inept and predatory government, fragments of traditional social institutions, drainage from the country of the profits from the enormous foreign investment in China, and the special protection that the unequal treaties provided for foreign interests, often directly against Chinese interests. Many Chinese businessmen, who enjoyed a boom while privileged Western competition was deflected by World War I, became in a sense revolutionaries, precisely because they were patriots and businessmen. They supported the Kuomintang in its bid for power, 1924–27, because of its program to abolish imperialism; to create an effective, modern, centralized government; and to campaign relentlessly against the shreds of the Confucian order.

During this period, strikes and other signs of labor unrest were widespread, especially in foreign-owned enterprises. The foreigners' customary retort that their labor was at all events much better paid than other Chinese labor was irrelevant. Chinese peasants coming to work in factories for the first time suddenly saw much greater gaps between poverty and wealth than they had ever seen before. The poverty, and it was still extreme poverty by any standards, was theirs; the wealth belonged to foreigners and to a few Chinese who could readily be labeled running dogs of the foreigners, and it was often displayed in a manner that could scarcely have been better calculated to offend.

This frustration was felt in many spheres of Chinese society. The professional diplomats of China, skilled though many of them were, made only limited and gradual progress toward abolishing the unequal international status that outraged Chinese of every political persuasion. The Japanese invasion of the mainland struck at the very core of China's national integrity, and the international complications of the war period left a tangled legacy of misapprehensions and misunderstanding. Western relinquishment of extraterritorial privileges during the war came far too late, and the continuing major role of the United States in the postwar period convinced many Chinese that the national government was incapable of independent action. To these Chinese, the situation seemed further proof that diplomatic resources, like economic resources, were useless to a weak government and that military power was essential to political effectiveness.

THE KEY ROLE OF MILITARY POWER

The new importance attached to military power was another major characteristic of modern Chinese history. Chinese had never been the pacifists that we often fondly imagined them to be, and it had been clear to them since their first contact with the military power of the West that only a country with strong armed forces could elect its own policies. For a century there was a steady sequence of military reorganization programs. Every program failed; never was the required fighting strength achieved; never was a war won. Yet what was accomplished in inadequate bits and pieces convinced nearly all Chinese that China need not forever be a pawn in world politics; that there were no insuperable obstacles to genuine great power status. Experience had shown that Chinese peasants could be trained to use modern weapons efficiently and that they could on occasion fight with unsurpassed valor. Why was the opposite so often the case? Experience had shown that the country had the natural resources and the technological aptitudes needed for a modern arms industry. Why had one not developed? China had a small number of skilled strategists and effective line officers. Why were they not better deployed, and why had not many times their number been trained? The popular feeling as defeat followed defeat was less one of despair than of anger at the waste of opportunity. To a desperate government, massive outside aid seemed the only answer. To many Chinese, so much foreign aid to so weak a government seemed bound to lead to spiraling dependence. The suggestion that this was the intention of the aid fell on ready ears.

EDUCATION

Some observers insisted that the Chinese attitudes described above were limited to a tiny and powerless fraction of the population. They failed to note how rapidly political awareness was spreading through education and propaganda. It would be difficult to find any period in the history of any country where education was expected to work the miracles it was expected to work in twentieth-century China, and very nearly did. The dominant Chinese tradition, in marked contrast to Western tradition, had always held that men are by nature good and that although their talents vary, the variation has nothing to do with class. Hence education, on which an enormous value was placed, was theoretically as desirable for the lower classes as for the upper. It had always been gratifying rather than terrifying to see the son of a peasant attain a high education with all its consequent rewards. His chance to do this was slim indeed, but the barrier was economic only.

With the twentieth century, the peasant's chance at education began to improve rapidly. The missionary schools and the new government schools provided only a fraction of the facilities that would have been required for universal public education. Even so, they were closer to such a system than they were to the traditional system of tutors and academies. The way seemed open in the not too distant future for every Chinese to be given a basic education and for the ablest Chinese to be given the highest education. But to attain this end, vigorous government action was needed. Successive governments made some contribution, but only under heavy pressure from the leaders of public opinion. Education had a low priority on all budgets, and as new ideas mushroomed, some of those in power came to cherish an illiterate population. Mass education movements found contrived obstacles rather than the support they needed. Too many schools remained under foreign control, and it was humiliating to realize how dreadfully the foreign schools were needed. There was almost no field in which China offered full advanced training, this despite the world renown of many of her scholars, once they were trained abroad.

THE CHANCES FOR DEMOCRACY

Thus in education as in other fields, progress led not to stable satisfaction but to a sharpening awareness of how much more had to be done, and, it was believed, could be done, if China had an effective and efficient government. There were fifty years of controversy over the kind of government China had and the kind of government she needed. The trends were frequently confusing, for in China political characteristics that the West regarded as inevitably associated were often in conflict, and others that the West regarded as mutually incompatible were sometimes fused.

During the first half of the twentieth century, the trend toward democracy was strong in China—in some senses of the word. Legally privileged classes had already disappeared, and as the upper classes continued to expand rapidly in size, there were in China millions of families of some little importance rather than a few hundred very powerful ones. The open classes of the traditional society became highly fluid during a period of such rapid change. The country had since early times been culturally homogeneous, vertically as well as horizontally. Of course there were popular cultures, elite cultures, and subcultures, but nothing resembling the cultural cleavage between classes that until recently characterized much of Europe. With the spread of modern public education, few cultural stigmata of class origin remained. Traditionally, popular opinion had been taken seriously by the government and after 1919 the media for its expression expanded like the burst of a Roman candle.

In all these meanings—and they are valid meanings—twentieth-century China was democratic, and increasingly democratic. Yet this trend toward democracy lacked two elements considered essential in the West. There was no trend toward the establishment of civil liberties and there was no trend toward government by majority decision.

Neither of the two major political movements—the nationalist and the communist—showed any real interest in civil liberties, or even comprehension of what they were. As in traditional China, whatever purported to be the interests of the group remained paramount. In the 1920's there were flurries of talk about civil liberties, mainly among intellectuals, but these were crushed from both left and right. In the 1930's and 1940's, internal crises and foreign aggression seemed to require unfettered action by a powerful government if there was to be a viable future for anyone Chinese. In such circumstances, it is not surprising that a demand for civil liberties came to seem a demand for a right to wilful self-indulgence. There was no thought that individual Chinese ought to be guaranteed some small but irreducible minimum of privacy and originality, an area that the state could never touch, however great the alleged public interest.

Nor was there any trend toward representative government in the first half of the twentieth century. In Chinese tradition there had never been any notion that the wisest decision could be reached by counting heads, even in a select group. Statesmanship had been the art of selecting, training, and indoctrinating a small corps of able men who could then be trusted to run every aspect of the public life of a vast empire. To secure popular assent to official decision was essential; to ask the people what the decision should be never remotely occurred to anyone. Within the official hierarchy there were intricate checks and balances, impeachments, conferences, and compromises, but no idea of majority decision. After 1912, the few efforts at a façade of parliamentary government were fiascos, and most Chinese of all political persuasions saw the main problem as the creation of a competent new political elite to fill the gap left by the collapse of the imperial system. The idea of military tutelage followed by political tutelage meant exercise of power on behalf of the people by a nonhereditary, authoritarian political corps. It was as basic to nationalist as to communist political thought. During the first half of the century, neither party relinquished its control to popular elections. In 1950, the promise of ultimate full democracy offered by either seemed remote.

18 *Second, let us consider the social process.*

FROM

Ideology and Organization in Communist China

FRANZ SCHURMANN

THE Chinese Revolution is for the latter half of the twentieth century what the Russian Revolution was for the first half. By transforming Chinese society, it has brought a great power into being which proclaims itself the revolutionary and developmental model for the poor countries of the world.

From the eighteenth century to the present, the world has been caught in a wave of revolutions. The industrial revolution in England started a process of economic transformation that has now reached to the farthest corners of the globe. The French Revolution sowed the seeds of a process of political revolution that has given rise to the modern nation-state. The results of these two revolutions have become the goals of the world's new countries: economic development and political integration. Above all, the new countries desire a national economy resting on an industrial-technological basis capable of creating wealth and power, and a national unity which arises from effective political institutions. It is symbolic that these two processes should have different points of origin, for most new countries have discovered that it is difficult to attain both goals simultaneously.

Economic development takes time; we may speak of it as a process of revolution. The British Empire and the world market were brought into being by a long series of developments which finally led to an economic system of great power and creativity. The present world market system, which grew out of the industrial revolution and became global in the nineteenth century, has shown the new countries a road to economic development: linkage to that world market system which will allow them to share in the wealth already created by the old countries. In so doing, they launch their own economic revolutions by becoming a part of a world-wide process of economic revolution.

Franz Schurmann, *Ideology and Organization in Communist China* (University of California Press: Berkeley and Los Angeles, 1966), pp. xxix–xliv. Reprinted by permission of The Regents of the University of California.

However, the choice of such a road often prevents the new countries from achieving their other great goal, national unity. Though modern cities, factories, schools, and communications networks arise within their borders, they are usually restricted to a few areas, frequently on their coastlines where they are in close relation to the world's trade routes. The regions of the interior, vital for the creation and maintenance of national unity, benefit little from these developments. Moreover, all the wealth and power of economic development do not give the new countries a sense of national identity through which political integration can be achieved. Thus they are often faced with the choice of ignoring the peoples of the interior and the poor of the cities in order to develop economically within the world-wide context or seeking their support for political integration but thereby sacrificing easily available economic gains.

Though France's history as a nation-state began long before the French Revolution, that revolution gave the people of France a sense of national identity, expressed in the words *patrie, citoyen,* and *français.* The political revolutions that have brought new countries into being in the nineteenth and twentieth centuries have almost without exception sought to create the same sense of national identity in their peoples as the French Revolution did for the people of France. In this sense, many of the political revolutions have succeeded, for they have been able to create unity where earlier it did not exist. However, unity has often been acquired at the cost of economic development, a price which France also paid with its belated industrialization and modernization.

Modern France came into being, not by a process, but an act of revolution which swept away more than an ancient political system; it destroyed an entire social class. The French Revolution was, in effect, a social revolution. De Tocqueville, in describing the conditions leading to the French Revolution, makes clear what may be the essence of all social revolutions: an act of destruction willed against a whole ruling class.

Though all new countries of the preceding and the present centuries have participated in the processes of economic and political revolution, not all have undergone social revolution. Germany and Japan, for example, were able to combine the processes of economic development and political integration without a social revolution. Many new countries of this century, however, face the possibility of social revolution as a consequence of their inability to achieve sufficient economic development and political integration. They may have some wealth and power and a sense of national identity, but not enough to still the forces of social revolution.

Revolutionary France is the world's first example of a modern social revolution. In 1917, Russia underwent its social revolution. And, in the late 1940's, it became clear that China had come through its social revolution, marked by the revolutionary struggle of the land reform. China's social revolution had causes deeper than its inability to develop economically and politically, but the shallowness of its economic and political revolutions made the social revolution inevitable.

A series of rebellions began in China toward the end of the eighteenth century, and continued until the advent and final triumph of Chinese communism. In retrospect, we can say that these rebellions began the process of revolution. Generally Buddhist or Taoist in ideology, they combined a revolutionary chiliasm with a hatred of secular authority. They occurred in certain inland areas of the country, many of which took on an endemic rebellious character. The greatest of these rebellions was that of the Taipings (1848–1864). There was much in the Taiping cry *ta-kuan*, smash the officials, which was reminiscent of the murderous hatred of the aristocracy during the French Revolution. The Taipings were crushed, but the process of social revolution did not end. Revolts continued to break out in the inland regions. The Communists succeeded in combining these forces of revolt into a mighty revolutionary movement. The military victories of Chinese communism took place at the same time that a revolutionary struggle was waged on the land against the rural gentry. A whole class was destroyed, not only physically but psychologically. Every act of land reform was climaxed by a drama where the landlord literally "lowered his head" (*tit'ou*) and so symbolically expressed his acceptance of defeat by the people.

All social revolutions are directed against elites, ruling classes. There has been a contemporary revival of interest in elites, for modernization and industrialization are seen as requiring leadership. But the elite concept involves more than leadership. An elite must not only be able to lead men in the organizational structures that criss-cross society, but must have legitimate status at the top levels of a social system. When an elite loses its capacity to lead and the legitimacy of its status, it reaps contempt and hatred from the people. The histories of social revolutions indicate that where an elite constitutes an entire ruling class, hatred can reach intense levels of collective fury.

Why the collective fury should have broken out with such ferocity during the Taiping Rebellion is not clear. The eighteenth century was a period of stability in China, for which it was widely admired in Europe. Toward the end of that century, extreme misery reappeared, but, as De Tocqueville indicates, misery is not the cause of revolution. During the Opium War of the early 1840's, China had sustained a stinging defeat at the hands of England. Not only was China as a country humiliated, but, more specifically, those who exercised authority in its name in Kwangtung, an area not far from where the Taiping Rebellion broke out. Whether the defeat China suffered in the Opium War had anything to do with the outbreak of the Taiping Rebellion is a subject for historical inquiry. However, humiliation at the hands of an external enemy who proclaims his moral superiority is particularly subversive to the authority of an elite. If this is paired with ineptness in domestic leadership, the conditions exist for social revolution. The stage is set for the act of class destruction.

China had its political revolution in 1911 and thus became a modern nation-state. The urban bourgeoisie eventually found a role in the emerging republic. But the landed gentry found no real role in the new government. Whether it would have if Chiang Kai-shek had been able to achieve political unity is a matter of dispute. Probably not. Few members of the gentry had much modern education, nor much understanding of the great things of the modern world which had an increasing attraction for the people of the country. The outcries of anger against "corrupt officials and lewd politicians, local landlords and inferior literati" began to erupt again. It was inevitable that the Communists, taught to look for revolutionary seeds in the cities, sooner or later would perceive the potential for social revolution in the rural areas. By the 1930's it was clear that China was moving toward a revolution similar to those of France and Russia. Chiang Kai-shek's dream of emulating the German and Japanese examples of nation-building was being gradually shattered. Nevertheless, by 1936 it appeared for a while that Chiang could succeed. The Communists had been reduced to a small band of stragglers holed up in the caves of remote Shensi, and the country enjoyed relative stability and prosperity.

One can argue *ad infinitum* whether the Chinese Revolution would have broken out if the Sino-Japanese war had not started. Even granting the wisdom of retrospection, it seems unlikely that a powerful Japan could have long coexisted with a reunited China, particularly with the mounting demands within China to recover Manchuria and the foreign concessions in China's most advanced regions. There was a growing student movement and a deep dissatisfaction within the corps of younger army officers. The Sino-Japanese war and the United Front between Kuomintang and Communists deflected revolutionary energies in the cities, but created conditions for a new revolutionary outburst on the land. If there had been no war, the revolutionary process would probably have started again within the cities and the Kuomintang. But there *was* war, and it sparked the dormant social revolution in China's rural regions.

France emerged from the revolution as one of the most highly organized countries in the world. The beginnings of political centralization antedate 1789, but the revolution and the first empire completed the process. Revolution followed by political centralization is a phenomenon repeated time after time in the wake of the French Revolution. It has been true of all Communist countries ever since the Russian Revolution. One can see it today in the newly emerging countries. Revolutions are followed by the creation of networks of organization.

Social system and organization must be viewed as two different things; a true elite is solidly imbedded in both. When a revolution destroys a social system, it also annihilates its elites. The new revolutionary regime can only pull society together again through organization. Political centralization is one of the forms that postrevolutionary organization has taken.

When a society has experienced political revolution and moves to resurrect organization, it looks for leadership, and naturally turns to its elites. But if its ruling class has lost the capacity to lead, that is, the capacity to strike out in new directions and to get men to follow them on the new road, then organization remains an empty shell. Nothing reveals the nakedness of a ruling class so starkly as its impotence in organization. When a social revolution destroys a social system, it is no longer possible for society to reach out toward its erstwhile elites for leadership, for they have ceased to exist. But the destruction of the social system makes organization more necessary than ever, for otherwise society would disintegrate into chaos. New leaders arise, whose primary qualification is their ability to lead. In time they may turn into a new elite by adding social status to their political positions. The system is reconstituted, but this time on a new basis. Both France and Russia have their elites today, though they are far different from the classes they replaced in the wake of social revolution.

The Manchus, when threatened by the West, did what all rulers do when facing the need to create and staff new organization: they turned to their traditional elite. The tide of social revolution which had erupted with the Taipings had subsided. There was no reason to suspect that the bureaucrats had lost their leadership abilities. The attempt failed. The Kuomintang tried a different approach. The destruction of the monarchy cleared the road for setting up all kinds of new organizational structures. The Kuomintang acquired a strong military streak during the 1920's, and military men have a keen sense of organization. But the Kuomintang persisted in staffing organization with old elites. What was left of the rural gentry moved into inland government positions. The urban bourgeoisie acquired powerful positions in the central government. Chiang Kai-shek, impressed with Germany and Japan, felt that strong military-political organization imposed from the top down, combined with civil government staffed by old and new elites, could accomplish the task of unification. It failed because of the inability of the elites to make civil government work. When the forces of social revolution revived, in the rural areas and within the Kuomintang itself (young army officers and intellectuals), Chiang attempted to suppress them. It was clear by the 1930's that the social revolution had eroded the social system. China needed organization to pull it together again. Chiang realized this, but he never understood that organization needs leaders.

The Communists, however, understood this very well. They recognized the forces of social revolution and made use of them. They not only saw revolution destroying a social system, but actively aided the process. While the revolution was still in the making, they already began to build new structures of military and civil organization. But, in great contrast to the Kuomintang, they knew that new organization needed new leaders. From the beginning of the Yenan period (1935–1946), their main organizational effort concentrated on recruiting and training new leaders. These became the cadres of the revolution and of organization.

The series of rebellions that broke out in China toward the end of the eighteenth century started a process of social revolution that, in some respects, has not yet ended. De Tocqueville's suggestion that economic factors were not major causative elements in the French Revolution could be generalized: the immediate factors that lead to acts of class destruction are not economic. Thus, when a country faces social revolution, economic countermeasures alone cannot prevent it. But in a more fundamental sense, the matrix from which revolutionary processes arise is economic. In China, it was not Western imperialism with its new business and industry which created the economic matrix of revolution, because Western enterprise did not come until the latter part of the nineteenth century, whereas the revolutionary process began late in the eighteenth century. Moreover, the impact of Western imperialism was largely confined to the coast and a few select inland regions, whereas the social revolution was an inland phenomenon. Although there was a brief period of revolutionary ferment in the cities during the second and third decades of the twentieth century, which clearly was linked to the economic changes produced by imperialism, the great continuing revolution took place in remote inland regions.

The Communist party was born in Shanghai, but its destiny was in the interior. Ping-ti Ho in his *Studies on the Population of China, 1368–1953* (Harvard University Press, 1959) indicates that far-reaching changes had occurred in China's economic and demographic situation toward the end of the eighteenth century: "The over-all opportunities for gainful employment in the nation began to be reduced amidst continual population increase and technological stagnation" (p. 226). This suggests that the traditional economic fabric had started to disintegrate. But "technological stagnation" is not a phenomenon of nature. It is a manifestation of incapacity on the part of those who hold economic responsibility. In China, the accusation of economic responsibility falls on the shoulders of the gentry. The rebellions that broke out late in the eighteenth century were ferocious, and they were repressed with equal ferocity. That thread of ferocity created a social and psychological climate which ultimately led to the revolutionary terror of the late 1940's. However, it was the ever more evident impotence of the gentry in the face of economic challenges that marked its fall from elite position.

The economic elements that played a part in the genesis of the French

Revolution arose from the transformation of post-feudal society, not from the industrial revolution which had just occurred in England. So it was in China. Ping-ti Ho's explanations of the growing tide of misery as due to population increase amidst technological stagnation sketches the terrible problem that has faced all Chinese governments since the end of the eighteenth century. No one has ever been more sensitive to this problem than the present leaders of China who have been trying to create a technological and economic base for Chinese society adequate for its population.

The period of peace and stability which China enjoyed during much of the eighteenth century was very different from a similar period of prosperity a thousand years before during the Sung dynasty. Then a new gentry had appeared on the scene; cities were growing; new ideas came into society. But the eighteenth century was different. The Manchus had allied themselves with an old ruling class that had strong local roots. Cities were mostly stagnant. And, except for a few new political ideas of the early Ch'ing, China's intellectuals had turned into tedious and plodding academics. Rebellion and internal migration in the late eighteenth century were warning signals that something was wrong with the social fabric. Western imperialism led to the rise of new great cities and thus provided new economic opportunities for the rural masses. But the rent in the social fabric had already taken place and could not be healed. The counter-revolutionary ferocity of General Tseng Kuo-fan in combatting the revolutionary ferocity of the Taipings created an atmosphere that made the final act of class destruction inevitable. Just as economic improvement in pre-1789 France and pre-1917 Russia failed to stem the tide of revolution, so periodic economic recovery and even progress in pre-1949 China failed to halt the social revolution.

The 1911 upheaval in China destroyed the monarchy and was succeeded by a republic which, in form, was quite modern. But by the 1930's it was evident that more had crumbled than the political system alone. The social fabric had disintegrated in much of rural China, yet the new patterns in the cities were too weak to exercise a commanding force over the country. The disintegration of the traditional economic system which began in the eighteenth century continued without interruption, yet the modern sector could not constitute an effective substitute. In the world of ideas and values, Confucianism was dying. The sharp cry of the intellectuals during the May-Fourth Movement, *fan li-chiao*, an untranslatable slogan which in effect announced that the old elite of the country had lost its moral charisma in the eyes of the young, signaled the disintegration of the value system. The Communists saw the trends of history and fought to complete the revolution. In the course of their long struggle, they looked to the future, and began to prepare for it with ideology and organization. When they triumphed, they replaced system by organization, and ethos by ideology.

The French and Russian revolutions were characterized by a seizure of state power which opened the floodgates of the social revolution. The waves of revolution spread outward from Paris and Petrograd to the provinces. Class warfare broke out and sent counterwaves back to the capital which pressed the leaders of the revolution into ever more radical directions. The Chinese Revolution was different. The seizure of state power was the climax of a revolution which began deep in the provinces. The social revolution had been burning for a century and a half. It remained relatively dormant during much of the early twentieth century, but broke out again in the late 1920's. The peasant jacqueries of the Kiangsi period were still reminiscent of the classical rebellions, despite the veneer of Bolshevist ideology. But in Yenan, the Communists began to use the dynamics of revolution and war to build organization. A dual process began to emerge. On the one hand, the drama of class destruction continued, reaching its culmination in the revolutionary terror of the land reform of the late 1940's. On the other hand, the Communists began to create the building blocks of their organizational network, which was to become the basis for their rule over the Chinese Mainland after final victory.

The French and Russian revolutions went from the top down. The apex of the political system was smashed with one blow, actually and symbolically, and this led to a disintegration of the social fabric at all points of the system. There were other revolutions from the top down which did not have this effect, because the revolutionary pressures within the social system were not as great. One of them was the Meiji Restoration. The shogunate was overthrown by a basically conservative cabal of feudatories, but soon thereafter leadership passed into the hands of a radical group. One can see the pace of radicalization moving fast during the first years of the Meiji era. A system of social stratification and political order that had taken centuries to construct was obliterated. But there was neither a revolutionary bourgeoisie nor a revolutionary peasantry. The transformation of the political apex did not open the floodgates of social revolution, despite the unsettling rapidity of change.

Why were forces of social revolution, comparable to those of France, Russia, and China not present in Japan? There was no absence of peasant discontent during the Tokugawa; there was discontent among a new group of inland merchants who fought against the entrenched privilege of the city bourgeoisie; there was a highly dissatisfied and highly educated body of minor nobility seeking a new role in society. But Japan was yet too feudal, an argument that De Tocqueville also invokes to explain the absence of revolutionary pressures in Germany at the end of the eighteenth century. But the French Revolution, like the Russian, was directed against the state and a ruling class closely identified with it. Feudalism had imposed a complex patchwork of social and political relationships on society. Processes of rationalization in France had long before the revolution done away with these patterns, leaving them only as vestiges of an earlier age. Russia and China never knew feudalism in its West European and Japanese senses.

Though China's social revolution was similar to that of France and Russia, it was also different. In the former countries, the ruling classes had lost that intimate involvement with local regions that remained so important in China. The French and Russian aristocracies became court aristocracies, living in cities and drawing their sinecures from their local possessions. The Chinese gentry did not live in the villages, but neither did it live in Peking. The court aristocracy in the nineteenth century was Manchu, an alien race. The 1911 revolution did away with the aristocracy, but left the gentry undisturbed. Thus one of the aims of the Taïping Rebellion had been accomplished. But not the other, the destruction of the traditional gentry. In France and Russia, the ruling aristocracies were destroyed by revolutions that seized state power. It was not possible to destroy the Chinese gentry in a similar way. One might say that the Chinese gentry had strong linkages to both state and society. After 1911, it lost its linkages to the state, and, to compensate for this, held on more firmly to its particular interests in society.

This was not the first time that an alien group had come to power leading to a temporary retreat of the gentry from the scene. Most gentry undoubtedly thought that sooner or later the state would require its services again. Indeed, it was not disappointed, for that is precisely what the Kuomintang did. The weakened tie to the state had its advantages, for it immunized the gentry from the constant political changes in Peking and Nanking. On the other hand, heightened commitment to its landed possessions made it more vulnerable to the pressures of social revolution. Revolutions are profoundly influenced by the character of ruling classes. The entrenched localism of gentry power made it inevitable that the Chinese Revolution, in contrast to the revolutions of France and Russia, would come from the outlying areas to the center rather than the reverse, and, moreover, that it would take a long time. The gentry was widely distributed throughout China, and could not be destroyed with one blow. The peculiar conditions of the social situation in China gave the Chinese Revolution a populist character, one which neither Trotsky nor Stalin understood. It retains that character to the present day.

The Chinese Communists claim that their revolution is prototypical for the revolutionary process now burning in the countries of Asia, Africa, and Latin America. They argue that revolution cannot be won by student seizures of state power, by occupation of a capital city; they preach the "building-blocks" approach; they argue for revolution as a long-term process; they see capture of state power as the last act in a long drama.

Are they right in their assessment of the world revolutionary situation? Our analysis of revolution suggests that the seeds of social revolution are present when a traditional elite is incapable of exercising leadership in organization and when its status disappears as the result of disintegration of the social system. Thus it loses power and authority. In traditional peasant societies, the elite derives power and authority both from state and society. By society I here mean a localized social system which operates in a district or a region rather than in the country as a whole. The ownership of land usually is an important element in the localized social system. The Chinese Communist doctrine of revolution states that the revolutionaries must strike against such local systems—that it is here where the revolution will be won.

Every old elite tries desperately to maintain its positions in state and society. It will try to staff government with its people, and it will hold tenaciously to its local interests. The lessons of history suggest that it cannot do both. The pressures for land reform force the elite to hold on even more tightly to the reins of government. If a liberal government accedes to demands for land reform, as did Alexander II in Russia, the elite demands in return control of decision-making positions. It is not accidental that the most liberal of bureaucratic administrators often come from the old elite, like Count Witte. On the other hand, if strange people move into government, then the elite must preserve its interests in society. Benito Juarez became president of Mexico, but the caciques maintained a tight grip on the land. The one part of the world that appears to constitute a testing ground of the Chinese thesis is Latin America. Most Latin American countries have old Hispano-Portuguese elites with strong roots on the land and close association with government. Social and economic reform alone will not resolve the problem, for the dispossessed elite will simply move into the cities and into government. This is exactly what emancipation in Russia did. No matter how liberal and reformist the old elite becomes, historical example suggests that revolutionary pressures will rise against it. Land reform may ease revolutionary pressures in the villages, but the presence of a discredited elite in the cities and in the structure of government creates revolutionary pressures in the cities. This would portend a revolution of the French or Russian type. On the other hand, if the elites rather surrender their hold on government than their grip on the land, a revolution of the Chinese type threatens. The Chinese Communists believe that this will be the pattern of revolution in the coming years.

The Sino-Soviet dispute is not only a conflict between two powers, but one between two different revolutionary models. These two approaches to revolution are reflected in the split that has appeared in revolutionary groups in Latin America. On the one hand, there are the old-line Communists who maintain their tightly disciplined, centrally organized parties, waiting for the day that a February Revolution will break out. On the other hand, there are the Castroites, spiritually akin to the Chinese, working for a guerrilla war of social revolution on the land.

Can social revolution with all its bloodshed be avoided in Latin America? Marx said that no ruling class departs willingly from the stage of history. Perhaps he is right: the chances of avoiding revolution would appear to be slim. However, the rapid emergence of a liberated peasantry on the land, and a new class of technocratic administrators and entrepreneurial managers in the cities could furnish a chance of avoiding social revolution. The old elite, tainted irreparably with ineptness and loss of charisma, would be replaced by younger men of ability, of mixed race reflecting the character of Latin America, and by men who can produce as well as consume. The new men would not only have to have real power, but would have to be visible, to stand out as the true leaders of the country.

After a social revolution has taken place in a country, there no longer exists a ruling class to constitute a source of recruitment for the leadership roles that organization requires. To survive, the revolutionaries need organization. China went through a social revolution in the third century B.C., which led to the disappearance of an old feudal aristocracy. The Ch'in empire emerged from that struggle as the most highly organized political entity known to that time in Chinese history, and armed with an ideology called legalism, which was in fact an ideology of organization. Triumphant revolutionary movements often tend to be military, not only because of the importance of armed struggle, but because armies are by their nature pure organization. The successful revolutionary movement has desperate need for leadership to direct the organization it creates. It recruits leaders from where it can find them. But the type of organization which a revolutionary movement creates in its formative phases, and the kinds of leaders which it recruits, have a decisive influence on the kind of society it builds up after victory.

In Russia, the tight conspiratorial organization of the Bolsheviks, and its direction almost entirely from outside of the Russian social context, influenced the type of organization and leadership that arose after the Russian Revolution. The revolutionary process in Russia had developed for a long time before the October Revolution. However, the Bolshevik party, because of its inability to operate openly in the country, could not become a true mass organization until the eve of the revolution itself. It was a highly centralized organization with a straight-line chain of command. Though the top leaders were intellectuals (as in China), the Party fighters were men of the working class. Despite the rapid regrowth of bureaucracy during the early 1920's, the new Party men were more managerially than bureaucratically minded. In the early 1920's, workers were put in positions of power to make certain that the proletariat ruled in organization. Subsequently, Stalin made great efforts to create a "workers' intelligentsia." Russia moved in the direction of great organizational centralization. Stalin wanted a phalanx of trained working-class managers to run that organization. Thus revolutionary Russia embarked on a process of political centralization, comparable to that of revolutionary France, but far more thorough. In contrast to the bourgeoisie that came to be the new elite in nineteenth-century France, in Russia organization was increasingly staffed by sons of workers.

The organization and the leaders that came out of the Chinese Revolution were different. Not since 1927 was the Chinese Communist party simply a conspiratorial group aiming to seize state power. In Kiangsi, it was mainly an army riding to power on the waves of a jacquerie. During the Yenan period, it turned into a political-military organization that sought systematically to use the forces of social revolution. The ideal nucleus of that organization was a small armed band that at times fought but at other times tended to agricultural production. The leaders of Communist organization during the Yenan period were the poor young peasants of the villages who centuries earlier had been recruited into defense brigades or roamed the hills as rebels. Out of this group emerged the cadres who led the revolution, fought the battles, took control of the production teams, and finally launched the acts of revolutionary land reform in the later 1940's. The Chinese Communists during the Yenan period wanted leaders first and foremost, and they sought them out wherever they could find them. The young peasant cadres had a military bent; for centuries their predecessors had gone forth to fight. War against the hated Japanese provided fertile ground for organizing. The village elders could not quarrel with the patriotic cause. But, as the land reform shows, the real target was the rural elite. The peasant jacquerie of the early 1930's broke out before the Sino-Japanese war. The revolutionary terror of the late 1940's burst forth after the Japanese had been defeated.

If any group in society is not an elite, it is the poor and the young. They have neither wealth, nor power, nor prestige. In China, the poor and the young peasants became the leaders of the revolution. But leadership could only be actualized in organization. Thus by destroying the social system and replacing it with organization, they created a role for themselves in the new society. What they sought was leadership and power, not status and authority.

The one great organizational product of the Chinese Revolution has been the Chinese Communist party. It is an organization made up of leaders whose one great purpose in life is to lead—at all levels of the structure. In its early years, it was a party of youth. Today, though older, it is still made up largely of workers and peasants. The Party has created an organizational context which gives them a continuing role in society.

Organization, in contrast to a social system, needs conscious efforts to survive. This is all the more so when organization cannot rely on a social system, such as recruiting its leaders from a solidly based status group. In wars, armies survive through the challenges of battle. The end of the war often has a demoralizing effect on military organization, as was the case with the American army after World War II. The Chinese Communists have understood this well, and thus "struggle" (*toucheng*) has become the watchword of the Party. This is not an abstraction, for the constant reappearance of "rectification" keeps the atmosphere of struggle alive, particularly when the leadership role of the Party diminishes. Ideology provides the moral cement that not only arouses commitment but creates the cohesive forces which prevent struggle from turning into disintegration. Cohesion through conflict is a problem with which both Western sociologists and the Chinese Communists have concerned themselves. For the latter, it has been a life and death matter.

When the Chinese Communists triumphed in 1949, there no longer was a social system to which they could turn for support, even if they had wanted to. There was no gentry left, and they distrusted the bourgeoisie. But there was a choice of directions. Should they construct organization along the lines they had developed during the ten years of Yenan or should they emulate the one model they respected above all: the Soviet Union? They chose the latter course, and thus for the first five years of the 1950's, China began rapidly turning into a second Soviet Union. The imposition of bureaucratic organization from the top down proceeded rapidly, symbolized by the elaboration of a vast planning structure. China appeared to be following the road to bureaucratic centralization. If centralization meant the emergence of a new professional elite, the changes in Communist party recruitment in the early 1950's followed the model perfectly. Large numbers of old and new intellectuals were recruited into the Party. Expertise became a prime qualification for Party membership. Untrained rural cadres were dropped from Party rolls. Managers were coming into their own again. A "new class" was in the process of coming into being. But the process was stopped in 1955. The purge of oppositional elements in Manchuria and Shanghai led to the elimination of large numbers of budding apparatchiks. In the summer of 1955 the Party struck against the bureaucracy. And finally collectivization led once again to radicalization.

The evidence indicates that there was a social core to this process. The demobilization of the army in 1955 saw millions of war veterans return to the countryside where they became leaders of the collectivization drive and rural Party cadres. The enormous jump in Party membership went hand in hand with political radicalization and collectivization. Despite the consolidation of 1956 and 1957, the rural Party organization continued to grow. Late in 1957, rectification once again struck the Party and the professionals. While the "regionalization of the Party" was opposed, decentralization nevertheless gave the local Party apparatus great power. When communization was introduced, a great ground swell of enthusiasm came precisely from the young rural cadres. Today, in the declining years of his life, Mao Tse-tung calls for the recruitment of a new generation of Party members from among young workers and peasants. These are the cadres with whom he made the revolution, and these are the young leaders who tried to implement his programs of rural reconstruction. China in the mid-1950's thus veered sharply from the Soviet model of organization which it so assiduously followed during the early 1950's.

China's social revolution has been long. The type of organization that has emerged from it has been much more directly involved with the masses of society than in the Soviet Union. The Chinese peasant, even in remote inland areas, has been drawn into political life. Mao's dream is the transformation of the Chinese peasant into a modern producer. Land reform destroyed the old rural elite. Collectivization deprived the peasant of his ownership over the soil. Communization changed the whole pattern of work organization. Was this the final act of liberation from which a new peasant will emerge? It seems almost inevitable that the forces of bureaucratic centralization will once again make themselves felt in China. It does not seem likely that a political semi-elite of worker and peasant cadres and a social semi-elite of professionals can long coexist in peace. Neither is it likely that the professionals will long be content to do staff work for their red executives nor that the red cadres will forego the chances of acquiring social status through education and professionalization. The lure of education is powerful. If, however, the "new class" emerges after society has been truly transformed, and if the peasant has been brought into the modern world, then Mao's dream will have been realized. Then institutionalization can set in once again. The revolution will then be over. A new society will begin to emerge. . . .

19

Third, there is the foreign embroilment.

FROM

Confucian China and Its Modern Fate: A Trilogy

JOSEPH R. LEVENSON

I T is said that the ancient Roman triumvir Crassus had both a private fire department and a private arson squad, and that he made many talents out of using the two in judicious combination. To an interesting degree, western powers in China, and perhaps elsewhere, appear to have played the part of Crassus in the last century. Their material interests seemed best secured when the Chinese government had a fire lit under it, the fire of at least partly western-inspired domestic rebelliousness; for in such a precarious situation, no matter how much they would ordinarily wish to withhold concessions from foreigners, Chinese rulers would have to make concessions, or confirm them, in order to qualify for the foreign aid which alone could save them at home. For both sides, there was one condition to the smooth working of this protection-system: the Chinese government should not become so helpless before its domestic foes that effective foreign aid must overtax the foreigner or overencumber the Chinese client; the former will not dispense more than his stake is worth, the latter will not repay more than he stands to lose.

In its ideal form, as a point of reference for our comprehension of later modifications, the system was established in 1860. The T'ai-p'ing Rebellion against the Ch'ing dynasty had already been raging for ten years. Nevertheless, the Manchu government had tried quite naturally, in the ancient manner, to be successfully anti-foreign and anti-rebel at the same time, and it had been reluctant to extend or even confirm the foreign privileges in China granted in the eighteen-forties, in the wake of the Opium War. But though the traditional Chinese world may have seemed the best of all worlds to the ruling group in China, it was no longer a

Joseph R. Levenson, *Confucian China and Its Modern Fate: A Trilogy* (University of California Press: Berkeley and Los Angeles, 1968), I ("The Problem of Intellectual Continuity"), pp. 147–155. Reprinted by permission of The Regents of the University of California and by permission of Routledge and Kegan Paul (London).

possible one. For when the government was defeated by the Anglo-French forces in the second western war against China (1856–60), and thereby weakened in its resistance to the rebellion, it was established for the next century that either domestic dissidents or foreign intruders had somehow to be accommodated. Both internal threats and external threats of despoliation could not be fought off at once.

Since in 1860 the foreigners sought only the dynasty's capitulation, while the T'ai-p'ings sought its extirpation, the dynasty's one recourse was to suffer the evil of foreign aggrandizement at China's expense, and to try to turn the loss to account; when it was hammered home to the Ch'ing that they had no hope of two victories, they became grudgingly reconciled to accepting the one defeat (and the lesser one) which could be put to use in staving off the other. New treaties, more favourable to foreign interests than the old ones, were concluded with western nations in 1860, and thus the latter, especially Britain, were bound to the service of the Chinese government by virtue, in effect, of their owning shares in it. British intervention in the civil war was soon forthcoming. It was worth the while of a western power to preserve the government which at last it had taught to be tractable.

The T'ai-p'ings, who had never been allies of the foreigners even when they shared the same Manchu enemy, now served the foreign interest by persisting in their enmity while the West abandoned hers. For the British, however easily, perhaps, they might have crushed the Ch'ing forces themselves and even taken over the government, were better suited by a client government—dependent, yet able to play the larger part in its own defence—than by the prospect of wars against a possibly unified, anti-foreign nation-at-arms. No Chinese government would yield bounty to foreigners unless pressures were being exerted upon it. The British had exerted their share (and would do so again, when usable rebels lay not so close to hand), but once their point had been made, it seemed more politic and probably more profitable to let the task of pressing the Ch'ing devolve on the excellent T'ai-p'ings, who were usefully dangerous but far from invulnerable, and whom the dynasty could never conciliate except by conniving at its own destruction. The British, therefore, by a relatively small expenditure in the form of aid to a Chinese agent, instead of a large expenditure in the form of suppression of Chinese independence, could work their will in China. The Ch'ing regime, in its T'ai-p'ing-induced extremity, sold out to foreigners what it once had fought to keep.

The situation, then, concerning the foreign stake in China may be summarized, *in a preliminary fashion,* as follows:

Foreign claims in China may be honoured by unpopular governments, which can be used, or by popular (i.e., generally accepted) governments, which must, however, be menaced or forced. For a government representing a general Chinese will would have to oppose foreign intrusion, but an unpopular government would be relatively docile, since acquiescence is the only key to acquiring from foreign sources the force that is needed to counter the force of opposition at home. Therefore, liberal western nations, often providing the inspiration for Chinese protests against Chinese rulers, tend to support discredited Chinese regimes; to see a regime discredited, then to step in as its only hope—that is the way to buy it. The West drains power from the Chinese ruling circles so that the West, for a *quid pro quo,* can give it back to them.

This is the ideal pattern for the western use of leverage against Chinese governments (a pattern depending on the logic of events, not on assumptions of flawlessly rational, cunning forethought in foreign chancelleries). But the pattern dissolves with the passing of time, for the situation is never static. Either the Chinese government, using its bought protection to good advantage, becomes domestically less in jeopardy, hence less inclined to continue to pay for protection; or on the other hand, the jeopardy grows, precisely on account of the government's possession by foreigners, and there is no longer a sort of tame loyal opposition, a steady but moderate resistance to the regime, which the powers can easily and perpetually exploit. They prefer to invest in a Chinese government which is always a little off balance. But either the government eventually tries to dispense with the West and to right itself (e.g., the Boxer movement, 1900), or it threatens to lose its balance completely and require more western succour, lest it fall, than its services seem to its western sponsors to warrant.

The latter description applies to warlord-foreign relations during the 'Nationalist Revolution' of the nineteen-twenties. From the foreign point of view, Chinese political forces were in an uneasy equilibrium. Chinese hostility to the Peking regimes of puppet warlords was indispensable to ensure their dependence on foreign powers, for the warlords had to replenish abroad the support they squandered at home. However, especially after May 30, 1925, nationalist hatred of the Peking cliques fed on the foreign support of them, and the hatred increased out of all proportion to the foreign aid lent to Peking to counteract it.

Obviously, for the powers, this had reached the point of diminishing returns. The foreigners might well find themselves the receivers of an entirely bankrupt regime, faced by a solid phalanx of Chinese opposition, so that only a total foreign commitment to war against the Chinese nation could protect the West's prerogatives. The ground the warlords stood on might vanish to a pinhead, and foreigners, instead of enjoying the favoured position of arbiter in a civil war, would find themselves faced with a full-fledged national war.

Some foreigners were willing to face this prospect. They saw China as it appeared in the middle nineteen-twenties, a land of two camps: nationalist or 'Bolshevik' (i.e., Kuomintang and communist parties together in an anti-imperialist, nationalist united front), and anti-nationalist. Seeing no hope for themselves in the first camp, the united front, these foreigners stood ready to bail out the warlords, whatever the cost. Other foreigners, assuming, like their compatriots, that Chinese nationalism was implacable, doubted it could be thwarted by the essentially limited western forces which properly might be charged with such a task. As long as Chinese nationalism was so gloomily assessed, as solid and inflexible— as long, that is, as the *North China Herald* continued to inveigh against the raging Bolshevik, Kuomintang leader Chiang K'ai-shek—the foreign community could see indeed only two alternatives: either invade China properly, or cut losses and get out.

But by the spring of 1927, when the insight was gained that not all nationalists were Bolsheviks—in short, to put it coldly, when the foreigners realized that civil war was still a possibility—a third, the old and the best, alternative emerged. The West could support a Chinese government strong enough to bear some of the burden of its own support, yet threatened enough from within to need foreign aid. When the Kuomintang, with foreign connivance, broke with the communists in 1927, the western powers had a new agent, neither uselessly weak, as the warlords had become, nor solidly, nationally secure (hence very hard to deal with), as Chiang K'ai-shek had seemed to be becoming.

Yet, the arrangement between Chiang and the West was not precisely the old one. The foreigners had to settle for a *faute de mieux*, retention of their treaty rights, but with some infringements and promise of others. There was not simply a change in hirelings, with the foreigners turning from one to another internally-jeopardized regime (as they had done in 1912, for instance, when the Chinese Republic was born). For Chiang was authentically a nationalist, and in the course of its struggle against warlords and foreigners, Chinese nationalism, in these twentieth-century parlous times for Chinese culture, had acquired so strong a position as a moral imperative that a new regime had to appear to be following its dictates. The foreigners were either changing an impossible control-system or they were not. If they were, they had to give their Chinese government such concessions as would prevent the communists simply capturing the title to nationalism. If they were not, they would make of the Kuomintang government just such an isolated, dependent warlord regime as those they had abandoned as bankrupt.

The West could mitigate the anti-foreignism of Chinese rulers by declining, otherwise, to bolster them against Chinese dissidents; that was like old times. But Chinese rulers could force the reduction of foreign pretensions by declining, otherwise, to break their alliance with dissidents (the most intransigent of anti-imperialists), an alliance which could prove for the foreigners a most expensive mischief; that was new. In effect, the West held up the spectre of communism to curb the Kuomintang, and the Kuomintang held up the same spectre to curb the West.

The Kuomintang's terms and the foreigners' terms were figuratively spelled out, each to the other. Implied the foreigners to the Kuomintang: 'If you want to get anything, stop trying to get everything, hence break with the left extremists; or we will block you ourselves with all our strength or leave you, at best, with no aid from us, to your ultimate communist reckoning.' Implied the Kuomintang to the foreigners: 'If you want to keep anything, stop trying to keep everything, thus forcing us into our communist alliance, which threatens to cost you dear.' In February, 1927, retroceding their concession at Hankow, far up the Yangtze, the British seemed to be heeding the other's warning. In March, at Nanking, nearer the sea, the Kuomintang seemed to be doing the same, as it dissociated itself from what it described as communist violence against foreign nationals. In April, at Shanghai, the foreign stronghold and the nationalists' goal, where a clear-cut decision had to be made, the Kuomintang and the foreigners met, extremes were softened, and the communists, by joint agreement, ruined.

A communist remnant survived, becoming a serious force again in the next decade. The Kuomintang government fought communist rebels, but in 1937 these factions formed their second united front. For a Japanese threat had intervened, a foreign menace of such proportions that civil war could not lend itself to foreign exploitation, but could only be set aside.

The British, principal targets of Chinese nationalism from 1925 to 1927, had hoped at best to hold their own in China, and would never really have ventured, at that late date in Sino-British relations, on full-scale war. Therefore, they could be reached by the Kuomintang, a bargain struck, and Chinese nationalism to some extent politically indulged, at the expense of its solidarity. But when the Japanese, not the British, posed the challenge to Chinese nationalism, a Kuomintang-foreign bargain was hardly possible. Since Japan was fully prepared to war on China and to monopolize power, not to share it, Chinese nationalism could be indulged not by bargaining but only by resistance; and real resistance precluded civil war. The British and Chiang K'ai-shek had had something to offer each other—relief from the prospect of communist expropriation. But the Japanese and Chiang had nothing to offer each other. Chiang could not force the Japanese to any self-denial, since whatever he had to sell they were ready to seize without incurring obligation. And the Japanese had no leverage on Chiang, since whatever part of his power they might save from communist raids they meant to pre-empt themselves.

Therefore, though the Japanese blatantly used the communist threat as a blackmail weapon to force Chiang to their side, in the end they lost him because they changed the rules for intervention in Chinese revolutions. What they wanted (and found in other quarters) was a Chinese agent to facilitate a wartime foreign conquest and the exercise of nakedly foreign rule, not a Chinese agent to facilitate a peacetime foreign remote-control. Chiang, in order to save the chance to break the communists in his own interests (not Japan's) in a later bout, had to join with the communists to clear the ring of the Japanese. As an anti-communist nationalist, he had to keep Japan from handing over the patriotic cause to the Chinese communists, from making nationalism and communism synonymous in China.

In short, Chiang's dearest wish was to eliminate both communists and Japanese from China. He deferred his pursuit of one of these satisfactions in order to seek the other, whose postponement would be fatal.

But with the entrance of the United States into the war against Japan, both of these ends for the first time seemed attainable together. A breach of the united front would no longer of necessity deliver Chiang to Japan, nor must it compromise his nationalism fatally, since the national objective, Japan's defeat, would presumably be provided for. So in the nineteen-forties civil war was prepared again for China, even before the end came to the general, national war.

Like other modern Chinese civil wars and pressures of dissent on the central government, this civil war was relevant to the preservation of a foreign stake in China. But the situation was complicated, in that the stake was more political now than economic. With Japan's defeat, the United States emerged as the strongest western power in the Far East, and what the United States wanted was the political support of a dependable Chinese government. By American definition, that meant a non-communist government.

But when such support was the prize the United States sought, no manner of aid to the embattled national government could guarantee that the prize would be delivered. To Chiang K'ai-shek, because of the difference in kind of the foreign stakes involved, the United States seemed to lack what Britain had held in leverage against him in 1927—the priceless option to withhold the aid with which he could break the left. It had been entirely possible for Britain to utter a plague on both their houses in the early nineteen-twenties, when communists and Kuomintang had seemed equally ready to confiscate the British assets. But it was inconceivable that the United States, whose treasure in China was of a different kind, could abandon Chiang to the communists.

Therefore, it was easy for Chiang to withstand American pressure for Kuomintang reforms. For the Chinese revolution which reform was supposed to block was just as dark a *bête noire* to the United States as to the rulers of China; and the latter, then, rather than dissipate through reform the advantages they wished to save against revolution, assumed that sufficient foreign support would always be forthcoming, no matter how much the need increased as domestic corruption strengthened the rebels' hand.

And so the Kuomintang, in its capacity as a foreign instrument, went the way of the Peking governments of some twenty years before, forfeiting popularity until the only strength it could offer its foreign sponsor was the strength the latter gave it. But this time there was no place for the foreigner to jump, no other possible Chinese protégé, and the opposition to the West's candidate got out of hand. The United States aided the only contender whose triumph would serve her purpose—a contender, however, whose chances of triumph were hopelessly prejudiced by the very inevitability of American aid.

By 1950 the wheel had come full circle. The West had exploited domestic threats to Chinese governments so as to redress the domestic balance and receive a *quid pro quo*. But domestic threats, partly because of the western intervention, grew so strong at last that rebels became the government, while the erstwhile government, with its American ally, became the threat. The Kuomintang, or the United States looming behind it, was converted into the ominous threat which made inevitable Russian aid to China for a time, as a prop to the threatened regime, and equally inevitable the Chinese payment of a *quid pro quo*—a phase of political submission, if nothing else—no longer to the West, but to Russia.

20
And finally—full circle—we have a consideration of past and present identity and prospects for the future.

Marxism and the Middle Kingdom

JOSEPH R. LEVENSON

I. THE CHINESE COMMUNIST VIEW OF CHINA AND THE WORLD

I N the late 1940's, Chou En-lai described the Chinese Communist movement in terms of precedent and change. He said that Chinese history
was basically a story of peasants' wars; the current war was a peasants'
war, too, but led by the working class. This would make all the difference. To Mao Tse-tung, though, the cause seemed more precariously
poised between old recurrent failures and new decisive success. The new
regime's choice, he felt, was between "killing the tiger and being eaten
by it." In one aspect, the tiger was 'imperialism'—in another, 'feudalism.'
In any case, the tiger had to be *killed*. The old Confucian society, in
which the key word was 'harmony,' had dissolved into a society of
'struggle.' The new China was still China, unmistakably emerging from
its own indigenous past; but it was unmistakably new.

The Communist regime came to power with broad support from the
intelligentsia. This reflected not only political desperation but cultural
disenchantment: both traditional Chinese assumptions and their Western
liberal challengers were equally challenged. In a dialectical sense, a
socialist 'people' might be released equally from a restrictive Confucian
past ('feudal') and an intrusive Western present ('imperialist'). This
formulation appealed to intellectuals who were seeking new departures,
yet Chinese continuity. The Chineseness of the Confucian order could
not redeem its modern moribundity; but the renovating force of the
Western influence could not redeem its alien provenance. Men felt a
passionate need, cultural as well as political, both to clear the ground and
to own the ground they stood on.

Accordingly, Communist historians in China took an interest in several
special motifs. For one thing (particularly through a flourishing archaeol-
ogy), they emphasized material culture, a countertheme to the old con-

Joseph R. Levenson, "Marxism and the Middle Kingdom," *Diplomat*,
XVII, No. 196 (September 1966), pp. 48–51. Reprinted by permission
of the editors.

cern with literary 'superstructure.' They emphasized, also, nonliterati or 'popular' activity in science, technology, and social protest. And there was an overriding concern with periodization, to banish the spectre of 'Westernization' by equipping Chinese history with the same Marxist stages as the West (primitive communist, slave, and the rest); these implied a line of development parallel to the West's, with a dynamic internal to China. Together, they lent assurance of equivalence and autonomy, the vindication of Chinese independence.

Individual heroes and institutions of the old culture might now be 'progressive' or 'reactionary.' Now that they were in, Communists could rehabilitate (in a sense) certain standard targets of an earlier generation of radicals; the latter, who were still out, had been more iconoclastic. A Marxist historicism, while being quite un-Confucian, could even restore Confucius—as a progressive influence in an ancient phase of transition —to a place of ambiguous honor. Honor, because Confucius colored *Chinese* history so strongly; ambiguous, because Chinese *history*, the redeemable but unrepeatable past, was the place where the honor rested. The Communists, revolutionary though they were, meant to annex the great tradition, not to yield it to their Chinese opposition. However, as new men, they still felt uncommitted to any primary reassertion of traditional values. The latter might be acceptable as a *heritage* for a new China, without surviving as living, present authority.

The Communists had confidence in their take-over bid for title to the heritage, and this finally led them to warn more sharply against 'bourgeois' sentiment, putatively pro-Western, than against 'feudal' Confucian reaction. When Confucianism could be relativized to 'history,' absolute condemnation was not required. What did have to be condemned, because it still was a live option, was a post-Confucian, yet non-Communist stance, pro-scientific but politically detached. Here was the root of the 'red and expert' issue. The regime needed experts, many of whom were Western-trained. Should political questions affect their employment? The prevailing answer, though sometimes fairly soft, was that redness is essential.

By 1960 the Chinese Communists, assured about their own hue and skeptical of the Russians', were claiming to preside over two heritages, not one—the national, and the international Marxist. Mao was named, over the Soviet 'revisionist' successors of Stalin, as the legitimate heir to the legacy of Lenin. At bottom, what set off the Sino-Soviet dispute was the question of the relationship between technical advance (i.e., atomic weapons) and international revolutionary action. The Chinese held, in literary theory and elsewhere, that man's role, not the machine's, is decisive. Therefore, throughout the world revolutions ought to be pushed, not restrained. Yet the Russians were urging restraint (the Chinese said), out of an apolitical awe of the history-making (or history-ending) potential of the atom.

What have we said so far? First, that Communism was a break with tradition and a way of compensating for the break—paying the cost of recognition that a break had to be made. Everything about modern history that had made a conservative happy-few of Confucian literati fade into a restless intelligentsia, everything that brought science and scientism to corrode the classical curriculum, made Communist China not a replica of something ancient and invincible, but a reaction to and a warrant of its passing.

Second, that China is not at a pole: neither a 'Chinese essence' nor an opposite 'Communist essence' sums up the situation. Change towards Communism does not preclude continuity from Confucianism—as long as *continuity* and *persistence* are not equated. History is process, not essence, and the past may be significant for the present without being reenacted in the present. The old Chinese autocracy, bureaucracy, and classics really lost their grip and their standing, lost them conclusively. The Communists (and adherents to other causes in modern Chinese history) responded to something real, and they really were responding, not repeating. The existence now of the Communist autocracy, bureaucracy, and classics has beguilingly suggested an eternal Chinese essence, but they came in a train of process, preceded but not prefigured in the past. They serve a regime certainly conscious of its Chinese identity, jealous of it, but its leaders propose to have Chinese history culminate in them, with their new kinds of power; their coming is not meant to be (and it is not) just the latest beat in an age-old rhythm of imperial-power withdrawal-and-return.

Mao Tse-tung, accordingly, is not an avatar of some old emperor, like Ch'ien-lung, even if both of them sent their armies to the Himalayas, and both of them were capable of a literary inquisition. Both seem formidably self-righteous, but their conceptions of the right are not the same. Ch'ien-lung, proclaiming that the imperial virtue was acknowledged everywhere, could write complacently to George III, "We are in need of nothing. . . ." Mao, however, knows how desperate the needs are—the intervening century and a half had ruined any complacency and the Confucian pretension to virtue that explained it—and his prescription to banish the needs is *science* (very far from Confucian values), most especially including a 'science of society.' The 'red' of 'red and expert' is not an eternally Chinese demand, whether Confucian or Communist, that officials profess to a world view transcending technical skill and specialization. It implies something else, that the modern world is incompatible with the Confucian, not congruent with it—so incompatible that science and technology are in the ascendant everywhere, and Marxism has to own them or lose its own ascendancy. And if it stays ascendant in China (while it fades in Russia), China deserves ascendancy in the world.

Then, when all is said and done, is it the 'Middle Kingdom' still, the center of the world?

2. THE PLACE OF CHINESE COMMUNISM IN CHINA AND THE WORLD

Or, to put it another way: is the combination of strident nationalism and internationalist pretensions the classical combination? Confucian China, too, after all, commended its way as the absolute Way itself, something more than merely relative to a nation among the nations. Mao's China commends itself, certainly, as the model for the 'under-developed' world. The model, though, is 'substructural,' economic, complete with political prescription for making the model work. It has no direct connection with the Chinese cultural heritage, which is a particularly national concern now, no longer a universal. Rather, for Communist China, the national culture is 'superstructure'; and when China seeks a constituency in Asia, Africa, or Latin America, it offers itself as the modern contriver of material progress from a standing (or prostrate) start, not as the ancient achiever of the only spiritual end. When it poses as a model to other nations, their common historical status, as economic and political victims, is the tie that binds, and their radically different cultures are of no account.

This is the difference between old and new: Confucian 'rule by example' implied (among other things) that the Chinese past, the treasury of sage examples, was the fountainhead of civilization, and that Chinese civilization, then, was Civilization itself, so that China was the world. Communist rule by example (to some), and by contradiction (to others), implies that China rides the wave of the future, and that China is a nation in the world. In either case, of course, there is a powerful sense of self-aggrandizement, and the link between the two is psychological: pre-eminence was a long-standing Chinese expectation. The Communist recipe was offered to men who remembered the old—*and despaired of its efficacy*—so that what they swallowed now in traditional spirit was new in substance, an old psychology smoothing the way for a new sociology.

Is it a Chinese eminence or a Red eminence that China seeks? The question confuses the issue. Li Ta-chao, one of the founders of the Chinese Communist Party and a strong influence on Mao, hailed the Russian Revolution in the following way—a way which permitted a Communist China to be eminently nationalistic, with Chinese identity prized, as of old, but in an utterly post-Confucian definition:

Call it Russian Revolution or call it twentieth-century revolution. Such mighty rolling tides are beyond the power of the present capitalist governments to prevent or to stop, for the mass movement of the twentieth century combines the whole of mankind into one great mass. . . . In the course of this world mass movement, all the refuse of history which stands in the path of the new move-ment—such as emperors, nobles, warlords, bureaucrats, militarism, and capital-ism—will certainly be destroyed.

Here, Li is doing two things.

First, he makes Marxism qualify for China, so as to assuage the pain of cultural break. He shifts the terms of cultural comparison from space to time, as one must do if the revolutionary impulse is to bring, not 'West-ernization,' but 'modernization'; the revolution itself is moved from a foreign nation to his own century, which his own nation owns as much as any other (though the very concept of 'century' came to China from abroad). And second, Li makes China qualify for Marxism, so as to make this first operation possible. That could be done only by theorizing China into a world combination, so as to make good China's own deficiencies in capitalist development, the necessary prelude to socialism. *Foreign* capital-ists (imperialism) become China's—or China *as a nation* becomes a class. It becomes the proletariat (better still, the vanguard of all exploited proletarian nations), in a single, integral, international class society, 'the whole of mankind in one great mass.'

Therefore, since the Western nations, the class enemies without, seek to keep their supremacy, the class enemies still within can be damned by Communists, through their class-analysis world view, in the language of nationalist invective: to betray the proletarian (read, Chinese) cause is to 'sell the nation.' When class denunciation and nationalist excommunica-tion are one, China can still be intensely China while the vision is international, intensely (if eccentrically) Marxist-Leninist as well—but not Confucian. Chinese may see the world as China-centered again, but China can never be self-centered again, as the only world that matters. If Communist China seeks to make inroads on the world, it is because the world, ineradicably, has made inroads on China.

3. THE PRESENT AND THE PAST

If Chinese see themselves as at least potentially a very great force in the world, one does not have to explain this as determined by invincible tradition. How could any people of such a size and so many talents, with hopes and plans for an industrial system to match, help but be self-assertive? Remembrance of things past, both triumphs and humiliations, surely encourages the claim, but a taste for power and influence, espe-cially where their attainment seems so plausible, is general, so general as to make a specific Chinese essence superfluous to account for it. The same holds true for dogmatism. ". . . the 'immutable *li* (principle)' of Neo-Confucian orthodoxy provided a precedent that makes it less difficult for the Chinese to subscribe to what the Communists call 'the universal truth of Marxism-Leninism.' " Perhaps. But why is there not an effective antidote in the skeptical Taoist doctrine of the relativity of all values, since the same author has described that doctrine, with its concomitant individualism and insistence on compromise, as "one of the most important ingredients of the Chinese spirit"? This Neo-Confucian–Communist version of radiation at a distance seems to be another expression of anti-historical essentialism, whereby logical sequence—philosophical affinity—is evidence of historical consequence.

As a matter of fact, one should be wary of speaking of 'the Chinese spirit,' as distinct from the spirit of these Chinese, or those. It is a cardinal historical error to interpret ideas and attitudes which are products of historical development as the ground of historical development. If the Chinese rejected Mo Tzu, who lived in the generation after Confucius, it was not because Mo Tzu flouted 'the perennial Chinese values' of reasonableness, harmony, and moderation. If Buddhism was ultimately worn down in China, it was not because 'the Chinese mind is normally' practical, skeptical, and this-worldly. These nouns and these adjectives, however applicable they may be to a long stretch of history, do not constitute an immanent spirit of the Chinese people. If they constitute a spirit at all, it is rather the reflection of a Confucian civilization, which was a historical, explicable experience; the spirit is not a natural endowment, to be simply accepted as given. Confucian civilization, long-lived but not eternal, was not there at the beginning of Chinese history. It had its own beginnings. And the experience of the nineteenth and twentieth centuries suggests that it could have an end. It could accustom people to holding a world view; but there are plenty of world views.

A world view is a whole. When fragments from one persist in another, the otherness remains. When Mao says, "All Communist Party members should study . . ." let us assume that the spirit of *Ta-hsüeh,* the Confucian classic of "The Great Learning" ("Be studious and constantly exert yourself . . ."), still lives. But the world view that encompasses it has changed. Study what? Mao: ". . . the theory of Marx, Engels, Lenin, and Stalin, study our national history, and study current movements and trends." Thus, the object of study has changed, even when the idea of a canon persists and when the Communists, like Confucianists (but with a quite different conception), proclaim the importance of history.

And let us assume that Confucius in the "Analects" and the Communist theorist, Liu Shao-ch'i, have a common (transmitted?) concern with the morality of service. "A superior man is one who in the service of his prince will lay down his life" ("Analects"). "When necessary, sacrificing one's own life to complete one's virtue and giving up life to attain righteousness are considered the most natural thing by Communist Party members" (Liu). Yet, for all the remarkable Confucian tone in the language, the Communist is defined by demands of the collective (cf. Liu's colleague, Ch'en Po-ta, in another Confucianoid, not quite right—though titillating—homily: "If we party members talk independently about our 'individual natures' apart from our 'party nature,' we will lose our Communist virtue"). But, in Max Weber's distillation of the character of the Confucian literati, the Confucianist saw himself, individually, as an aesthetic end in himself.

If we move from the character of cadres to comparative institutions, we can stay with Weber for a bit. Let us note some similarities between historical Chinese society and the Communist one. They show some common divergence from capitalist modes of society. For example, the concept of private property, weak, of course, in Communist systems, was under many forms of pressure in the unreconstructed Chinese world. And in the nineteenth century, when tentative steps were taken towards industrialization, mandarins, not merchants, dominated the enterprises. Indeed, as the most inclusive and aggressive theory of Chinese society, the 'Oriental Despotism' theory, would have it, the Confucian-imperial state was generally 'stronger than society.' Must we not assume that an essential China shines through Communist lineaments?

There is something wrong with that. This same Confucian society, whose anti-capitalism ostensibly set the stage for Communism, might be deemed, just as plausibly, potentially capitalist, with a stronger potential in this respect than feudalism. The promise of Communist potential in Confucianism rests on no firmer base than the capitalist promise—whose base was the existence of certain anti-feudal features, such as channels of social mobility and assaults on primogeniture, pertaining to both Confucian and capitalist Weberian ideal types. Yet, despite the fact that so-called 'fetters of feudalism,' which should have been obstacles to capitalist development, were far from prominent features of Confucian bureaucratic society, European feudalism, fetters or not, evolved to capitalist forms while the process was abortive in China. Capitalism was not furthered in China by Confucian persistence or affinities—quite the reverse. Then we have no grounds for assuming, with successive social systems, that an affinity of fragments establishes the basis of succession. The Confucian type and the capitalist type share fragments; but the second did not succeed the first in China. The Confucian type and the Communist type share fragments; if there was succession in China here, the affinity of the fragments is not the necessary key.

4. CONCLUSION

What is it all in aid of, this nagging concern with continuity? It relates to the problem of how we relate to contemporary China. If we think we see imperial China *redivivus,* we commit ourselves to either a condescending complacency or a fantasy of terror. It may seem merely a dumb show, an empty ritual protestation of virtue. Or it may seem ready to strike us dumb, for how can a Son of Heaven help but assume that all of us under Heaven must be his subjects? It is much too late in the day to respond with the old correspondences: ignoring a remote China whose pretensions did us no harm, or doing harm to its pretensions by crashing through the walls.

We need an end to 'essences.' It is China still, but not the essence of China—Communist China, but not the essence of Communism. Communism is not simply an inessential tool, put to eternal Chinese uses; China is not an inessential vehicle, bearing a transhistorical creed around the world. The determinism implied in anyone's convictions about a never-changing China (hence, with a never-changing ecumenical drive) is mitigated when we see it change in Communism. And the determinism implied in Communism, whose real and significant force we must acknowledge, is mitigated by its domestication to China. Chinese needs may well divert the juggernaut of history. The ends are open. Minds should not be closed.